A GUIDE TO SUPERNATURAL SITES
FREQUENTED BY GHOSTS, WITCHES, POLTERGEISTS
AND OTHER MYSTERIOUS BEINGS

BY

ANTONY D. HIPPISLEY COXE

With photographs specially taken by Robert Estall

PAN BOOKS LTD
LONDON AND SYDNEY

Haunted Britain

First published 1973 by Hutchinson & Co. (Publishers) Ltd
This edition published 1975 by Pan Books Ltd,
Cavaye Place, London SW10 9PG

ISBN 0 330 24328 4

Designed and produced by George Rainbird Ltd,
Marble Arch House, 44 Edgware Road, London W2

House editor: Penelope Miller
Designer: George Sharp
Cartographer: John R. Flower
Indexer: Gerry Miller

Text typeset and printed by R. & R. Clark Ltd, Edinburgh
Colour printed by Impact Litho Ltd, Tolworth, Surrey
Book bound by Robert Hartnoll Ltd, Bodmin, Cornwall

FOR

ARAMINTA

REMEMBERING

THE OCCASIONAL ALARUMS AND

MANY EXCURSIONS

WE HAVE

SHARED

Contents

List of Colour Plates

All the colour photographs are by Robert Estall
except for Hall Well on page 125 which is
included by courtesy of Derbyshire Countryside
Limited.

Preface

This is a guidebook to places about which people hold some strange belief. They are convinced that a certain house is haunted; they are sure that water from a particular well will improve their eyesight; they are positive that a ritual performed on a special spot will make their wish come true. I have included a few peculiar customs which are either the last vestiges of pagan faith or possibly a magic ritual. I have also added one or two legends – such as King Arthur's birthplace or buried treasure – but only when they are concerned with places.

Of course there are many sceptics, and there are also people who will not admit their beliefs to strangers because they are a little ashamed of them. They are ashamed of being thought superstitious, not realizing perhaps that many of those who ask questions are themselves seeking to believe. In this age of disillusionment it is our faith in mundane things that has been most noticeably shaken. Some people, tired of what they consider a sick civilization, become anarchists; others join the Flower Folk or follow older, and sometimes less worldly, cults.

I do not think anarchists will find much of interest in this book, except, maybe, the hint of Guy Fawkes's ghost and the rites of the Bonfire Boys; but I hope that others will, for they, together with the rest of us who try to make the best of life, are all seekers.

I would like to state my own thoughts about the kind of places described in this guide. If people have believed something strongly for many hundreds of years, it seems to me possible that a part of that belief may have left its mark. To deny this, I suggest, is tantamount to refuting the efficacy of prayer on the one hand, and on the other the results of the experiments carried out at Duke University by Drs J. B. and L. E. Rhine. I certainly do not believe that the hauntings I have described will be apparent to all, nor that any of the healing wells will provide as reliable a cure as a doctor, although it is conceivable that a well may succeed where a doctor has failed. I have no doubt that what people call supernatural phenomena – even miracles – do occur; and when scientists are able to explain them they will cease to be considered strange or frightening or miraculous, and become accepted as quite ordinary.

I am convinced that the way to the supernatural lies through the natural. I do not know how warts can be charmed away, any more than a doctor knows what causes new tissue to start forming in a wound and to stop when the wound is healed. Auto-suggestion obviously has a great deal to do with certain cures and also with some of the rituals that are still performed. The part it plays in psychic phenomena may be greater than one thinks. If some apparitions are hallucinations, which means that they are created or made manifest in the mind of the beholder, though not necessarily by him alone, then they must be studied in a different way to those ghosts which are said to appear before you. I am not conscious of ever having seen or heard a ghost myself. In the garden here in Devon I often feel that someone is watching me, but when I look round I am always just a fraction too late to see who it is. This is more frustrating than frightening.

Time must have a great deal to do with psychic manifestation. I cannot understand why people should expect ghosts to abide by our time scale. They certainly do not conform to other measurements. In this respect I am not the first to point out that the calendar was changed by Pope Gregory in 1582, a year which consisted of 355 days, October 5 becoming October 15. England adopted this system in 1752. The reason for this change was that the old division of the year was slightly inaccurate so while the equinoxes obviously remained the same the days on which they were supposed to fall had slipped out of phase. This means that you will find references to Old Midsummer's Day and New Midsummer's Day. However, had the old calendar been maintained the date at the present time would have slid even further from the actual solstice, by about two and a half days. This leads me to suppose that if ghosts who originally appeared on certain anniversaries before the change seemed to adopt the new calendar, then those who wanted – consciously or subconsciously – to see them were responsible for conjuring them up. In other words, hauntings do not just happen. It is not merely by chance that you are there when the ghost walks. A physical presence is needed not only to see the apparition but perhaps to cause it to appear. Just as one can focus a camera and calculate distance or vice versa, so maybe people can focus time, without knowing it. Exorcism might well affect visitors to a place as well as – or even instead of – the spirits which are said to inhabit it. I find this far easier to understand than the idea that a religious ceremony can prevent the ghost of a man, who might have practised a completely different religion when alive, from haunting his earthly habitat. Exorcism has frequently been found to lose its power, and may in fact always be temporary.

Not many of us understand time although we are governed by it. I once heard that the Marquis de Sade was almost as interested in time as he was in his own peculiar pleasures, and that it was, oddly enough, one of his experiments with time which those two British school-mistresses, Miss Moberly and Miss Jourdain, stumbled upon at Versailles and described in *An Adventure*. I think of time as a disc on a record player. The stylus traces the present; but there is no reason why another stylus should not simultaneously pick up the music to come, or that which has passed. Our time seems to be governed by the clock; but a clock's relation to time is even less significant than that of a metre measure to the Atlantic Ocean.

Time, ghosts, faith – all these require much more study and considerably more space than could possibly be given to them in a guidebook. To me the most interesting and plausible explanation of hauntings is that given by T. C. Lethbridge in his book *Ghost and Divining Rod*. As dowsers know, different substances have different 'fields'. They are found, for instance, around woods and springs. In fact everything has its 'field'. It seems possible that some very strong force could impress itself on one of these fields; maybe the force which originally led to a certain grove being regarded as sacred, or a well as capable of healing. When a weaker field, such as that of a person in a drowsy state, finds itself in a stronger field, the impression held in the latter may leak into the former. There is, of course, very much more than this in Lethbridge's theory. To me its fascination lies in the way he explains how his basic concept fits so many strange phenomena, from dowsing to poltergeists, including those places which are not necessarily haunted but which have powerful atmosphere. When my wife and I have been looking for somewhere to live, both in England and abroad, many a house has been scratched off the agent's list because the place did not feel friendly. Some we found downright evil, while others (including one in which my wife lived in Edinburgh) had a very sympathetic ambience yet were definitely haunted.

While working on research for this book, I have again come across evidence that some people who appear to be genuinely interested in psychic phenomena from an utterly detached, scientific point of view and who seem determined to remain absolutely objective, fail in the end to observe the strict standards that they themselves set up. Some have to deceive them-selves if things do not work out, and occasionally stoop to trickery. Read *The Most Haunted House in England* and *The End of Borley Rectory*, both by Harry Price, by all means; but when you have finished them, read also *The Haunting of Borley Rectory* by Eric J. Dingwall, Kathleen M. Goldney and Trevor H. Hall. It presents a different picture. Should you visit Ballechin House in Perthshire and hear of the psychic investigations carried out by Adah Goodrich Freer at the end of the last century, read, on your return, *Strange Things* by John Campbell and Trevor Hall. Such books are admirable correctives to romantic over-indulgence.

There are many books you should read to get the full flavour of some of the haunts. All there is room for in this book is a concise version, and ghost stories are rarely improved by condensing. You will find that many of the more famous hauntings mentioned in these pages are splendidly elaborated in the books listed in the bibliography.

This guide could not have been compiled without recourse to such books, and to publica-tions such as *Notes and Queries*, newspapers and magazines, and the journals of the various folklore societies. I would like to thank all authors and journalists, those mentioned in the bibliography and those without a by-line, who have provided such fascinating reading, and also those who have so painstakingly collected the more ephemeral accounts, particularly the

British Tourist Authority (B.T.A.) Information Library. My appreciation is no less due to those who talked about their experiences, providing new material and elaborating on old themes; among them the curators of museums, keepers of castles, priests, publicans, their patrons, and, particularly, librarians. Some of the stories have been taken with a grain of salt. People with knowledge of haunted places usually fall into one of two categories: those who will tell you little or nothing because they do not want 'hordes of tourists' invading their privacy, and those who, because they rely on public patronage, are inclined to exaggerate. I have tried to keep a balance, but when visiting a site readers may sometimes be deliberately misled by local directions, or occasionally overwhelmed by accounts of psychic phenomena. I have suffered both.

After the collection of information came the selection, for which I must accept sole responsibility. Some 2000 sites have been cut by nearly half. I have tried to present a reasonable mixture, bearing the tourist in mind. Most holiday-makers spend more time in London, Edinburgh and the West Country than they do in, say, Cardiff, Newcastle or the Potteries. I have therefore tended to give tourist areas priority, not because industrial districts lack fascinating sites, but simply because I do not think they will appeal to as many visitors. However, I would very much like to hear of any site within the compass of this book, whether urban or rural, which I fail to mention, so that it may at least be recorded and possibly find a place in some future publication. Sites of great historic interest, and also of mystery, are disappearing at an alarming rate.

When I first started to compile a list of the sites we had to visit, I intended to give meticulous instructions on which road to take from one place to another. I found, however, that too many words were used in providing itineraries. Furthermore, as readers may well want to visit other places, which are not mysterious, on the way, I decided that the maps should be based on the points of the compass, leaving the reader to decide if he should take the most direct route or include diversions to other places. It should be noted that although the book is arranged county by county (following each other logically rather than alphabetically) some sites from one county are occasionally included in the tour of a neighbouring county for the convenience of the traveller.

To many people – particularly foreign visitors – a guide such as this must be considered as a supplement to the more tangible attractions which Britain has to offer. However, I do suggest that one-inch or half-inch scale maps will not only make your trip easier but much more enjoyable. I would also advise buying the latest editions of *Historic Houses, Castles and Gardens* (an ABC Travel Guide) and *Ancient Monuments and Historic Buildings open to the Public* published by H.M.S.O. An increasing number of houses are opened to the public every year, although some, like Brede, are closed. For a small expenditure you can avoid disappointment.

The inspection – in order to try to ensure that some site had not been razed to the ground or did not lie at the bottom of a new reservoir by the time this book appears – proved the most formidable task of all. As it now stands, over eighty per cent of the sites have been substantiated – but the figure of more than 1000 places would not have been achieved if it had not been for the help of Mr Kemmis Buckley, Mr Steve Clarke, Mr St John Couch, Mr Anthony Fleming, Mrs Harry Warman, Mrs Derrick Seebohm, Mrs Dudley Usher, Mrs M. Reynolds, Mrs Pat St John, Miss Josephine Pullein-Thompson, my sister Mrs Alan Rae Smith and my wife Araminta who, if ever I suspected her of being a witch, must have used her broomstick to cover so many sites during the last two years. For checking the typescript I am especially grateful to Mrs Miller of Rainbird, whose keen and questing eye found many inconsistencies and solecisms. To all these kind, helpful people who made the checking so much easier my warmest thanks are due.

I would like to make it clear that although positive statements are made – 'The castle is haunted by a Grey Lady', for instance – it should be taken to mean that the site is reputed, supposed or believed to be so haunted.

Finally, I would like to recount my favourite ghost story. I believe it to be true because as a small boy I read it in some magazine and was so excited by it that I rushed to tell it to my mother, only to find that she knew the people to whom it actually happened. What is more, she finished the story for me.

It starts with a Navy lieutenant who, from the day he married, spent his serving life overseas. During this time his wife, who was always with him, frequently dreamed of a certain house. As the children grew up 'Mama's dream house' became a family joke. The time came for the father to retire; he came home and they started to look for a house in the country. Sure enough, as they approached one place on the house agent's list, the mother said excitedly, 'But we're coming to my dream house'. This was met with derisory scepticism until she told them precisely the route they would take, although none of them had been there before. They were met by the agent who showed them over the property. Every so often the mother would remark on some change. 'But surely the stairs used to come down here? Oh! yes, I remember now, they were altered when we were in Hong Kong; that would be about fifteen years ago.' She was right every time. The children were thrilled, and as it was an old house asked if it was haunted. 'Yes,' replied the agent, 'there is even supposed to be a ghost.' Of course they had to buy the house. Some time later the mother met the house agent who asked if they were happy there. 'Perfectly', was the reply, 'it is so wonderful to be settled at last. The children love it too, although they are a bit disappointed that they have never seen the ghost.' 'I did not think they would,' said the agent; 'you are the ghost. I have seen you here many times.'

I was going to ask if any reader could provide the name of the family and the place. Then I read Alasdair Alpin MacGregor's excellent survey of strange hauntings called *The Ghost Book*. He describes how Mrs Boulton knew every inch of Ballachulish House from dreams before she visited it. He also quotes André Maurois' *La Maison*, which is about a house in the Rhône valley, to let because it is haunted, and found by the flesh and blood ghost. I do not think that these stories invalidate my own version. In fact they tend to confirm its veracity. It would be most suspicious if this phenomenon had happened only once.

Ackworthy
Hartland
Devon
1973

A. D. H. C.

Note

Key to Symbols

This book is arranged mainly by counties but occasionally a site in one county is included in the tour of a neighbouring county for the convenience of the traveller. Readers should refer to the index – which lists sites alphabetically – for easy location. Cross-references within the text mention only the name of the site referred to if it comes within the same section, but add the county name if it is to be found in another section. For example, in the entry for **Shervage Wood,** Somerset, the cross-reference reads: 'See Fiddington; and Wayland Smith's Cave, Berkshire.' (Fiddington is, like Shervage Wood, in the Somerset section.)

Many of the sites mentioned in this book – such as churches, bridges and beaches – are obviously open to the public; houses, castles and ancient monuments may or may not be. Useful booklets giving opening times are recommended in the Preface. To help the reader further the following initials have been inserted in the text where appropriate:

O.P. (private property but open to the public at certain specified times)

O.P.A. (private property open only by appointment)

N.T. (National Trust)

N.T.S. (National Trust for Scotland)

D.E. (Department of the Environment, formerly Ministry of Public Building and Works)

Other abbreviations used in this guide are:

O.S. (Ordnance Survey)

B.T.A. (British Tourist Authority)

⊛ Hauntings, ghosts and poltergeists

✿ Holy, healing and wishing wells; sacred magic and mysterious places

☗ Witchcraft, sorcery and curses

🐾 Spectral and mythical beasts; the Little People

◉ Strange customs and festivals

🐎 Legends (including Arthurian) and odd stories

⚒ Buried treasure

Overleaf Forde Abbey (Somerset section). The Great Hall is the most likely place to see a sixteenth-century abbot.

England

CORNWALL

The Duchy is as packed full of beliefs as a can is of Cornish pilchards. A chough is a red-legged crow, and bad luck comes to anyone who kills this bird. King Arthur's spirit entered a chough after he died at Slaughter-bridge. In the tin mines underground spirits can be heard knocking and singing carols; they are the ghosts of the Jews who crucified Christ. If you want to become a witch, touch a logan stone nine times at midnight. Such legends are common all over Cornwall. We are, however, concerned with places, and I suggest using Launceston and Truro as bases for excursions. If you enter the county by the A39, you will go through Kilkhampton and Stratton. Then on your right you will come to:

⊙ **Binhamy Farm** (derived from Bien Aimée). Through a couple of fields you will find, with Mr Jose's permission, all that remains of Blanchminster Castle. When Ranulph returned from the Crusades he found that his wife had married again, so he became a recluse. He was a great benefactor to Stratton and his body is buried in the church, but his ghost still haunts the moat of

his castle. There is also an odd man-made amphitheatre here, thought to have been a cock-fighting pit.

About 4 miles further along the A39 turn left for:

⊙ **Penfound Manor.** For years its owners welcomed visitors, but at the time of writing, this haunted house is no longer open to the public. April 26 is the most likely day for seeing Kate Penfound's ghost, but strange things happen at other times. Kate was in love with a neighbour, John Trebarfoot; but his family were Roundheads, her parents Cavaliers. Her father caught them trying to elope and killed John. Arthur Penfound's ghost is also said to haunt the place. He was a famous smuggler and killed more than one preventive officer.

In another 5 miles take a right-hand turn to:

✿ **St Gennys Well**, which lies alongside the church, inside which you will find the history of St Genesius.

Now go south-east to:

⊙◉ **Launceston.** The churchyard is said to be haunted by a Kergrim or ghoul. A stranger belief is that if a man has a stiff neck, he should go – on May 1, 2 or 3 – to the grave of the last woman to be buried there, and, after passing his hand from the head to the foot of the grave, apply the dew to the afflicted part. The same ritual applies to women, but they should go to the grave of the last deceased man.

Two miles north of Launceston lies:

⊙ **Yeolmbridge.** The Wild Hunt haunts this spot. It was once seen by a man crossing the bridge and he was told by the Master that if he ever got in the way of the hounds again he would be struck dead. For years he steered clear of the place, but one day he begged a lift from the driver of a carriage. He never arrived home; his body was found on this bridge next morning.

From Launceston the 3254 leads to South Petherwin; fork right here for:

⊙ **Botathan.** The ghost of Dorothy Dingley has been seen here by a number of people, including the Rector of St Mary Magdalene, Launceston, in 1665. His detailed account was rewritten by Daniel Defoe. The ghost first appeared to young Bligh of Botathan in a field then known as Higher Brown Quartils,

Left Launceston churchyard, the haunt of a ghoul, but also a place for curing stiff necks

Right Cotehele Bridge is marked by an indelible bloodstain

and also on a nearby road. One of the fullest descriptions of an exorcism is given by Parson Rudell of Launceston. The ritual included tracing out pentagrams, inserting rowans at the points in a 'magick tradition' and conversing in Syriac, which is, or was, 'used where such ones dwell and converse in thoughts that glide'. Strange words – and deeds – for a parson! He claimed to have exorcised the place, but the ghost of Dorothy Dingley has subsequently been seen on a number of occasions.

South of Launceston is:

🏹 **Hingston Down,** where buried treasure – or minerals perhaps – lie:

> Hingston Down, well y-wrought,
> Is worth London Town, dearly bought.

☆🦌 **Callington.** Dupath Well (D.E.) (signposted) cures whooping cough. It marks the site of a legendary battle between Sir Colam and Gottlieb for the love of a lady, in which both died.

South-east lies:

🦌 **Cotehele** (N.T.). This house of the Edgecumbes, on the banks of the Tamar, is approached by a bridge near which a treacherous warder was slain by his master. An indelible bloodstain marks the spot where he died.

North-west, just south of the 395, is:

☆ **Laneast.** In the valley below the church lies St Sidwell. It is best to ask the way as you must go through a farmyard to reach it. It is now said to be boggy and overgrown, but was once held in high esteem as a wishing well.

The next village to the west is:

☆ **St Clether.** Directions for finding the well are given in the church. It lies about ¼ mile away, but is well worth the walk as it is set in a baptistry which has recently been repaired.

West, across the A39, is:

🦌 **Slaughterbridge** where, according to Cornish legend, King Arthur received his fatal wound.

North on the coast is:

👕 **Boscastle** where you will find one of the two witchcraft museums in the United

Left Pengersick Castle has two ghosts

Right, top Tingtagel: possibly King Arthur's birthplace, certainly a windswept haunt of his spirit

Right, bottom Dupath Well, Callington, cures whooping cough

Kingdom. This contains as strange a mixture of exhibits – often frightening, occasionally ludicrous – as any witch's recipe.

South-west lies:

🦌👁 **Tintagel** (D.E.). Whether or not you believe that King Arthur was born here and that Camelford has a connection with Camelot, this is a fascinating place, whose aura of mystery has not yet quite disappeared under tourist trappings. One of the many legends tells how Gorlois, King of Cornwall, sent his wife Igerne from Dimilioe to

Tintagel to protect her from the amorous advances of Uther Pendragon, King of Britain. Merlin, however, enabled Uther to impersonate Gorlois so well that even Igerne was taken in and seduced. Of that union Arthur was born. (See St Dennis.) His spirit is said to haunt the ruins of Tintagel.

A mile or so to the east, along the 3263, you come to a rocky valley; at its head is:

⚘ **St Nectan's Kieve** where the hermit is said to be buried (although he was murdered at Hartland, North Devon, q.v.). In the nearby cottage two mysterious ladies lived as recluses in the early 1800s. In spite of any local stories you may hear, they were *not* St Nectan's sisters. They were a Cornish counterpart of the Ladies of Llangollen.

Take the 3314 for:

☆ **St Minver** where a famous well cured sore eyes.

A little further on, at:

☆ **Rock,** there is a fifteenth-century baptistry over a well which cures whooping cough.

East, across the A39, is:

☆⚘ **St Breward.** In a valley near Chapel Farm, on a public footpath, is St Breward's well. It is easily accessible but in poor condition. It cured sore eyes and pins were offered. St Breward's Feast Day is on the Sunday nearest to February 22, when special buns are baked, blessed in the church and distributed among the villagers. The Revd Browning can give further details.

North of Leaze Farm, on the north bank of the de Lank river, is King Arthur's Hall, actually built about 2000 years ago by the Beaker People.

The next site, across the Camel estuary, is:

◉☆ **Padstow.** 'Baiting the Hobby Horse, on May 1, is a pagan custom, if ever there was one,' says Daphne du Maurier. At one minute past midnight on Mayday, the landlord of the 'Golden Lion', who keeps the Black 'Oss (made of canvas and wood), is woken up and the dance begins. The 'Oss is baited by the Teaser whose club bears the initials O. B. which are thought to be Celtic, but why, no-one remembers. The tempo of the dance varies and the 'Oss sometimes lies down, then gets up again and continues until at the end of the day he dies. At one time the 'Oss used to end up in Traitor's Pool on the outskirts of the town, and water was sprinkled on him and the bystanders. This was probably a rain charm, complementing the sunworship origin of the baiting. There is a rival 'Oss, but the ritual and origins are the same.

Down the estuary there is a well, where, some say, Jesus landed on his way to Somer-

Top Three of the girls turned into the Nine Maidens of stone at St Columb Major

Above Roche Rocks and St Michael's Chapel, where the persecuted Tregeagle can be seen

set (see Priddy, Somerset), though it is dedicated to St George.

To the south, on the A39, is:

✿ **St Columb Major.** The Nine Maidens are monoliths erected to face a tenth, the Fiddler. Legend says that these were girls turned to stone for dancing on the sabbath, which is doubtless a Christian explanation for what was originally a pagan rite performed here.

🐾 **Castle-an-Dinas,** 2 miles to the east, is reputed to be the site of King Arthur's hunting lodge.

South-west of St Columb is:

✿ **Colan,** and Our Lady of Nantes' Well, a divinatory well which should be visited on Palm Sunday, with a palm in one hand and an offering in the other. If the palm sinks the thrower will die during the next twelve months. St Pedyr's Well is marked on the O.S. map by Melancoose Mill.

East, across the A39 and the A30, you will find:

✿⊛ **Roche.** Near the station is a divinatory well known locally as the Holy Well. Girls may still throw in pins and pebbles on Maundy Thursday and the Thursday following, before sunrise, to see the bubbles reveal their fortunes. I doubt though that lunatics or 'frantick persons' are now immersed in the water as they once were. Roche Rocks contain a hermit's cell and St Michael's Chapel (1409). The publican at the Rock Inn is most informative. The chapel is one of the haunts of Tregeagle, the Cornish Bluebeard. He is doomed to many impossible tasks, such as emptying Dozmary Pool (q.v.) with a limpet shell and making up a truss of sand with a sand rope. He is constantly chased by the Devil till he finds sanctuary here.

To the south-west is:

🐾 **St Dennis.** Here it rained blood in the graveyard of St Dionysius at the very moment that St Denis, the patron saint of Paris, was murdered in the French capital. A similar manifestation is said still to warn the village of impending disaster. This village is the Dimilioc of Arthurian legend, and the fort in which the church now stands was the Castle of Gorlois. (See Tintagel.)

Using Truro as your base, I suggest you first tour the south coast, working clockwise round to the north of the peninsula. You can then travel back, through the south-eastern part of the Duchy. At:

✿⊙ **Perranarworthal** there is a Men-an-Tol, a stone known as the Cornish Pebble, balanced on two supporting stones. If you wish to cure rheumatism or sciatica, you must crawl round the stone on all fours, from east to west, and squeeze through the aperture in May. Pin offerings, laid crossways on top, reveal the future.

Ask the way to the Irishwoman's Grave, off the green lane from Perranarworthal to Mylor. Who she was, no-one knows. Two stones and a mound can be seen. M. Chetwynd-Stapylton refers to the Irishwoman's Garden in Mylor parish. She is thought to have been flung from her carriage when her horses took fright. But why is she buried here?

To the south is:

⊛ **Penryn** where a ghostly coach, drawn by headless horses, appears just before Christmas. Some people believe that unless they avert their eyes the coachman can spirit them away.

To the south-west, just before the turning to:

✿ **Constantine,** you will find, east of the road and almost opposite Trewardreva, Pixie's Hall, an underground passage or fogou with granite walls.

Continue south. Three miles before you reach the Lizard take the Cadgwith road to:

✿ **St Ruan.** Here the canopied St Ruan's Well lies in a field hedge, with access from a farm lane and also from the Cadgwith/Lizard road. It once had miraculous properties and its water is still used for baptisms.

Further north of Cadgwith is:

⊛ **Croft Pascoe Pool** in the Goonhilly Downs, where a ghostly ship with lug-sail spread has been seen.

⚓ **Kennack Cove,** north-east of Cadgwith, is one of the two sites where the buccaneer Avery is reputed to have buried several chests of treasure. The other site is:

⚓ **Gunwalloe,** which lies west of the 3083 on the west coast of the promontory north of Mullion. At Church Cove, nearer Mullion, the King of Portugal's treasure was lost in the *St Andrew* in 1526, and so was that of another ship wrecked in 1785.

North at:

⊚ **Helston,** on May 8 (unless this falls on a Sunday or a Monday), the famous Floral or Furry Dance takes place. The long-gloved, top-hatted dancers and their escorts are a very sedate relic of a Roman saturnalia, although the dancers still wend their way in and out of houses and can at least demand a kiss. The Hal-an-Tow, which follows the first Furry Dance, is more colourful, as those taking part wear the costumes of the characters in the song they sing. The Floral Day Association can produce full details.

Due west is:

☠🐗 **Pengersick Castle** which is haunted by at least two ghosts. One is that of a Mr Millington, who bought the place in the reign of Henry VIII. Some say he tried to murder his wife by poisoning her, but she exchanged the goblets and they were both carried off by the Devil.

The story of an older ghost is the perfect fairy tale. A Crusader forgot the wife and son he had left at home and married a foreign king's daughter. Although she gave him a magic sword he forsook her too, so she followed him back to Cornwall with her infant son. He threw them both into the sea: she was drowned, but her spirit entered into a white hare; the child was saved by a passing ship. The evil baron then married a witch, who was very cruel to the firstborn. One day a ship was wrecked nearby and the only person saved was a boy who bore a marked resemblance to the heir. He was, of course, his half-brother. Guided by the white hare the two boys found the magic sword. The baron was thrown from his horse and killed when it shied at the white hare. The boys, who had mastered the occult arts and discovered the elixir of life, lived for several generations.

More mundane is the fact that the 'wreckers' here were even worse than those on the north coast:

God keep us from the rocks and shelving sands,
And save us from Breage and Germoe hands.

🏊👣🐚 **Cudden Point** marks the site of more sunken treasure. It is also the haunt of mermaids.

Inland at:

👁 **St Hilary** an eccentric ghost – that of the Revd John Penneck, early eighteenth-century Chancellor of Exeter – flies into rages and raises great storms.

👁🐗 **Marazion** is the next port of call. Although referred to as Market Jew, it is probably derived from Marghaisewe, meaning Thursday's Market. At what was known as Marazion Green, a ghostly lady in white would jump up behind a horseman, pillion fashion, and ride as far as Red River. On the beach here Sir John Arundell, Sheriff of Cornwall, was killed while leading an attack to reclaim St Michael's Mount, seized by Richard de Vere, Earl of Oxford, in 1471. This death fulfilled the prophecy of a shepherd, who considered he had been wrongfully imprisoned by Sir John. He made a habit of fixing the sheriff with a steely eye and chanting:

When upon the golden sand,
Thou shalt die – by human hand.

Inland you come to:

✡ **Ludgvan,** passing the Giant's Grave. Here there is said to be the Well of Colurion, 'sacred before the saints'. It cured sore eyes, and anyone baptized in its waters could never be hanged with a hempen rope.

✡ **Chysauster** (D.E.) lies north-west. This place of mystery was an Iron Age village 2000 years ago and was more recently used as a Methodist preaching ground. There is also a ruined fogou.

To the south lies:

✡◉ **Madron.** There are, or rather were, two wells here, north-west of the village. Take the Morvah road and in less than a mile turn right. This lane leads to three gates. Along the cinder track to the right is the site of the divinatory Doom Well, but the water has been diverted. The track straight ahead leads to a grove with a baptistry in which is St Madron's Well. This cured nightmares, difficulties in breathing and afflictions of the limbs. After bathing in the water you must sleep on St Madron's Bed, a nearby stone. The first Thursday in May is most propitious; or, for rickets, the first three Sundays in May. In this case the child should be dipped three times while the parents face the sun, then passed nine times round the well from east to west. The parents must then tear a rag from the child's clothes and hang it on a tree in silence.

🐗👁 **Penzance.** There is a legend that a coach and headless horses rattle through the streets and if you should meet them death will follow. It seems probable that this story was put about by smugglers. However, Chapel Street is haunted by Mrs Baines who was shot by the guard she had placed in her orchard, when she tried to catch him out. The bay south of the town is known as Gwavas Lake, and only became sea when the great flood covered the land which joined Cornwall to the Isles of Scilly.

West of Penzance is:

✡◉ **Sancreed** where St Euny's (Uny's or Eurinus's) Well cures ailments, dries humours and heals wounds on the last day of the year and on the first three Wednesdays in May. Children should be dipped and dragged widdershins through the water.

South at:

👁 **St Buryan** there is a Quaker burial ground, said to be haunted by the Wild Hunt. Some people think that this is the place haunted by Kenegie. His spirit was laid by a

Top A phantom ship sails mysteriously inland at St Levan

Above At Cudden Point mermaids play round sunken treasure

parson who condemned him to count the blades of grass in an enclosure at Castle-an-Dinas.

Near the headland you will find:

🜨👿 **Treryn Dinas** which is haunted by witches.

✵👿 **St Levan.** At Parchaple Well any child christened Joanna will be a fool and ill-omened, because a lady of that name once reprimanded the saint for fishing on Sunday. More mystifying is the ghost ship which has been seen sailing straight towards the shore and almost half a mile inland before disappearing.

The southernmost headland, west of St Leven, is:

🜨 **Hella Point.** It used to be called Nancy's Garden. Nancy, daughter of a farmer, fell in love with a boy who went to sea. Day after day she would stand at this point scanning the horizon for his ship. One night she dreamed she heard him call her. She went out and was never seen again. It was subsequently learned that the boy had been drowned that night. Her ghost, or his, may well still haunt the spot.

The sea-bed between Hella Point and Land's End is called:

🜨👿 **Lyonesse.** It once stretched to the Isles of Scilly and contained 140 parish churches, so they say. When the flood overwhelmed the land, the only person to escape was the founder of the Trevelyan family; and the only animal was a white horse, perhaps the origin of the water-horse legends. Several people, including Miss Edith Oliver, have seen the crenellated battlements, towers and spires of Lyonesse, well out to sea.

👿💀 **Sennen Cove** was once much frequented by mermaids, and also by a manifestation known as the Hooper. This took the form of a cloud of mist which rested on Cowloe Rock and emitted hooting noises by day and showers of sparks at night. It was looked upon as a guardian spirit until one day a foolish fisherman and his son beat their way through the mist with flails. Neither they nor the mist were ever seen again.

Just south of Cowloe Rock is the Irish Lady, a rock which acts as a memorial to an Irishwoman, the only person to scramble ashore from a wreck. Unfortunately no boat could reach her and she finally fell into the sea, but her ghost still clings to the rock.

At the top of the Penberth valley, east of Sennen, lies:

🜨 **Penrose,** once the seat of the family of that name. Three hundred years ago Ralph Penrose, a smuggler, on the death of his wife, took their seven-year-old son to sea, leaving the estate in the care of his brother John. Ralph, with his cousin William and his son, ran into a storm and were wrecked on Cowloe Rock, while John watched them, making no effort to go to their rescue. The heir managed to get ashore only to be murdered on his uncle's instructions. William also managed to survive but lost his memory. One day, by chance, he found himself back at Penrose and heard a boy's voice saying, 'My uncle bade the captain murder me, I lie beneath the dead tree in the orchard. Dig, and bury me.' William traced the murderer who confessed. John hanged himself. But William found Penrose so haunted that he could never live there.

St Just. A mile or so north of the village, at Kenidjack, is the hooting cairn, haunted by witches led by Old Moll. Under it lies the Gump, where the Devil hauls lost souls and demons fight. Mortals can get pixie-led here.

There are stone circles, logan stones, quoits, menhirs and many mysterious relics of prehistoric man all over this part of Cornwall. If you follow the road to Morvah and turn right, in a little over a mile you can turn left down a lane which will lead you to:

Men-an-Tol, a round stone with a hole in the middle, between two upright stones. Crawl through the hole nine times against the sun, and the stone will 'blacken disease'. You will be cured of any 'ailment or nightmare or weight in your chest'.

Continuing along the coast you will come to:

Zennor, site of the most famous 'merry-maid' legend of them all. It tells how a mermaid was lured ashore by the beautiful singing of Matthew Trevella in Zennor Church. He, in his turn, became so bewitched by her that he was inveigled into the sea and never seen again, although a few years later a mermaid complained that the cable and anchor of a ship in Pendour Cove were preventing her reaching her husband Matthew and her children. See the carved pew-ends in the church.

Follow the same road on to:

St Ives. On stormy nights the bay is haunted by a white lady with a lantern, forewarning of a wreck. At St Ives Head a ghost ship has been seen, but disappeared when fishermen tried to board her.

The Knill Monument is a folly built in 1782 by John Knill, who left a bequest that a band of ten maidens, two matrons and a fiddler should visit it on July 25 every fifth year and dance round it singing the hundredth psalm. This should happen again in 1976.

South-east, on the other side of Hayle, is:

Leedstown where a ghost

> . . . runs up and down stair
> And sits and weeps and sleeks her hair.

This is the spirit of a woman whose lover refused to marry her till she gave him the title deeds to her property. When she did so he promptly sold them and went to America.

South lies:

Godolphin House (O.P.). The King's Room and the King's Garden were designed to allow King Charles II to escape by one of five routes, but it is a White Lady who emerges from a sealed-up closet and walks along the terrace.

Nearby Jew's Lane is haunted by the ghost of a Jew who hanged himself from a tree and is buried beneath the road. The ghost is said to take the form of a bull and a fiery chariot, a mithraic pagan symbol, which suggests a mingling of legends in folk memory.

The next site is:

Redruth. According to Robert Hunt in *Cornish Legends*, no child baptized in water from St Ruth's Well will ever be hanged. St Ruth wore a red cloak, hence the place name.

North-east, inland from Perranporth, is:

Perranzabuloe. There have been three churches here. The most modern one stands by the main road and inside you will find the history of the 'lost church'. This lies in the dunes near the golf-course, and is signposted. It was buried in the sand for many years, and is one of the oldest places of worship in Britain, to which people came on pilgrimages 1000 years before the Reformation.

St Cuthbert's Well is in Holywell Bay, $2\frac{1}{2}$ miles to the north, and is reached via the village of Cubert. This well cured itch, scurf and dandruff. It is situated in a cave on the beach and visitors climb fifteen steps up and slide down into the water. There is said to be another well at Trevornick Farm, between St Piran's and St Cuthbert's.

You can now return to Truro and start on the southern tour. Inland from Gerran's Bay is:

Veryan. If the church clock strikes on a Sunday morning during the singing of the hymn before the sermon, or at evensong before the collect against devils, then there will be a death in the parish before the following Sunday.

Due north of Veryan, on the 3078, near the turning to Tregony, is a milestone known as:

Robin Long which marks the grave of a smuggler and pirate of that name, who was caught, then hanged in chains and buried on this spot in the mid-1600s.

St Austell. The Menacuddle Well is about $\frac{1}{2}$ mile from the town in the woods off the Bodmin road. It cures ulcers and is also a wishing well. Bent pins are the votive offering. The name is derived from Maen-a-coel or Stone of the Hawk. Nearby is a granite 'chair' or 'bed'.

The 390 takes you to:

🐚♿◉ **St Blazey** and the road is reported to be haunted by a strange animal which looks like a bear but sounds like a horse. The inhabitants however, are strangely reticent about it.

The Feast Day of Blaize, who landed at Par from foreign parts, is celebrated on February 3. A candle, which has previously been burning on the altar of his church, should be applied to aching teeth and the saint's aid invoked. He has been instrumental in curing sore human throats, and diseases in cattle.

A few miles north lies:

☠✿ **Luxulyan.** The garden of the vicarage is said to be haunted by the ghost of an eighteenth-century incumbent named Cole. Behind the village pump and down some steps is a fifteenth-century baptistry over St Cyr's Well.

Going north you will reach the A30 just south of Lanivet (where St Benet's Well lies under a stone in a farmyard). Turn right for:

✿ **Bodmin.** Scarlet's Well provides special 'heavy water' with iridescent colours, which was thought to be very efficacious in curing most diseases.

East, on the moor, you will find:

◉ **Warleggan** where there is apple-was-sailing on Christmas Eve. (See Carhampton and Dunkeswell in Somerset.)

✿ **St Neot.** Upstream is St Neot's Well. It will be found in a meadow down a lane to the right of a garage. St Neot is said to have been: (i) a dwarf; (ii) brother of Alfred the Great; (iii) a monk from Glastonbury; and (iv) all three. He was particularly kind to animals, especially those which were the quarry of the hunt. This curative well is most effective on the first three mornings in May.

Now take the St Cleer road and turn left for:

🐾◉ **Dozmary Pool.** This lake, a mile in circumference and lying high on Bodmin Moor, is not fed by any stream. Into its depth Sir Bedivere is said to have flung King Arthur's sword Excalibur (see Llyn Ogwen, Wales). It is haunted by the ghost of Lord Robartes' wicked steward Tregeagle (see Roche), who is condemned to empty it with a limpet shell. The chill of evening is not the only thing to send a shiver down one's spine in this mysterious, brooding place.

If you drive past the west side of the pool, you will reach the A30 near Jamaica Inn. You can then turn back along the east side of the pool, past King Doniert's Stone (D.E.), to:

Top The silhouette of the Knill Monument, St Ives

Above During Sunday services, Veryan Church clock may strike a knell for a parish soul

☆🐎 **St Cleer.** Here there is a famous bowser or ducking well, once used in curing lunatics and epileptics. The well is in a baptistry 100 yards below the church. People here were particularly credulous. A century ago house-maids at the nearby vicarage refused to kill any spiders because they firmly believed that their deceased master, Parson Jupp, had been reincarnated as one.

To the north, on Bodmin Moor, is:

☆ **The Cheesewring,** and below it is Daniel Gumb's cavern. Gumb, a stone-cutter and amateur mathematician, lived as a hermit until his death in 1776. He chiselled diagrams on the huge stone slab which formed the roof of his retreat.

The next five sites take you south towards the coast:

◉☆ **Liskeard.** St Martin's Well – in Well Lane – had a lucky stone on which engaged couples had to stand while drinking to ensure fertility. It has now become Pipe Well; the middle pipe is still thought to be curative. There is another well in Lady Park, but this is private property, so permission should be sought before visiting it.

☆🐎 **St Keyne.** The saint was a beautiful and holy virgin, daughter of King Braganus (Brechin) and aunt of King David. Her well is one of the most famous and lies south of the village where three roads meet. After a wedding the first one of the bridal couple to drink here will be the dominant partner.

☆ **Duloe.** At the edge of the village towards Sandplace is St Cuby's (St Cuthbert's or St Kilby's) Well in a baptistry.

☆🐎 **Pelynt.** At Hobb's Park Farm is St Non's (St Nunne's or St Ninnie's) Well. It is also known as Piskie's Well. A farmer once tried to take the round granite basin to use as a pig's trough, but it broke loose from his grasp and rolled back into position. From that day he suffered misfortune. Pixies are placated by pins thrown into the water.

☆ **Polperro.** Here a well, visited fasting three mornings before sunrise, cured sore eyes and other ailments, as in Chaucer's *Pardoner's Tale*:

If the goode man that the beast oweth
Wol every wike er that the cock croweth
Fastynge, drink of this well a draught
As thilke holy Jew oure elders taught
His beestes, and his stoor shall multiplie.

🐇 **Looe.** A white hare, which is sometimes seen running from Talland to the 'Jolly Sailor', is believed to be the ghost of an unhappy girl who committed suicide. Or is this yet another rumour set about by smugglers?

SOUTH DEVON

I have divided Devonshire into three parts. Dartmoor is treated as an area on its own. Sites to the north are far-flung; those to the south are sparse. Finding suitable centres to cover an interesting group of sites is not always easy, but I decided on Buckfastleigh as the base from which to cover both South Devon and Dartmoor, and Torrington for North Devon.

In *The Shell Guide to England*, Euan Bowater says, 'Dartmoor for wildness, Exmoor for beauty'. I agree, not only from a scenic point of view, but from a supernatural one as well. The earthiness of Dartmoor is almost ferocious, a remorseless reminder of elemental powers. The dominant spirits here are not ladies in grey wringing their hands, but hairy fists wrenching at steering wheels, and demons who haunt mine-shafts and re-gurgitate Christian corpses, while the Wish Hounds of the Wild Hunt answer the horn of the Devil more often than that of the squire's ghost. In the centre of the moor rises the river that gives it its name, and epitomizes the awe in which the whole region was once held – and still is by many. Originally a sacrifice was made to meet the river god's demand, as two bits of doggerel, handed down from generation to generation, testify:

> Dart! Here's man
> To chill
> Or to kill.
> Now let me over
> To go where I will!

and, more regretfully:

> Dart! Dart! Cruel dart!
> Every year thou claim'st a heart!

But before visiting the cradle of this infamous river, I propose to cover the area to the south. First:

☿ **Buckfastleigh** itself. The unimpressive abbey is said to be haunted by pre-Reformation monks, who were seen ten years before the present monks returned.

Towards Totnes you will come to Shiner's Bridge where you turn left for:

☿ **Dartington Hall.** This is a place of profound atmosphere. It is not so much a place of mystery as a place where mystery is reconciled. Its White Lady and other ghosts, I am sure, rest quietly in the peaceful wisdom of the place.

This is not the case at:

Berry Pomeroy, east of Totnes. A mile beyond the village in the castle ruins, the spectre of Lady Margaret Pomeroy beckons to wayfarers, luring them to her tower. If they are tempted in they fall to their death. Either Lady Margaret or, more probably, the ghost of a kinswoman wanders sadly about, bemoaning the death of her baby whom she murdered because the child was incestuously sired by her own father.

South-east at:

Dartmouth the Royal Castle Hotel is on the British Tourist Authority's list of hotels 'reputed to be haunted'.

Brixham. The Black House lives up to its reputation. Despite an *art nouveau* stained-glass door, the house dates from the fourteenth century and was built or used by monks at that time. Doors get locked quite inexplicably. The owner has been locked out of the bathroom and even out of the house itself. Bolts, however, are not shot. The ghost is said to be that of Squire Hilliard, whose son, 400 years ago, fell in love with a country girl from Cheriston. The father forced the girl to marry another, and his son, riding through the woods, saw her coming out of the church on the arm of the man his father thought more suitable. So young Hilliard hanged himself from a tree and the horse came home riderless. His father's ghost searches for his son to ask forgiveness.

Torquay. Montpellier House, former choir school, is the haunted vicarage of St John's Church. The ghost is either that of Henry Ditton Newman, who died in 1885, when the organ played by itself at his funeral, or that of a man who committed suicide in 1953.

Compton Castle (N.T.), which lies 3 miles west of Torquay, is said to be strangely haunted.

North, along the 380, just beyond Newton Abbot race-course, is:

Kingsteignton. This place has become famous for its ram-roasting on Whit-Tuesday, although the ram may now be a deer. It is a relic of a sacrifice made to propitiate the river god in pagan days and to offer thanks for the renewal of life. The ritual killing was abandoned fairly recently, but that old fertility symbol, the maypole, is still in evidence.

East, on the 3192, is a site marked on the map as:

Little Haldon. On the right-hand side of the road, between the farms of Smallacombe and Lidwell (Our Lady's Well) there is a chapel and a well. I think this must be the

Top Do not be tempted into this tower at Berry Pomeroy by Lady Margaret's beckoning ghost or you will fall to your death

Above The Black House – in reputation if not colour – at Brixham place haunted by the Mad Monk who, in the fourteenth century, lured travellers into his cell to hear their confessions, then murdered them and threw their bodies down the well.

☙ **Exeter.** In the cathedral cloisters the ghost of a nun appears at 7 p.m. in the month of July. She emerges from the south wall of the nave and disappears through the south wall of the Church House. The deanery is also reputed to be haunted.

Towards Exmouth, less than a mile past Exton, a road on the right leads to:

☙ **Nutwell Court,** the home of the Drakes *after* the death of Sir Francis yet still said to be haunted by him. Along the main road you may see the ghost of Eliot Drake who challenged a friend to ride a race to a certain inn. His horse fell; both animal and rider broke their necks. This spectre is supposed to appear on the anniversary of the race.

Back down the Plymouth road you will come to:

☙ ✦ **Chudleigh Knighton** where a ghostly dwarf is supposed to lead those who will follow to buried treasure. New Bridge, crossing the Teign south of the village, is haunted by the Dewar or Devil, and there are also reports of a haunted bridge over the river Bovey near Stover where, in 1961, a woman experienced 'something waving its arms and running alongside her'. When Stover was a private house the servants would never go near this bridge at night. Mrs St Leger-Gordon, the authority on Dartmoor folklore, thinks that this may well have been Jew's Bridge. It may be that some poor Jewish pedlar was murdered here.

To the north-west is:

🐾 **Bovey Tracey.** At the Riverside Hotel you can see a sword which may be the one that killed Thomas à Becket. The original Tracey came over with William the Conqueror and was given land in Devon; his grandson, William, was one of Becket's murderers. According to legend he built the church and, as a gesture of remorse, broke his sword and threw it into the river. The pieces were found and welded together, as you can see. (See Lapford, North Devon.)

This completes the eastern half of the region south of Dartmoor. The first of the sites to the south and west of Buckfastleigh is:

🐾 **Dean Combe** where you will find the Pool of the Black Hound. It is haunted by a dog who in real life was a weaver from Dean Prior called Knowles. On his death his spirit refused to leave his body and was transmogrified by the village priest – in a rather un-Christian fashion – into a Black Dog, destined

to empty this pool with a leaky walnut shell before finding salvation.

South of the 385 is:

☙ **North Huish,** where the manor house, now the rectory, is haunted by a bearded monk in a brown habit.

Off Bigbury-on-Sea is:

☙◉ **Borough or Burgh Island.** The ghost of Tom Crocker, a pirate who made this his lair, walks in the third week in August, when the anniversary of his death by hanging in 1395 is celebrated by some locals and many holiday-makers.

North, across the A38, just short of Cornwood, is:

🐎 ✦☙ **Fardel Hall,** now a farm. The Fardel Stone (in the British Museum) was once used to form part of a bridge here. It is inscribed in the Celtic Ogham script which, according to Conway in his *Magic, an Occult Primer,* some believe to have been the written language of Atlantis. Between the house and this bridge is a field, reputedly uncultivatable, which is said to contain buried treasure guarded by a lady in dark and rustling silk, who glides up and down the road at night. Sir Walter Raleigh is said to have lived in the Hall at one time.

🐾☙ **The Tamar river's** banks are haunted by a pack of hounds whose ghostly master is a renegade priest called Dando, seen only on Sunday mornings.

🐎☙ **Plymouth** is inextricably associated with Sir Francis Drake. His adventures were so miraculous that he was thought – and some still hold this opinion – to be in league with the Devil. This is the reason why the southernmost point of the city, west of the docks and the Hoe, is called Devil's Point. It was here that he and other sorcerers conjured up the storm which dispersed the Armada. It is here, too, that the spirits of Sir Francis and his brother magicians (who surely have as just a claim to be called white as black) can still be seen and heard muttering their incantations. More of his haunts will be described later. (See Combe Sydenham, Somerset.)

North, beyond Tamerton Foliot, you will find:

☙ **Ashleigh Barton,** where for generations a ghost has glided through the upper rooms to warn the inhabitants of an impending death in the family.

North again lies:

🐎☙🐾 **Buckland Abbey** (N.T.) which teems with ghosts and legends of Sir Francis Drake, because this was his home. The extensions he made to the Cistercian abbey, which was originally built in 1278, were, it is said, completed in only three nights with the help of the Devil. For invoking Satan's aid, Drake's spirit is condemned to drive a black hearse, drawn by headless horses and followed by headless hounds, along the old road from Plymouth to Tavistock, which passed this place. Tradition also says that a certain box could never be removed from the abbey. Whenever it was placed on a cart, the horses or oxen became paralysed until it was replaced in the house. Here, too, you can see Drake's Drum. A roll on the drum will conjure him from the dead to come to England's aid in time of peril. Many believe that his spirit was made manifest in both Nelson and Blake, and there are people living who heard the drum beat during the Battle of Britain.

The last site on this tour is:

☠🎬 **Tavistock,** scene of one of the best authenticated ghosts in Devon. Kilworthy House was the sixteenth-century home of the Glanvilles. It was rebuilt about 1800 and is now a boys' school run by Father John, who is the latest in a long line of people who have seen the ghost of Judge Glanville's daughter. She was in love with a sailor, but her father wanted her to marry a goldsmith in the town. The girl, her servant and her lover killed the goldsmith and were brought to trial. The judge was her father. He sentenced them all to death. Father John saw the outline of Judge Glanville's daughter in cloak and hood, standing by his bed. On other occasions the ghost has been seen by Father John's sister, by a matron at the school and by a workman. A door to the courtyard (where the Great Hall once stood) will bang violently on the calmest evening when no-one is near, and many have heard the rustle of silk on the stairs. Father John has been asked to perform an exorcism, but he says that as there is nothing evil or frightening about the ghost he does not think it necessary.

An exorcism

DARTMOOR

Setting out from Buckfastleigh you could make a pilgrimage on foot right across the moor from Buckfast Abbey by means of:

👁🚶 **The Abbot's Way.** It enters the moor proper at Cross Furzes, 3 miles west of Buckfastleigh, along the road past Wallaford. This end is haunted by Squire Cabell and his great Black Hounds. His tomb, outside the church, lies in a porch, especially built to keep the stone slab and its occupant safely in place.

◉ **Holne** is past Cross Furzes, where the remains of yet another sacrificial rite can still be observed. Until fairly recently a ram was brought from the moor before daybreak on Old Midsummer's Day, tied to a menhir about six feet tall in Ploy (Play) Field, then killed, roasted whole and cut into slices, for which the inhabitants scrambled. The feast remains.

◉ **Buckland in the Moor** has the same story, but in this case the blood of the animal was sprinkled on those present.

🚶 **New Bridge,** which lies between Holne and Holne Chase, is still believed to be the haunt of pixies.

🎬 **Poundsgate.** Here, on the occasion mentioned immediately below under Widecombe, the Evil One was entertained at the Tavistock Inn. He paid in money which turned into dry leaves after he left.

🎬 **Widecombe in the Moor.** The story of how a bolt of fire did much damage in 1638, and its connection with a stranger who had cloven hoofs, is described in the church. It will also be remembered that it was from Widecombe Fair that the ghost of the grey mare comes in the famous song.

It is a far-flung sort of place, so it would be best to ask how to get onto the Postbridge road, which runs past Blackaton Manor, not to be confused with Blackaton Brook further north. In 1½ miles, to the south of the road, is:

🚶 **Cator Common** where there is a rare apparition – a *white* phantom dog.

👁 **Postbridge.** Turn south down the 3212 towards Two Bridges. This is a very mysterious stretch of road. Drivers of cars and riders of bicycles have had their steering-wheels or handle-bars seized by hairy hands and wrenched to cause an accident.

A mile and a half west of the bridge over Cherry Brook lies:

☆🚶🎬 **Wistman's Wood,** an extremely ancient place, best approached up the valley

Squire Cabell's tomb at Wallaford on the Abbot's Way

from Two Bridges. There is something ominous in the very name of this wind-tortured copse of stunted oaks. I wonder if there is any connection between 'Wist' and 'Wish', for the Wish Hounds are heard here in full cry. It must have been this pack which a moorland farmer saw, riding home from Widecombe Fair. He had done well and celebrated with several mugs of cider. It was a cold night and he topped up with a nip of spirit to keep himself warm. No doubt this gave him courage to address the Master when, nearing his farmstead, he met the phantom pack. 'Heh there, Old Nick!' he cried, 'D'yew have a good run then? D'yew kill?' 'Aye!' said the ghostly huntsman, 'Here's one on them!' He threw the farmer the corpse of a small child. The farmer caught it and to his horror saw that it was his own son. Frantic, he raced home only to be met by his distraught wife who told him that their only child was missing from his cot. It is interesting that the Wild Hunt is sometimes called Herod's Hunt.

The Lych Way is a track (marked southwest of Devil's Tor on the one-inch maps) along which the dead were taken from moorland homesteads for burial at Lydford churchyard. Monks in white and phantom funeral processions have frequently been seen here.

Between Wistman's Wood and Two

Bridges, on the east side of the valley, you will find:

Crockern Tor. According to legend, Old Crockern's ghost can still be seen riding a skeleton horse.

Drive down the road to Princeton and turn left by the side of the chapel. This road runs to Whiteworks which is about a mile's walk from:

Childe's Tomb, the site of one of the most famous legends of Dartmoor. It lies to the south-east, across the treacherous Fox Tor Mires. In the reign of Edward III, Childe, a hunter from Plymstock, got caught in a blizzard. He killed his horse and disembowelled it so that he could shelter in the carcass from the freezing snowstorm. But he died of exposure just the same. He is supposed to have left a message saying that:

The first that brings me to my grave
My lands at Plymstock he shall have.

This caused a greedy rush by the monks of Tavistock to bury the body first. Between the two world wars, two girls, who were complete strangers to Dartmoor, saw monks carrying a bier at this place.

Take the 3212 to Dousland and turn south-east for:

Marchant's Cross. This marks a branch of the Abbot's Way along which Drake, rather than the Devil, hunts the Wish Pack.

Sheepstor is a mile or so to the north-east. By the church, running eastward, there is a lane. If you look up towards the rocky hill you will see a cleft in the ground. This is Pixie's Cave. It also sheltered members of the Elford family during the Civil War. A pin offering is made to the pixies.

Take the road out of Sheepstor which leads round the east side of Burrator and up onto the moor. This should bring you within a few hundred yards of:

Crazywell, Clasiwell or Classenwell, a place shunned by local inhabitants at night, because of a mysterious voice which comes from the middle of the pool and announces the name of the next person in the neighbourhood to die.

The next trip covers the north of the moor. It is a zig-zagging itinerary and you may prefer to cut corners. About 1 mile past Poundsgate is Leusdon, where you will find:

Bel Tor. In a farm enclosure south of the road is a logan stone. On its surface is a basin about a yard square. Good fortune awaits all those who see the reflection of the rising sun in the water which may have collected there.

North-east of Widecombe (already mentioned) and a mile or so south of Manaton is:
☆ **Great Hound Tor,** a place which a number of people find unbearable. Some, who have tried to overcome their inexplicable fear, have fallen into a trance, yet no-one knows why.

Less than 2 miles west, but a little difficult to find, is:
☆ **Jay's or Jane's Grave.** It is on the left of the road although it is marked on the *right* on the O.S. map. This road is a continuation of the 3344 which runs up to Chagford. Kitty Jay was an eighteenth-century orphan, who was seduced by a farmhand, became pregnant and killed herself at Canna's Farm up the road. Like so many pathetic suicides she could not be buried in consecrated ground and so she lies at the junction of three parishes, Manaton, North Bovey and Widecombe. Kitty's last resting place is always mysteriously decorated with flowers, like the Gypsy's Grave near Newmarket (see Cambridgeshire).

Follow the 3344 to its junction with the 3212. Turn left and in about 2 miles you will reach:
🐗 **Warren House Inn.** A traveller, finding himself snowed up, decided to stay the night here. In his bedroom he opened a chest and found a corpse inside. Convinced that he had discovered a murder, he rushed downstairs to tell the landlord, who replied calmly: "Tis only feyther. Us zalted 'n in, 'gainst the time we can get'n up-along Lydford graveyard.' Another story tells how a corpse was salted down with the bacon, which reminds me that to the south-west of Warren House Inn lies:
🐗 **Merripit Hill.** According to local legend, it is haunted by a phantom sow and her hungry litter, who hear that there is a dead horse at Cator and set off to eat it. But when they get there they find nothing but skin and bones, so return to Merripit to start the sad little ritual all over again.

To the east are the tin workings on Challacombe Down. Here is:
🐗 **Chaw Gully,** the 'Roman Mine', which contains buried treasure guarded by a monster somewhere down the shaft and at the top, a raven (which some say is the original one from the Ark). The bird warns the monster when anyone is about to descend the mine to search for the treasure, and it then cuts the rope. However the body is usually found next day lying on the grass near the mouth of the shaft, regurgitated by the monster because he cannot swallow Christians.

The 3212 which leads back to Moretonhampstead is haunted by the ubiquitous Black Dog, and there is something particularly mysterious at:
☆ **Shapley Common,** two miles north-east of Warren House Inn. Just before it is joined by the road from Grimspound, the 3212 crosses one of the headstreams of the Bovey. It is little more than a trickle, carried under the road by a conduit. According to Mrs St Leger-Gordon there are two dips in the road, close together, and it is at the second one that people sometimes feel ice-cold, dogs cringe and shiver and there is an atmosphere of intense fear, for no known reason.

⊛ **Gidleigh.** A stone bridge crosses the Blackaton brook and not only are the sounds of a bloody fight heard here but nearby the ghost of a woman who drowned herself has been seen.

⊛ **Scorhill Circle** is on Gidleigh Common. Faithless wives and wantons had first to wash in Cranmere Pool (q.v.) then return and run round Scorhill three times. They next went down to the river Teign and passed through the Tolman (a holed stone, reputedly good for rheumatism as well as virtue), then up to Grey Wethers where each woman knelt and asked forgiveness. If the stones remained standing all was well, but if they fell – and some did as you can see – the woman would be crushed to death. Grey Wethers lies south-west near Sittaford Tor.

⊛ **Wonson** is situated just north of Gidleigh. At the manor four Cavaliers are sometimes seen playing cards, a reminder of the time when the owner of the manor gambled away his property. In a bedroom unseen hands have tucked people into bed and smoothed pillows.

⊛ **Drewsteignton.** At Bloody Corner a thin trickle of blood is said to seep under the door of a cottage where, many years ago, a murder was committed. There is also reputed to be a field about a mile away in which no animal will stay.

About 3 miles west is:
⊛ **The Spinsters' Rock,** three huge granite slabs, originally forming a cromlech, supposedly set up by spinsters or spinning women. Nearby is Bradford Pool, haunted by a ghost that lures you to your death.

West, and just north of Wonson, lies:
🐗 **Throwleigh.** From Petticoat Lane to Throwleigh village the sound of phantom ponies is heard and the rush of wind is felt as they gallop by; but they are never seen.

The road over the moor will take you to:
🐗 **Okehampton.** The castle (D.E.) is haunted by a Black Hound. I do not think that this is the same animal that follows the 'Coach of Bones' because, according to legend, that

31

The Spinsters' Rock

animal is – like the vehicle it accompanies – a skeleton. The seventeenth-century coach is said to be constructed of the bones of the four husbands of 'the Wicked Lady Howard', all of whom she murdered. According to S. Baring Gould's description of the apparition:

> Human skulls supply the place of those balls which once ornamented the four corners of its roof. Lady Howard rides in it, a pale and sheeted spectre, as her skeleton hound runs before her to bring nightly a blade of grass from Okehampton Park to the Gateway of Fitzford, a penance doomed to endure till the last blade of grass shall be plucked, when the world will be at an end.

Who was the Wicked Lady Howard, and who were the husbands she is supposed to have murdered? Did she in fact murder them? In searching for the answer to this mystery one comes across some strange historical facts. Lady Howard was Mary, daughter of Sir John Fitz of Fitzford, a man with large estates

in Devon and Cornwall, whose house was situated on the southern outskirts of Tavistock. He died early in the seventeenth century when she was nine years old, leaving her an heiress. This no doubt led to the Earl of Northumberland's buying her wardship for £465, although he was no relation and the girl's mother was apparently still alive. Northumberland then sent his brother, Sir Allen Percy, down to the estates at Tavistock and Walreddon to fell sufficient timber – her timber – to pay for the wardship. Within three years Sir Allen had married her (she was twelve years old while he was thirty-one) but the marriage was never consummated. About three years later, in 1611, he died. The Earl of Suffolk then considered her a suitable match for his second son, Sir Thomas Howard; but she eloped with another Thomas, the son of Lord Darcy and afterwards Earl of Rivers. When her second husband died, a few months after their marriage, she married Sir Thomas Howard's younger brother, Sir Charles. They had two daughters before he died in 1622. Her fourth and last husband was Sir Richard Grenville, grandson of the famous naval commander, a tiresome and quarrelsome fellow who spent much of his time either in prison or abroad. Mary then lived at Audley End with the Earl of Suffolk and he may have been the father of her son who was called George Howard. Though her marriages did not last long, there is no direct evidence that she murdered any of her husbands; yet the legend persists, perhaps because there have been children capable of murder throughout history, and Mary Fitz seems to have had some justification. The story of her ghost and the Coach of Bones is told in a ballad which the Keeper of Okehampton Castle may be persuaded to show you. He may also tell you of how his deputy saw the Wicked Lady Howard sitting on a stone, combing her hair. All there is room for here is a verse from Baring-Gould's version:

> My Lady's coach hath nodding plumes
> The coachman has no head
> My Lady is an ashen white
> As one who long is dead.

But do not look for the Coach of Bones on the present Tavistock-Okehampton road, as this was only constructed in 1817. It travels the old road, the King's Way across the moor.

Six miles south of Okehampton, lying between the heads of the Okement and Dart rivers, is:

🌀 **Cranmere Pool,** haunted by the ghost of Bingie Gear (Benjamin Gayer) who, in life, was four times Mayor of Okehampton (1673–1684). His spectre sometimes takes the shape of a mis-shapen dwarf and sometimes a black colt. His spirit was transmogrified into these shapes at an exorcism attended by twenty-four clergymen (one of whom, it is recorded, spoke Arabic). Within living memory people believed that his ghost could be conjured up by reciting the words:

> Bingie Gear, Bingie Gear,
> If thou art near, do ye appear

while walking round a table with the right hand stretched towards it.

South-west of Okehampton on the A30 at:

☺ **Bridestowe** the ghosts of Lady Howard and her coach have been seen, but more often heard, outside the Royal Oak.

☺⚰ **Lydford** is due south. The castle (D.E.) here was described in an Act of Henry VIII as 'one of the most annoius, contagious and detestable places in the realm'. Many suffered here. For

> I have often heard of Lydford law,
> How in the morn they hang and draw,
> And sit in judgment after.

Judge Jeffrey's ghost must feel at home in such surroundings. He is kept company by Lady Howard, whose ghost here takes the form of the Black Hound. In Lydford Gorge there is a haunted pool known as Kitty's Steps, where the ghost of an old woman with a red kerchief on her head is sometimes seen.

To the west lies:

☺ **Lewtrenchard House,** which is haunted by the ghost of an eighteenth-century Mrs Baring-Gould, according to her famous descendant, Sabine. His full account will, surprisingly, be found in *Folklore of the Northern Counties* by W. Henderson. It contains this rather strange description: 'My mother has often told me how she heard the step at night, as though proceeding from high-heeled shoes, and, thinking it might be my father coming to bed . . .' Sabine Baring-Gould himself heard the crunching of unseen carriage wheels on the drive, followed by peals of mocking laughter when any poor mortal looked out to see who was arriving.

Although we have left Dartmoor, it seems a pity to omit a site which lies to the west across the A30 at:

☺⚰ **Stowford.** Hayne Manor is haunted by the ghost of a page-boy murdered by a butler, a man with his head under his arm who foretells the death of the owner, and a Black Dog.

But Black Dogs belong more to North Devon.

NORTH DEVON

The north of Devon can be toured from Torrington, but to get there you pass several sites and can follow the track of one manifestation right up to the town itself. This is the Black Hound of Torrington, investigated by Mrs Carbonnell. All along a straight line from Copplestone to Torrington, she found people who had seen, heard or heard of the Black Hound. Others gave her what, as she says, Devon folk call the 'sideways look' but said nothing. I have checked the route myself; it ends a few miles east of my house and is easily traced on the one-inch scale map. It runs from **Copplestone** through **Down St Mary, Thorne, Stopgate Cross, Blackditch Cross, Wembworthy, Hollocombe, Beaford Moor** and **Allen's Week** near St Giles-in-the-Wood. Mrs Carbonnell's remarkable researches and collected evidence on the Black Hound are given fully in J. Wentworth Day's *A Ghost Hunter's Game Book*, and should on no account be missed.

☺⚰ **Torrington** has another ghost on Castle Hill. It is a soldier killed at the Battle of Torrington in 1646. But the Hound dominates the spectral scene. People have seen it in recent years on the Torrington/Bideford road, where it skirts the Torridge near:

☺ **Weare Giffard Hall,** which has its own two ghosts: Sir Walter Giffard who died in 1243 and who walks from the gatehouse to the church in search of his wife; and a loutish phantom who says, 'Get you gone!'

Although you have now arrived at Torrington, following the run of the Black Hound has led you to miss another site. If, instead of turning off to Down St Mary, you continue along the 377 from Copplestone, you will reach:

☺ **Lapford** where – again according to Mrs Carbonnell – St Thomas of Canterbury gallops through the village at midnight on St John's Eve (December 27), on his way to Nymet. I think this is Nymet Tracey rather than Nymet Rowland because Sir William de Tracey was one of Becket's murderers and is said to have built the church there as part of his penance (see Bovey Tracey, South Devon; and Braunton Burrows). But why Becket appears on December 27 when he was murdered on December 29 is puzzling. Nymet, incidentally, is derived from the Celtic word meaning sacred grove.

Top The crooked cross on the tomb of a murderous rector, wrongly buried in Lapford churchyard

Above St Nectan's Well, Hartland, where the saint walked after being beheaded

Lapford has another ghost as well. In the middle of the last century the rector murdered his curate but was acquitted at his trial because his parishioners 'had never hanged a parson yet, and weren't going to start now'. The rector lived several years more and left instructions that he was to be buried in the chancel, or he would haunt the village. The authorities refused permission and he was buried outside the vestry door. The cross on his grave cannot be kept straight, as you can see, but I was unable to find the hole which cannot be filled in, through which his ghost makes its escape from the tomb to tour the parish.

Clovelly lies between Bideford and Bude, and between Clovelly and Hartland you will find:

◉ **Velly Farm.** Ask Mrs Clark, who lives in the old home of the Velly family, if she is frightened of the ghost of a Cavalier which haunts the place, and she will reply, 'But he is my friend, and has been for more than sixty years!' He walks through the sewing room at the back of the house, and Mrs Clark pointed out to me the chair she puts ready for him, should he want to sit down.

◉🐾 **Hartland.** The parish church, dedicated to St Nectan, is at Stoke, 1½ miles west of Hartland. The road runs beside Hartland Abbey, and the valley from here to the church is said to be haunted by a ghostly procession of monks. At Stoke a small lane on the right, beside a white cottage, leads to St Nectan's Well. St Nectan (son of Brechin), landed at Padstow from Wales, and spent some time at St Nectan's Kieve (see Cornwall) before moving to Devon. At Newton Cross, on the road to Elmscott, he was set upon by a band of robbers and beheaded. However he miraculously picked up his head and walked to St Nectan's Well, which is why the church was built here. This legend may well have been invented to explain the reason for transferring the place of worship to Stoke from St Leonard's (about ½ mile from Newton Cross) where there are still the remains of an ancient chapel.

Continue along the road from Newton Cross till you reach a crossroads where you turn right for:

☆ **Philham.** In Farmer Pengilly's field lies St Clare's or St Cleer's Well, with an image of the saint inside it. This well may originally have been dedicated to St Nectan's brother or nephew. When I first visited the place I knew nothing of holy, curative or wishing wells; yet I felt a strong desire to wish or pray and make some offering; and that led to this book.

South, almost on the Cornish border is:

◉ **Tetcott.** Although the fine Queen Anne mansion was pulled down when the last of this branch of the Arscotts left the place to their cousins the Molesworths, much of the original manor house and buildings remain. As W. G. Hoskins writes in *Devon*, here we feel:

> Impalpable impressions in the air –
> A sense of something moving to and fro.

It is not surprising that this place is haunted by the last of the Arscotts (1718–1788), who

Wistman's Wood on Dartmoor: a run of the Wish Hounds

was above all a great huntsman and so is obviously associated with the Wish Pack. The story of Arscott the Huntsman is told in an eighteenth-century ballad:

> When the full moon is shining as clear as day,
> John Arscott still hunteth the country, they
> say,
> You may see him on Blackbird, and hear in
> full cry
> The pack from Pencarrow to Dazzard go by.

(Strangely enough the same story is told of Dunsland – that fabulous National Trust house which was burned down a few years ago – which was originally the seat of a senior Arscott line.)

Arscott was a very odd character and kept a tame toad named 'Old Dawty' which came when he called and took food from the table. It was thought to be his familiar, but was killed by a pet raven. He took a bottle of flies to church to feed the spiders, and threw apples at the parson. He lived with a lady called Thomasina Spry, whom he may have married on his death bed, but they had no children.

The strangest member of the Squire's household was a dwarf jester called Black John, who once dreamed he was in hell and, when asked what it was like, replied, 'Much as here at Tetcott, with the gentlefolk nearest the fire'. One of Black John's least endearing entertainments – and there were many – was to tie string to the legs of live mice, lower them down his gullet and then pull them up from his stomach.

They say that John's forebear, the Wicked Arscott, 'still pays the penalty in an old oak tree near Tetcott church'. And at the church you will find Black John's tombstone, almost indecipherable, propped up against the side door. The church is reached through the park gates, and lies in front of the house.

North-east you come to:

◉ **Shebbear.** A Christianized pagan custom takes place every year on the evening of November 5. Bell-ringers make as much clamour as possible to frighten away the Devil; then they leave the church, and amid shouts of encouragement, turn the Devil's Stone, which lies just outside the churchyard. If it is not turned annually, calamity will befall the village.

South-east, through Sheepwash, is:

✡◉ **Hatherleigh** where there are two wells. St Mary's is nearly 2 miles north-west of the town. Take the Torrington road, turn west

The last jester in England is buried in Tetcott Church

at Strawbridge, and ¼ mile past Lewer (or Lower on the map) there is a copse to the north. The path has long been overgrown, but 'the old folk' will show you the way. It cured sore eyes. St John's Well is east of the town, on the moor.

The George Hotel is haunted, though the landlord is a sceptic. Before he took over, a tough paratrooper and two other down-to-earth publicans experienced intense cold and saw a naked female phantom.

The 386 will take you back to Torrington. Setting out on the final tour of Devon, go due north to:

✡ **Horwood** where, in the grounds of a

white house, is St Michael's Well, once known for curing sores and eye troubles.

Beyond Barnstaple, on the north bank of the estuary, is:

Braunton Burrows. Here William de Tracey's ghost is condemned to twist ropes out of sand (see Lapford). Just as he manages to succeed, a Black Dog appears with a ball of fire and burns through the strands. But may not this be 'Old White Hat', or is he another ghost? Where the Taw and the Torridge meet, there is a rock called The Crow, and on a spit of sand Jack White Hat paces, calling for a boat to ferry him across to Appledore. Vernon Boyle of Westward Ho! reported that Captain Rice knew a woman in Bideford who was Old White Hat's grand-daughter, but I have yet to find out why he was so anxious to cross the river that his ghost still haunts the place.

Continue to Ilfracombe. On the outskirts is:

Chambercombe. In the manor house (O.P.) a room used by Lady Jane Grey is haunted.

The last site in Devon is just south of the 361 and off the road from South Molton to Torrington. It is:

☆ **Chittlehampton.** Here you will find St Teara's cottage. Alongside is her holy, healing and wishing well, overconcreted and with a pump.

Taunton Castle – where Judge Jeffreys held his Bloody Assizes – is haunted by many of his victims

SOMERSET

✗ *next time* –

I suggest you make Taunton your base for four tours, and then move north to Bath for the fifth (see North Somerset).

To the north-east lie Glastonbury and the Mendips, with their early Christian and Arthurian legends, which lead one down to Cadbury, almost due east of the county town. Just south of the main road from London you can take in the sites which are omitted from Dorset, because they are more easily reached from here. To the south of Taunton lie the Blackmoor Hills and due west the Vale of Taunton Deane. Then there are the Brendon Hills and Exmoor, the Quantocks, which are full of mystery, and finally Bridgwater and Sedgemoor with all their troubled memories of Monmouth and Judge Jeffreys. Each district has its own atmosphere and its quota of ghosts, wells and beliefs. One could divide this legend-laden land historically rather than geographically, and arrange an Arthurian tour, a Monmouth itinerary, or a Christian pilgrimage. But I will leave the reader to select the subjects that interest him and the route he wants to take. I have arranged four looping journeys, each starting and finishing in Taunton, and it is possible to join the first and the last together. All the sites are within thirty miles of the town, but if the weather makes you hesitate to go far afield there are interesting places to visit in Taunton itself.

Taunton. From St George's Church, Wilton, Hammett's Walk runs to Upper High Street beside the Wilton stream. It is haunted by a ghost with green hair.

Taunton Castle echoes to the tramp of Monmouth's men and their captors, who were tried here by the loathsome Judge Jeffreys. A figure in Caroline dress, booted, bewigged and gauntletted, with a sword by his side and a pistol in his hand, has been seen on a landing. The County Museum is located in the castle and includes the Great Hall in which were held what were perhaps the bloodiest assizes of all. The curator has experienced strange phenomena. He has been clutched by a pair of ghostly hands, and has seen the figure of a fair-haired young woman in seventeenth-century dress. There have also been strong poltergeist manifestations. The Castle Hotel includes a part of the original castle, and the Fiddler's Room is not the only place where ghostly music has been heard. At the Tudor

Tavern, Judge Jeffreys' room is haunted, and a photograph appeared in *The Field* on 15 October 1959.

The first tour, I suggest, is one which encircles the Quantocks to the north.

Kingston St Mary. About 2 miles from the centre of Taunton you will come to Tainfield House on your right. Squire Surtees haunts the drive on Old Christmas Eve, riding a grey horse, accompanied by a rattling of chains. Why, no-one seems to know.

To the west is:

☆ **Bishop's Lydeard** where there is a cursing well. The Devil's Whispering Well can be reached either through the churchyard or down a side turning to the left just beyond the church. Past the Bell Inn you will find the well on your left. The last person I saw using it gave an offering of a pin.

At the foot of the Quantocks lies:

☆ **Cothelstone.** Here is the antithesis of a cursing well: a wishing well (O.P.A.), particularly patronized by lovers. It is believed to have been designed by the wife of a former squire. She was a very devout lady and dedicated the well to St Agnes, which was her own name. To reach it you must go past the manor gates (where two of Monmouth's men were hanged, sentenced by Judge Jeffreys), continue along the road past the farm, through a wicket gate on your left, and over the stream, and you will see the well about 50 yards away, on your right.

The road continues up on to the Quantocks. It is patrolled by the Wild Rider, but I would not advise seeking him out. To hear him is unfortunate, to see him disastrous. If you are of a nervous disposition, it would be as well to retrace your steps to the main road at Bishop's Lydeard and drive north. A turning to Stogumber, will lead you to:

Heddon Oak. The tree stands at the junction of the road with two lanes. It dominates the scene, with a great branch jutting out over the road from which several of Monmouth's soldiers were hanged. The sounds of hard-pressed men are heard – hoofbeats, creaking leather and heavy breathing – followed by strangling noises. There are people in the village who will tell you that they always feel a choking sensation when passing this tree.

☆ **Stogumber** is haunted by the Wild Hunt, which rides through the streets with baying hounds, trotting horses and jingling bridles. Some say it rode through as recently as 1960, but no-one dared to look out of the window when the sounds were heard.

Here you will also find Harry Hill's Well.

There is a presence in Judge Jeffreys' room at the Tudor Tavern, Taunton

Turn left down the hill in the village, and then turn left to Springfield Maltings where the well is to be found. Harry Hill was a leper who was cured at this well; more recently it has cured other maladies. The well is in poor repair, but the water is still sweet.

To the west is:

Combe Sydenham (O.P.A.) on the 3188. Along this road the ghost of Sir George Sydenham comes galloping northwards. The white figure rides a headless grey horse. Sir George turned against Sir Francis Drake. Drake was engaged to Sydenham's daughter (the wedding actually took place eight years

39

Sir Francis Drake

later) but he spent so long at sea that Sydenham decided to marry her off to someone else. Drake somehow got wind of this, although hundreds of miles away, and fired a cannon-ball which landed at Stogumber Church just as the bride was arriving. This so unnerved everyone that the wedding was called off. The cannon-ball was, in fact, a meteorite about the size of a croquet ball, which was kept for many years at Combe Sydenham.

These last sites have been taking you away from the Quantocks; if you prefer, they can be included in the Exmoor tour.

Across the 358, north-east towards Quantoxhead, lies:

Weacombe where a ghostly dog, of friendly disposition, leads those who are lost back to safety.

North again is:

Staple. On the hills round here a ghostly figure known as the Woman of the Mist appears, and has been seen quite recently. A local solicitor will vouch for her; she appeared to him in the form of an old woman carrying a bundle of sticks.

St Audrie's Bay is on the coast to the north. From:

St Audrie's Farm to Perry Farm the road is haunted by a Black Dog. Some even say that the whole four-mile stretch of road from St Audrie's to Holford is haunted; not only by a Black Dog, but also by a grey shapeless Thing, and sometimes a coffin is seen lying in the road.

At:

Holford, further east, the Plough Hotel is said to be haunted by the ghost of a Spanish traveller, murdered there in 1555.

Nomansland lies near Dodington, between Holford and the Castle of Comfort. Every Christmas Eve at midnight a coach and four black horses drive up, turn, and drive away again. Some say that a ghostly lady walks from Holford to Nether Stowey: at other times she rides in the coach.

Shervage Wood will be found south of the road, between Holford and the Castle of Comfort. This place maintains a vestige of the Wayland Smith legend. (See Fiddington; and Wayland Smith's Cave, Berkshire.) Wayland's Pool is where he cooled the horseshoes he made for the Wild Hunt. Local farmers will tell you that any horse will stand quietly here, even if the rider dismounts and walks away. This wood was also once the home of a dragon known locally as the 'Gurt Vurm'.

Walford's Gibbet is south-east of the Castle of Comfort. The path leading to it is haunted by John Walford, a twenty-four-year-old charcoal-burner who dearly loved Ann Rice, but whose remote and lonely occupation led to his being forced to marry a slut called Jenny because she hung around his hut until she found herself carrying his child. He married her on 18 June 1789, and killed her seventeen days later. He was a dark handsome man – some said a Gypsy – and popular. The judge, Lord Kenyon, wept as he sentenced him to death, and so did many others on the day he was hanged, first by the neck until he was dead, and then in a cage for all the world to see, for a year and a day. The strange thing was that for a week after the hanging his face did not take on the horrible look of most hanged men. It remained dignified and handsome, perhaps due to the prayers of Ann Rice, with whom he had a touching reunion on his way to the scaffold (under which his body lies buried in its iron cage). There are people who say the putrid smell of rotting flesh hangs on the air.

At Dead Woman's Ditch the ghost of Walford's wife Jenny has been seen, although some believe she was not murdered there.

The high hill to the west is:

Dowsborough. This was the site of a Danish camp, and on wild autumn nights the sounds of soldiers carousing, then fighting

Right Walford's Gibbet

can be heard. One can also hear the voice of one little Danish boy who was saved from the English, singing.

☆☠ **Nether Stowey** must at one time have been a centre for cures. St Peter's Well is probably the same as Stowey Blindwell. It was known as being good for the eyes. The well is on private property; it is in good condition and the water is excellent to drink. At the house there is the ghost of a monk who walks from the church to the house for vespers. He has been seen quite recently by a guest who knew nothing of the story.

There are references to other wells in the vicinity: St David's Well and Seven Well's Combe lie just beyond Adscombe. Less pleasant is the 'galley-beggar' at Over Stowey crossroads who, shrieking with demoniacal laughter, sits on a hurdle, takes his head in his hand and slides downhill past Bincombe to Nether Stowey, surrounded by a strange luminous light.

Eastwards, and to the north of the Bridgwater road, you will find:

🐴 **Fiddington.** At Keenthorne Corner Wayland Smith is said to have worked and it was he who shod the Devil's mount (see Shervage Wood). Horses still behave strangely at this spot.

👹🐕 **Stogursey** lies north-west. There are many stories here about witches and Black Dogs. Certainly within living memory there was a witch who lived in a house in Cock Wood and, if anyone displeased her, would 'spell' them so that their carts overturned as they passed the house. Some say that in 1960 a motorist threatened to sue the owner of a Black Dog which jumped out at him, but he was met with an enigmatic smile and a 'sideways look'.

Just north is:

☆🐴 **Wick Moor.** This is now the site of the Hinkley Nuclear Power Station. In the middle is a barrow known as the Pixie's Mound, where a man found what he thought was a broken toy spade. He mended it and left it by the barrow. The next time he passed that way he found the spade gone and a plate of cakes in its place. These he ate, and ever after enjoyed good fortune. When the Power Station was being built, local inhabitants warned the constructors that if they built over the barrow nothing would work. They took this advice; the mound is untouched and surrounded by barbed wire.

East of Stogursey is:

☆👹 **Combwich,** on the banks of the Parrett, a river which is still believed to demand as an annual sacrifice a man, a woman and a child

in turn. Across the river on the Pawlett side a phantom coach has been seen.

Between Combwich and Cannington is:

👹👁🐕 **Cannington Park** where there are the remains of a Danish camp. It is said to be haunted by witches, and a headless rider on a black horse has been seen. Some people believe that the Yeff Hounds – or Wild Hunt – ride out from here through Dowsborough (q.v.) to Crowcombe Heathfield.

👁☆ **Wembdon,** once a village, is now almost a suburb of Bridgwater. On the hill appears the ghost of a woman in a gauzy shawl and with glaring eyes. There is also a holy well here (now on private property). It was an eye well but rather more elaborate than some, being situated in a little baptistry with stone seats. The water is still pure.

South-west is:

⚔🐕 **Ruborough Camp,** sometimes described as Roman, which, since it is triangular, is most unlikely. There is a legend of buried treasure here, which has to be dug for when the moon is full. It is guarded by a ghostly horse and chariot which are liable to run you down. One wonders if these were ever depicted on the hillside as on Gog Magog Hill in Cambridgeshire (q.v.).

And so, back to Taunton.

To get the full flavour of the strange flat land where the Battle of Sedgemoor was fought, and the mystic quality of Avalon, on your second tour you should leave Taunton on the 361 Glastonbury road. After 11 miles you turn left towards Bridgwater on the 372. One mile north of Westonzoyland lies the bloody battlefield of:

👁 **Sedgemoor.** A signpost in the village will lead you there. The river Carey turns into the King's Sedgemoor Drain at this point, and here a ghostly band of soldiers is to be seen, while voices are heard crying, 'Come on over!' These are the pathetic remnants of Monmouth's brave army. On July 3 Monmouth's ghost is seen, but never heard, escaping from the battlefield. One of the saddest stories of the battle is how a famous local runner was captured and told that his life would be spared if he could keep up with a horse. Bets were made and the race was run. The man did keep up with the horse; but his captors killed him just the same, and his sweetheart drowned herself on Sedgemoor Levels. Her ghost is seen, accompanied by the sound of his running feet and laboured breathing, and the galloping hooves.

Now make your way north-east across the A39 to:

The Duke of Monmouth's spectre can be seen on July 3 on Sedgemoor

☆ **Edington.** The road you take to the village is called Holy Well and you should follow it down past the church to a T-junction. Turn right and the well is a few yards further on, on your right. It is set in a large baptistry and is still used. The smell of sulphur is quite noticeable.

The next site is due north, bordering Axbridge:

☺ **Shute Shelve Hill.** At the Hanging Field there are three ghosts, two male and one female – an unholy trinity – who were executed for the murder of the woman's husband.

North-west at:

☺ **Banwell,** the abbey has been haunted for years, but there is more recent evidence of the supernatural in one of the nearby houses. Footsteps are heard descending the stairs accompanied by the sound of sobbing and the rustle of silk.

🐎☺🐕 **Locking** lies to the west, just off the main road. A legend says that Sir John Plumley joined Monmouth; after the disaster at Sedgemoor he managed to escape and hid either in a coppice on his estate or in his own manor house. He was unwittingly betrayed by one of the family dogs. He was hanged from an elm tree which was still standing at the beginning of this century. His wife then took her pet dog in her arms and drowned

herself in the well. These two are said to haunt the yew trees at the end of the manor walk. Sir John and his dog have also been seen.

Now take the southern side of the Mendips to:

🐎 **Priddy.** This is where Christ is said to have spent part of 'the lost years' – that period of His life between the ages of twelve and thirty about which nothing is known. People may wonder why there is no evidence of His visit but it is possible that at that time many young men came here with the traders from the eastern Mediterranean who were dealing in tin from Cornwall and perhaps lead from the Mendips. I have found quite a lot of people who believe that Joseph of Arimathea was a tin trader who visited the Cornish mines between A.D.13 and 30 and brought Jesus with him. Joseph is also thought to have been the uncle of the Virgin Mary. (See Glastonbury; Padstow, Cornwall; and Kidwelly, Wales.)

🐎☺ **Wookey Hole** lies south. The stones at the entrance to these caves are said to be the Witch of Wookey and her demons, turned to stone under a curse uttered by a young monk from Glastonbury, whose love affair had been blighted by her spells. Early this century a woman's skeleton, with a dagger, and that of a goat were discovered ten feet deep in the cave.

A Victorian cottage nearby is reputed to be haunted by the ghost of an old woman with clutching hands, smelling of mould. An attempt at exorcism was made, I believe, in 1912.

South again, you come to that heartland of legend:

🐎☆ **Glastonbury.** You will find most of the fabulous stories in the guidebooks. Under the spring on the Tor lies the chalice used at the Last Supper – the Holy Grail sought by King Arthur and his Knights of the Round Table. It was put there by Joseph of Arimathea on a visit in A.D. 63 or 64. He also thrust his staff into the earth, praying for a miracle which would convert the Druids to Christianity. The stick took root and grew into a thorn tree that flowers every Christmas Day. (The original stem is said to have been hacked down – typically – by a Roundhead vandal, who, I am delighted to say, cut off his own leg at the same time.) King Arthur and Queen Guinevere were buried, or reburied, here.

Fact and fable are inextricably mixed, and the fact is sometimes the more mysterious of the two. Obviously much of the legend is pre-Christian. For the Celts, Glastonbury was the Glassy Island, where the souls of the dead were separated from their bodies and received by Gwyn, King of the Fairies, and Leader of the Wild Hunt. Much of the uncovering of the ruins was based on a manuscript written in medieval script, apparently by a monk but actually by an officer in the Royal Marines, automatically, while in a trance. He knew nothing of either the subject or his method of conveying the message, and I can remember my parents, who had inspected the original documents, telling me that he was not interested in what he had written.

The spring which rises at the bottom of Chalice Hill is endowed with miraculous properties. Some people believe that the water is actually impregnated with the Precious Blood. It has certainly wrought miracles, particularly among those suffering from asthma. On 5 May 1751, 10,000 people visited the well. There is another well, dedicated to St Mary, in the abbey crypt.

Weary-All Hill also has its legends, but there is no space to tell them here.

The first site on the third tour is south-east of Taunton.

Curry Mallet. Here clashing swords are heard in the banqueting hall, the rustle of silk upstairs, and footsteps going up to the Minstrel's Gallery; but on 20 July 1962 it was suggested in *The Times* that 'the ghosts in the house were nothing to those in the garden'.

To the east, south of Langport, is:

Muchelney Abbey (D.E.), the setting of a sad and haunting story. An impecunious young man fell in love with the daughter of a rich knight who forbade their marriage. He became a monk and eventually prior at Muchelney, where he found his love, who had become a nun. They planned to elope but were overheard and betrayed. He was sent to a monastery far away; and she, waiting for her lover in a secret passage, may be there yet, for they walled her up and let her starve to death.

Continue east to Sparkford, where a road leads north to:

South and North Barrow. An ancient causeway used to run between these two villages, and on Midsummer's Eve the ghosts of King Arthur and his Knights ride out, accompanied by foot soldiers whose spears and lances are tipped with flame (see Cadbury Castle). If you drew a straight line from Cadbury Castle to Glastonbury, you would find it passed between these two villages.

Just north of Castle Cary lies:

Ansford where St Andrew's Well has long held a reputation for curing eye troubles, but is now only a muddy pool which lies across a field behind the church.

To the north-east is:

✡ **Bruton.** St Patrick's Well in Patwell Street is the best known, but also reported are Ladywell and Combe Hill Well. Still others are mentioned.

The road north to Milton Clevedon leads you to:

☻ **Creech Hill.** It is thought wise to take a lantern and a staff of hazel tipped with iron if you travel this way at night, as protection from a tall ghostly figure who makes the surroundings hideous with maniacal laughter.

You can now visit the North Dorset sites which you will find more easily approached on this trip. South of Wincanton is:

☠ ⛏ ☻ **Purse Caundle.** At the manor (O.P.) you may hear the chanting of plainsong. You may also be told the story of how, 100 years ago, the old staircase was removed by a fairy. The ghostly huntsman's horn, accompanied by the baying of the spectral hounds of King John's pack, is heard on the Bowling Green on Midsummer's Eve.

🗡 ☻ **Sherborne.** Osmond, one of William the Conqueror's knights who became Bishop of Sarum, made Sherborne Castle (O.P.) over to the Church with a curse on all who should take it out of ecclesiastical hands (see Battle Abbey, Sussex). Lay owners who have suffered misfortune include the Duke, and, at a later date, the Earl of Somerset, Sir Walter Raleigh (who built the new castle) and Prince Henry. The present owners, the Digbys, seem to have escaped the malediction. Sir Walter Raleigh's ghost is said to appear on St Michael's Eve (September 29). He strolls through the grounds of the castle and sits under the tree which bears his name. It was here, while smoking a pipe of the first tobacco brought from America, that he was 'extinguished' by a terrified servant who doused him with a pitcher of beer.

Go north and you will come to:

☻ **Poyntington.** A young Royalist called Baldwin Malet led a pathetic band against the Roundheads here in June 1646. They were slaughtered; Malet's body lies in the churchyard, but the others were buried where they fell and you can still see the mounds in a meadow near the stream. A hundred years ago, no villager would go near them at night for fear of seeing the ghostly band of headless soldiers accompanied by one poor girl who somehow got mixed up in the slaughter.

Sherborne Castle carries a curse for most lay owners

Top Sandford Orcas has fourteen supernatural tenants

Above The Chilton Cantelo skull is quieter in a cupboard than a grave

North-west lies:

Sandford Orcas. The history-drenched manor (O.P.) here belongs to the Medlycotts and is rented by Colonel Claridge, who says it has fourteen ghosts. There are, among others, a Lady in Green in the south bedroom; the Lady in Red silk (she is sometimes just a cold breeze) whose presence is felt on the stairs at 11.50 a.m.; a dog; a monk; a yokel who hanged himself in the gatehouse; Sir Hubert Medlycott; an Elizabethan lady in the courtyard; the sound of a spinet; and the ghost of a seven-foot-tall rapist, who only appears in the presence of virgins. He is thought to have been a footman who seduced a number of maid-servants, which, according to Colonel Claridge, is why it is now impossible to keep any living-in staff. However, he adds that since a Judas tree in the garden fell down, the rapist has not been seen.

Returning north to Somerset you will pass:

Cadbury Castle which can be approached by a lane in South Cadbury. Although there is not much to see, this is the most likely site of King Arthur's Camelot. 'Cam' is found in place-names hereabouts and there is a local tradition associating the king with a wishing well (there are two wells near the site), a palace, and a 'hunting causeway'. His ghost and those of his knights have frequently been seen and heard, which seems to belie the legend that they ride out of the hill only every seven years. (See South and North Barrow.)

To the south-west is:

Chilton Cantelo. At Higher Farm, opposite the church, is a skull that refuses to be buried. It belonged to Theophilus Broome who died in 1670 and requested that his head should be kept in the farmhouse. Many attempts have been made to inter it, but those who try are, according to the inscription on the tomb, 'deterred by horrid noises, portentive of sad displeasure', not to mention broken spades and other mishaps. The present owners, Mr and Mrs Kerton, are most willing to show the skull by appointment.

South of Yeovil is:

East Coker. At Westwells, near the road leading to Coker Court, is a holy well, good for the eyesight. From time to time a ghostly coach and horses drive up to Coker Court, pick up a passenger and drive away. There are villagers today who have both seen and heard it.

Due west is:

Merriott. At the manor house another ghostly coach and four have been heard rumbling up to the front door, or maybe this is the same coach which runs between the two houses. It would be interesting to know if they were connected in any other way.

Crewkerne. The main road between here and Chard is haunted. Horses are heard galloping hard, and a phantom fight has been seen between smugglers and preventive men, among them a wounded customs officer who is heard gasping for breath.

Chard. In 1662 a very odd occurrence took place here. On July 12, towards evening, two suns appeared in the sky. Two days later at 10 p.m. three moons were seen. Then on July 19 two suns again appeared. Some people think that these strange manifestations were U.F.O.s.

There is one more excursion into Dorset. To the south-east lies:

Forde Abbey (O.P.), originally built in 1142–8 to house twelve Cistercian monks. At the dissolution of the monasteries, the abbot was a man called Thomas Chard, and his ghost still haunts the place he loved. He is most often seen near the table in the Great Hall.

Back past Chard to the north-west is:

☆ **Whitestaunton** where St Agnes's Well has been famous for centuries for curing sprains and broken bones. Apparently it has been used by the boys of Taunton School who injure themselves at football.

On the 3170 one comes across a geographical mystery. On the o.s. map there are two sites, a mile apart, but with the same name:

Robin Hood's Butts. These are two barrows. The first one on the left of the road is easily accessible, but the second is more difficult to find. The story goes that under one of these barrows is a hoard of gold, but it is useless to try to dig it up, for the faster one digs the faster the earth falls back into the ground, being thrown there by unseen hands. Robin Hood or 'Hodekin' was established as a forest elf in pagan times, and presumably this name was taken by the famous outlaw of Sherwood forest as a pseudonym.

Holmans Clavel is to the north, and the inn here is haunted by a poltergeist who plays skittles in the middle of the night.

To the west is:

Churchstanton. At Merlan Corner a white mist is seen which sometimes transforms itself into a headless rider, but whether mist or apparition, the sound of trotting is heard.

To the north is:

Corfe where a ghost known as the White Rider has been seen. This could be the same spectre who appears at:

Duddlestone as a phantom headless rider in a flowing cloak on a grey horse.

This ends the third tour from Taunton.

The final tour covers the Vale of Taun Deane, Exmoor and the Brendon Hills. Ma your way south-west to the Wellington Monument; to the west is:

Park Farm. In the copse above the farm is a muddy pool, thought once to be the entrance to Hell. It was here that Sir John Popham's ghost (see Littlecote, Wiltshire) crawled out of Hell and was allowed to make its way to the family vaults in Wellington Church, but only by one cock's stride a year. As he died in 1607 his ghost would still have a long way to go, but according to legend, things are even worse. Apparently the ghost reached a farm where the haunting caused such a disturbance that the farmer got a white witch to send Popham back to the pit. His ghost then had to start its journey all over again.

You could now visit two sites in Devon. If you are here on the Eve of Epiphany (January 6) you should go to:

Dunkeswell, north of Honiton, where, on this date, they wassail the apple trees (see also Carhampton; and Warleggan, Cornwall). The farmer, accompanied by his farm workers, carries a pail of cider with roasted apples floating in it, to the orchard. Each person takes a cup of cider and says or sings:

> Health to thee, old apple tree,
> Well to bear pocketsful, hatsful,
> Pecksful, bushelsful!

The cups are then drunk and the remainder thrown at the tree (a libation for the tree's spirit) while all shout 'Huzza!' Similar rituals take place in both Devon and Cornish villages. Sometimes guns are let off to scare away witches.

Multiple suns and moons appeared over Chard in 1662

The second Devon site lies north-west, across the A38, but is of academic interest only. The house at Samford Peverell, frequently mentioned as the scene of poltergeist manifestations was burned down some twenty-five years ago.

Now go back into Somerset and make your way northwards to:

Langford Budville. The Squire of Norton Fitzwarren once dined with friends after a hard day's hunting. As he rode home late at night, a couple of stray hounds caused his horse to shy and fall. Both horse and rider were killed and their ghosts haunt the drive leading to the squire's home, now the site of an army camp, just west of Taunton. There are other versions of this story. One says that the hounds which frightened the horse were a part of the Wild Hunt and that the Devil, as Master, had claimed another 'kill'. Some consider the squire was 'a fearless horseman from up along Waterrow' who, after dining at Chipley Park, rode home at midnight along Langford Heathfield where he met the Wild Hunt who caused the accident. Anyhow, the place is haunted.

A few miles to the west is:

Bathealton where there is an eye well used to this day. It is on Yeancott Farm, owned by Mr and Mrs Cottrell, who willingly allow people to visit it. Mrs Cottrell managed to cure her family's eye trouble with this water, but, she says, it must never touch your hands or the properties will be destroyed. A very clean bottle should be held directly under the flow.

West of Milverton a turning off the 361 leads to Fry's Quaking House; a few yards past it is:

Friends' Burial Ground, an old Quaker graveyard, haunted by a man in Quaker costume. He must be a benign ghost for the place is filled with a sense of ineffable peace which alone makes it worth visiting.

Now go west and north to:

Dulverton. On the edge of the village is a housing estate called Bathwater. Immediately opposite a large garage is a field – behind the houses – which is the site of an eye well, the offering being a red rag hung on a nearby tree. There are signs of a ruin in the top corner of the field which may have been a bathhouse. The name Bathwater suggests total immersion rather than bathing the eyes.

Take the road to the moor by Higher Combe, and you will come to a crossroads; a few yards to the north lies:

The Caratacus Stone. Nobody knows its origin although it is thought to be fifth

The Caratacus Stone

century. It is haunted by the ghost of a foolish carter who tried to uproot it to get at the treasure which supposedly lies beneath. The stone crushed him to death. The apparition is both seen and heard on foggy nights.

The moor road leads north-west over Winsford Hill past:

Wambarrows, haunted by a Black Dog guarding buried treasure.

Now go through Simonsbath and take the 3358 towards Challacombe. In about 5 miles there is a valley on your right. From here you must walk to:

Pinkworthy Pond. The footpath is well marked by yellow arrows and squares. This man-made pond lies near the dreaded bog known as The Chains. It is haunted by the ghost of Farmer Gammon, a widower from Bowley Barton, who drowned himself here in 1889 because when he wanted to remarry, the woman turned him down.

The road which runs north from Exford through Edgcott and Hillhead Cross is haunted from:

Chetsford Water to Hawkecombe Head. Horses shy, jib, sweat and refuse to move forward. No Exmoor ponies are *seen* here after dark, although the clatter of hooves and strange whinnies are heard.

To the east is:

Porlock. The steep road down to the town is haunted by ghostly grey horses, possibly the spectres of a runaway team which were killed on this notorious hill.

Porlock Weir. The bodies of three sailors, one a Negro and one a boy, were washed ashore here and buried in the Marsh Field, 100 yards from the beach. Their ghosts have been seen both by local inhabitants and visitors. M. Chetwynd-Stapylton reports that the gravestones have been taken and one of the graves has recently been disturbed.

Here you could make a diversion if you wish. If you leave Porlock by the A39, a turning on the right will take you through:

Horner to Luccombe. Between the two villages is a wayside chapel dedicated to St Dubricius where there is reputedly gold buried beneath the altar.

To the south-east are:

Cutcombe and Timberscombe. This is another badly haunted stretch of road, particularly on the sharp bend at Sully where accidents have been attributed to a phantom hearse without a driver but with four headless black horses. At Cutcombe there is a healing well dedicated to St Luke.

If you do not want to make this diversion, continue along the A39 and turn north for:

Selworthy. The road from this village to Tivington crosses the A39 about a mile further on. The phantom Black Dog seen here is said to be the spirit of a suicide.

Continue along the A39 to:

Minehead. A Hobby Horse Festival is held here at Maytide – April 30, May 1 and 2. The teasers – at one time called gullivers – have disappeared (they remain at Padstow, Cornwall, q.v.) but shreds of the old fertility rites still exist.

In the seventeenth century this town was the site of a haunting which became a *cause célèbre*. Mrs Leakey's ghost was known as the Whistling Spectre; she appeared in the street,

on the shore and even at sea, whistling up the wind.

Dunster to the south-east, has St Leonard's Well for the eyes. It lies in a baptistry $\frac{1}{2}$ mile from the town centre. Cross St George's Street to Conduit Lane and go up a sloping path to find it.

Carhampton, on the A39, is where they wassail the apple trees on Old Twelfth Night (January 17). (See Dunkeswell.) Toasted bread, soaked in cider, is put into the forks of the branches.

Withycombe. Opposite the south door of the church is an ancient tombstone, said to be that of Madam Joan Carn of Sandown Manor, a famous North Somerset witch, who murdered three husbands. She was drowned by being flung into the Witch's Pool at Sandhill Farm, east of Withycombe. Madam Carn's ghost has been exorcised from Sandhill, but she is supposed to be returning to Withycombe churchyard at the rate of one cock's stride a year. She is said to have been buried here in 1612. But was she? There is a story that after this woman died, mourners saw her coffin buried, yet on returning to Sandhill found her frying eggs and bacon in the kitchen.

You could see the pool at Sandhill by taking the small back road out of Withycombe and then continue along it till you get to:

Rodhuish. Here lived a red-haired butcher's boy who wanted to frighten a youth from nearby Croydon who was visiting the village. He dressed up in the skin and horns of a freshly killed animal, to impersonate the Devil, and jumped out on the visitor from behind a tree. The youth attacked what he took to be the Evil One, and ran back to Rodhuish crying, 'I've killed the Devil!' The villagers, guessing what had happened, ran to the spot but all they found were the animal skin and horns. The boy was never seen again. Some people say that the Devil claimed his own and that the boy's ghost can be seen riding behind the Prince of Darkness on Croydon Hill, where his screams and groans are heard.

Now make your way to the coast at Blue Anchor. The road to Watchet runs down:

Cleeve Hill, haunted by a pack of Yeff Hounds.

Continue through Watchet to:

Williton, where you will find St Decuman's Well, once famed for curing scurvy and much patronized by sailors. It is down the lane by the side of the church and is a series of stone basins one below the other, approached by a flight of stone steps.

The elegance of Bath is unsurpassed; it also has some intriguing ghosts, so it is the obvious base from which to visit the sites of North Somerset.

✗ ☙ **Bath.** Next to the Theatre Royal stands the Garrick Head Hotel which has two ghosts at least. It is said to have been a gaming-house run by Beau Nash, and linked by a secret passage to the theatre. Near the entrance hovers the ghost of a Regency rake. Some think he is responsible for the strong smell of scent in the cellar, while others suggest that this emanates from a lady who committed suicide when her lover lost a duel in which she was the stake. Then there is a Grey Lady who threw herself out of the window. She is also seen in the Theatre Royal, sitting in a box. Her story remains a mystery.

There is a ghost in Grosvenor Place. The exact building remains unrecorded but should not be difficult for the diligent ghost-hunter to find (in September 1953 the second-floor flat was inhabited by a Mr Brinworth). The apparition takes the form of a woman in an old-fashioned dress and bonnet.

✿ **Bathford** is almost a suburb of Bath, situated 4 miles to the north-east, off the London road. Here St Anthony's Well is reputed to cure sore eyes.

From Bath you may like to visit:

✿ **Bristol** where in St Anne's Park you will find St Anne's Well. It is curative and has been patronized by royalty. Henry VII and his queen visited it.

Take the 370 south, out of Bristol, which will lead you to:

☙ **Brockley** where a road goes up to Brock-

A dragon flies between Dolebury Hill and Cadbury Castle

ley Combe. This is a very haunted place. First there is a phantom coach, driven hell-for-leather, which has caused many accidents. Then there is the ghost of a wicked parson called Hibbetson who rescued the Squire of Chelvey when he was injured, nursed him back to health and then, having made him change his will, murdered him. Brockley Manor is said to be haunted, and this may be connected with the old woman whose ghost brings madness or death to all who see it. Luckily it appears only every twenty-six years and is not due again till 1990.

Cadbury Camp. Beltane rites on May Day and Midsummer rituals were performed here in this century, and black magic ceremonies more recently still. There is also a tradition of buried treasure here:

> If Cadbury Castle and Dolebury Hill down delved were
> Then all England [or Somerset] might plough with a golden share.

Dolebury Hill lies 4 miles to the south. There is a Cadbury Castle and Dolebury Hill in Devon, and the same rhyme applies. A dragon flies between the castle and the hill in both cases. The matter is further complicated by the other Somerset Cadbury, thought to be Camelot.

South-east of Cadbury Castle, at:

✿ **Wrington,** is the mysterious Waterstone: the remains of a neolithic burial chamber which have become endowed with magical properties. Milk and primroses were offered to some unknown god. The top of the stone has a hollow in which water collects and never dries up. It is difficult to find but Mr H. C. Smith, an erudite local historian, is very willing to give instructions. Another legend says that when full moon falls on Midsummer's Day, the stone dances.

Further east still, along the 368, is:

☙ **West Harptree.** To the south is Harptree Combe. This contains the ruins of Richmont Castle, haunted by a Gournay who previously owned the place. This may be the same ghost who, in a long cloak and black hat, has been seen at the wishing well. At Devil's Batch, a labourer, returning home late from work, saw a dark knight who said, 'Past midnight, and time you left this place to whom it belongs!' Gournay Court once belonged to a cousin of mine, and when I stayed there I heard that in the Long Gallery there was the ghost of a lady who went out onto the balcony, which you can see from the road, in the centre of the façade.

To the south-east you will find:

✿ **Masboro' or Maesbury Castle** alongside

the golf-course. It is said that if you go up
here on Easter Morn, you will see a lamb on
the face of the rising sun.

☻ **Cannard's Grave Inn,** south of Shepton
Mallet, is at the intersection of five roads.
Giles Cannard was an innkeeper who made a
fortune out of dealing with highwaymen and
smugglers. He stooped to forgery though, and
was found out. Rather than submit to the law,
he hanged himself and was buried at the crossroads where once his gang of footpads used
to lie and wait. His ghost now frightens
travellers brave enough to pass that way in
the dark. His portrait swings from a gibbet
on the inn sign.

East of Shepton Mallet is:

✿ **Doulting.** Here there are two wells. St
Aldhelm's and St Agnes' Fountain. The
first had a reputation for curing ailing and
spell-bound beasts. It can be found by taking
a path from the cul-de-sac leading to the
church and then following a footpath on the
right. It gushes out of a wall behind what was
once the vicarage garden. St Aldhelm used to
sit here and read the psalms while suffering
from an illness in 709. St Agnes' Fountain
cured paralysed cattle 'as long as they were
not stolen'. It may be where a pump can be
seen on the left of the approach to the church,
but people seem to have forgotten.

South-east is:

✿ **Witham Friary** where St Dunstan's Well
once had a great reputation for curing epilepsy.

North of Frome is:

🐾 **Orchardleigh** (O.P.). There is an interesting legend here. The Lake Lady is believed
to be half-ghost, half-fairy.

☻ **Beckington** lies to the east. In 1872
Beckington Castle, which is in the village, was
advertised for sale, and among the desirable
characteristics listed were ghosts and subterranean passages.

✿ **Rode** is barely 2 miles to the north. Puck's
Well cured eye ailments. It is on the Bradford
road, 50 yards from the crossroads at the top
of Rode Hill. There was 'the devil of a row'
about it a few years ago when one farmer
tried to enclose it and another to cut off the
supply. The Water Board, I was told, stepped
in. Also marked on the o.s. map is the Devil's
Bed and Bolster, but I have not yet discovered
its significance.

North-west, on the way back to Bath, a
small detour will take you to:

☻ **Wellow.** Here in a cottage garden you
will find St Julien's Well. It is haunted by a
White Lady whose appearance, according to
one story, is reputed to foretell the death of
the Lords of Hungerford.

Top Cannard's Grave Inn sign

Above The water from Puck's Well, Rode, cured
eye complaints

DORSET

I have chosen Dorchester as a centre because it is the hub of an area which is full of mystery: within a radius of twenty miles there are more than two dozen sites. One can also slip over the border for one or two places which are more easily visited from this base. Ghosts predominate, and they are as good a collection as you will find anywhere. First:

☺ **Dorchester.** St Peter's Church is said to be haunted by Nathaniel Templeman, one-time rector. He appears only in order to remonstrate when some evil deed is done. He literally put the fear of God into two churchmen who, exhausted by putting up the Christmas decorations, thought they would refresh themselves with Communion wine.

In the Old Malthouse in Fordington, at the junction of High Street and High East Street, ghostly footsteps are frequently heard.

South-west is Chesil Beach, and at the north-west end you will find:

☆ **Abbotsbury.** On top of the hill, overlooking the village, is St Catherine's Chapel; check at the Post Office that the door is unlocked before you make the 250-foot ascent. In the south doorway are wishing holes. In less sybaritic days one would put one's knees in the lower hole and the hands above, then wish. Now all you have to do, I am told, is drop a pin inside a pillar.

To the north-west lies:

☺ **Litton Cheney.** Here you will find Baglake House, the home of William Light who committed suicide in 1748. His spectre is sometimes joined in the drawing-room and summerhouse by another ghost in rustling silk. Telekinesis has also been reported.

Follow the A35 to:

☺⛪🗡 **Lyme Regis.** The Angel Inn is haunted, and strong manifestations have been reported in the last decade. The Great House, or Chatham House, in Broad Street, is said to be haunted by Judge Jeffreys, wearing his robes, wig and black cap and carrying a bloody bone. Some of the assistants at the International Stores, which now occupy part of the building, can give details. Strange things have been heard, if not seen, recently, though the ghost has been renamed 'Annie'.

Here, too, the Black Dog legend is found. The spectre is said to lead one to buried treasure. The phantom hound knocked down the corner of an inn called the 'Black Dog'.

Although the next site is in Devon, it is easier to approach it from here. Take the 3070 for:

☺ **Uplyme,** where the rectory is haunted. Soon after the Revd Brooke de Malpas Egerton was granted the living in 1873 he saw an old lady sitting in an armchair by the fire. He thought this was a hallucination and sat down on the apparition which disappeared. But the next day he met the same figure in a passage and when he saw her for the third time he decided to get in touch with the sisters of the previous incumbent. 'Oh! that must be our mother,' they said; 'when we were there she was constantly appearing, but we did hope that when we left she might find rest at last.'

You must now make your way to the site of one of the most famous Dorset legends:

🐎 **Bettiscombe** (O.P.A.). Although it is so famous, directions for finding it are surprisingly inaccurate, but if you continue north from Uplyme and cross the 373, you will be on the 3165 which will take you through Marshwood to Birdsmoor Gate. (On the left is an inn where the landlady may be persuaded to give her version of the legend.) Turn right down the 3164 towards Broadwindsor. In 600 to 700 yards you come to Horse Mill Cross and then turn right again. Down here lies Bettiscombe Church, and a lane at the side leads to the farmhouse. The legend of the Screaming Skull of Bettiscombe starts with two brothers called Pinney who supported the Duke of Monmouth. One of them, called Azariah, was condemned to death by Judge Jeffreys at the Bloody Assizes but reprieved, enslaved but freed (both by the efforts of his sister, Hester) and finally transported to the island of Nevis in the West Indies, where he prospered. His grandson, John Frederick, came back with considerable riches and a Negro servant, whose skull, according to one version, is still kept at Bettiscombe. It would appear that this Negro swore that his spirit would never rest till his body was buried in his homeland. When he died he was first interred in the Bettiscombe churchyard, but such terrifying screams came from his grave, and there was such a banging of doors and rattling of windows in the house that the corpse had to be exhumed. In the course of time, head and body got separated, maybe the body was shipped to the West Indies, but the skull remains. Another version says that the Negro's

Forde Abbey

master was a priest and they had a quarrel which ended fatally for one of them, and either the murderer's or the victim's skull screams in death agony or remorse. There is a third and more probable, though less romantic, version which states that it is not a Negro's skull at all, but one from a barrow on the Dorset Downs, and its purpose is to warn the family of impending death. Although I can trace no direct descendants of the original brothers, the house came, through their sister, to the Pretor-Pinneys. For some time its tenants were farmers – it is still known as Bettiscombe Farm – but the Pinneys are back there now.

It is best to ask your way to:

☻ **Higher Filford Farm** which lies to the east. A very persistent ghost is reported here. He appears to be an old soldier and haunts the room where they used to ripen cheese.

North-east at:

☻ **Beaminster** St Mary's Church is haunted by a pathetic boy called John Daniel, who was murdered in the eighteenth century. His ghost, seen by many of his schoolmates, came to denounce his murderer, but as no-one was brought to justice, presumably he still appears. June 27 is the relevant date.

East again, and south-east of Batcombe, you will find:

☆ **The Cross and Hand** or more properly the Cross *in* Hand. No-one knows its origin, but Gypsies will tell you that this mysterious post is a Wishing Stone.

☆◉ **Cerne Abbas** lies south-east. It is dominated by the virile figure of the Giant, cut into the chalk on the hillside. As you enter the village a road on the left will lead you to the Giant's Hill, where a path leads up to the Giant himself. People who want to have children have been visiting him for 2000 years, and a girl who actually sleeps on the Giant will be blessed with many children. This pre-Christian fertility rite has stood the test of time better than many others, perhaps because some of the people of Cerne have been stubbornly pagan throughout history. With the advent of Christianity the legends were bowdlerized and anyone visiting the wishing well in the churchyard had to turn his back on the phallic figure before he made his wish. Yet the old knowledge persisted, thanks be to Priapus. Why else should the couple, whom I saw on my last visit, solemnly put on their

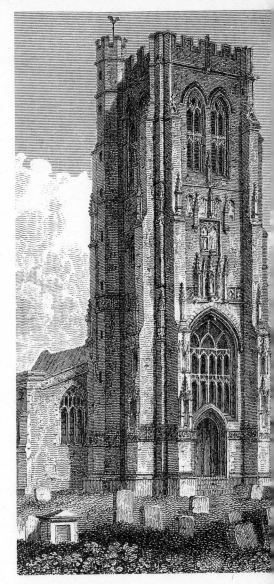

The churchyard at Beaminster

rubber boots and climb the hill hand in hand in the pouring rain?

Half a mile south of Charminster is:

☻👤♿ **Wolfeton House** (O.P.A.), built by Sir Thomas Trenchard in 1505, and haunted by three ghosts: one of his descendants who drives a coach and pair up the staircase; the wife of another, who cut her throat and now roams about what was once the Great Chamber as a headless lady in grey; and the spectre of a priest in the gatehouse.

When you set out from Dorchester again, take the Blandford road and go through the

John Frederick Pinney's portrait hangs behind the Screaming Skull of Bettiscombe

Top The Cross and Hand wishing post

Above Three ghosts haunt Wolfeton House

town. About 1½ miles along the 3082, the road passes:

🐎 **Down Wood,** where phantom horses are still seen and heard.

To the west of Blandford Forum is:

🐎 **Bryanston,** once the home of the Portmans, now a school. A phantom coach can be seen driving out of the gates. Rodney Legg tells how the old saying, 'It's unlucky to uncover a ghost', could apply to the Portman family. Aunt Charlotte used to haunt the

old house, but this was pulled down and she was 'uncovered' so that the new house could be built. There was a legend that when the white and coloured peacocks left Bryanston, the Portmans would soon follow. The third viscount sold the birds and died shortly after, in 1923. It was not long before the estate, too, was sold.

👁 **Hanford House,** to the north, was built in 1603 and is now a school. It was haunted nearly 100 years ago when my grandfather stayed there. A phantom woman in brown would curtsey to visitors on the stairs, and sit by the beds of children staying in the house till they went to sleep. In the room beneath that in which my grandfather always slept, the night was disturbed by what he described as 'hummocking about'. He would bang on the floor with his boot, asking why the devil 'it' could not allow 'us poor mortals' to get some sleep. He could not understand how that extremely civil woman in brown could turn into such an absolute fiend at night. It was many years before a psychic guest, without knowing of the stories, said immediately on entering the house that two ghosts were present.

East of Fontmell Magna the road runs down to:

✩👁 **Washer's Pit.** Before the present road was metalled, there was a barrow here. It had some very special significance because a cross cut in the turf was always scoured. The air at that time was filled with the strange gibberings of ghostly creatures called Gabbygammies. It is said that when the barrow was destroyed they migrated up the road to the pond at Ashmore.

At Washer's Pit there is also the memory of the woman who tried to hang herself, but was cut down just in time.

South-east lies:

👁 **Chettle Down.** Here a bloody skirmish took place between keepers and poachers, in which a man lost his hand. The hand was buried in Pimperne churchyard, but the body in London. The ghost of the hand is constantly seeking to be re-united with the body, and is most frequently seen at Bloody Shard Gate.

South-east, on the far side of the 354, is:

👁🐎 **Thickthorn Down.** The ghost of the first Lord Shaftesbury may be seen here, driving in a coach with a coachman who carries his head under his arm. No-one knows why he should haunt this part of Dorset.

To the west, just outside the village of Tarrant Gunville, is:

👁🐎 **Eastbury.** Built by Vanbrugh, it is now less than half its original size – only

Top Bryanston, base of a phantom coach

Above A headless coachman drives a team of headless horses along Eastbury drive

Blenheim and Castle Howard were larger. The north wing alone remains. It passed into the hands of Lord Temple whose steward, William Doggett, was a great scoundrel. He defrauded his master and, on the eve of discovery, committed suicide. Some say that he hanged himself from a tree in the drive, others that he blew his brains out in the house; but all agree that a headless coachman, driving a headless four-in-hand, stops to pick up the ghost of Doggett, whose knee-breeches are tied with yellow silk ribbon, and rattles over

the cattle-grid at the beginning of the drive, under the yews and up to the house. There is said to be an indelible stain where Doggett shot himself, and he is supposed to haunt the house as well as the drive. He was buried in Tarrant Gunville church (which is rather surprising for a suicide) and when the church was rebuilt in 1845 Doggett's corpse was exhumed. On opening the coffin it was found that his legs were tied together with yellow silk ribbon, and, more sinister, his face was rosy and his body showed no sign of decay. The villagers of the time were convinced that he had continued to prey on them after death – as a vampire.

South of the 354 and east of the 3081 you will find:

☠🦽 **Bottlebush Down.** Prehistoric ghosts are rare, but many people, including a highly respected archaeologist, have seen the Bronze Age horseman who haunts these parts. The 3081 crosses first the old Roman Road, and then the Cursus. On your left you will see a barrow and this is where the ride of the ghostly horseman ends, but continue to Squirrel's Corner and you may see him coming towards you. This is one of the best substantiated ghosts in Dorset.

The next five sites lead you south:

☆ **Knowlton.** A Christian church of Norman origin stands inside a pagan temple, circa 1800 B.C. The temple is remarkably well preserved, but the church is in ruins. *The Shell Guide to Dorset* says: 'This place is magical and said to be haunted. The ditch is inside the ramparts . . . to prevent the egress of spirits rather than defend. . . .' The yews and blackthorn both add to the mystery, but the Department of Environment keeps it trimmer and primmer than it used to be.

The road between here and:

☺ **Hinton Martell** is said to be haunted by a nun. The Old Rectory at Hinton is also reputed to have a ghost.

☺ **Wimborne Minster.** King's House, West Borough, is haunted by the Revd Percy Newall, who owned the house around the middle of the last century. He appears at 6 a.m. and, with a Bible tucked under his arm, opens what used to be a door on an upper floor.

☺ **Poole.** The Crown Hotel in Market Street was described in 1966 by the *Dorset Herald* as 'the latest in a long line of local premises plagued by poltergeists'. At the hotel, audible, visible and telekinetic phenomena have been experienced. They include the sound of a body being dragged across the floor, and the appearance of a 'fluorescent mist'.

Top Lulworth Castle

Above Lawrence of Arabia, whose motorcycle is still heard before dawn near Clouds Hill

Now make your way to the Isle of Purbeck and:

🌀 **Corfe** where the manor house is reported to be haunted.

On the outskirts of Swanage:

🌀 **Godlingston Manor,** an 800-year-old house, is haunted by an unknown lady.

The next site lies west, near Lulworth, and is only open to the public in August as it is Army property. Make your way to:

🌀 **Worbarrow Bay.** About 300 years ago a smuggler was trapped here by revenue men and stoned to death. His cries, as he flounders about in the water, hemmed in by the rising tide and trying to avoid the stones, are still heard at the moon's waning.

🌀 **Bindon Hill** lies at the west end of the bay, separating it from Lulworth Cove. A ghostly legion of Roman soldiers marches over the hill from Flower's Barrow. The abbey at Bindon was demolished in 1588 to provide building materials for:

🏚 **Lulworth Castle,** near East Lulworth. For years a luminous spot on a bedroom wall withstood all attempts to remove it, even rebuilding the masonry was of no avail. The castle was burned down in 1929 and is now a ruin.

North, on the 3071, you will find:

🌀 **Wool.** Next to the bridge stands the Elizabethan house of Woolbridge, once Turberville property, as was the manor house at Bere Regis, 5 miles to the north. Between the two houses runs a ghostly coach and four, which is said to be visible only to those of Turberville blood. There are enough of the family left to see it today, and some may be more surprised to find whose blood runs in their veins than they are to see the coach.

North-west lies:

🌀 **Bovington Camp**, an unlikely place to find a ghost, but it also happens at Tidworth (see Wiltshire section). In the camp you will find the Tank Museum, a brick building with windows high in the walls. The lowest panes are at least eight feet from the ground. Yet through these windows a German officer has frequently been seen, peering at the Tiger tank he commanded – and in which he may have died – in World War II. Guards at the museum know all about the ghost, whom they call 'Herman the German'.

North of Bovington is:

🌀 **Clouds Hill** (N.T.), T. E. Lawrence's cottage, prim and whitewashed amid the rhododendrons. The noise of his Brough Superior is heard in the stillness before daybreak. His figure, in Arab dress, has been seen. John Harries reports that Lawrence is well on the way to becoming a latter-day Drake, who returns when Britain is in danger (see Buckland Abbey, South Devon). I wonder if, instead of Drake's Drum, we shall hear the 'vroum-vroum' of his motorcycle.

North-west near Puddletown is:

🌀 **Athelhampton Hall** (O.P.), the site of six hauntings. The Spectral Ape, in life the pet monkey of the Martyn family who once lived here, has not been seen for some time, but the Grey Lady, the Black Priest, the Phantom Cooper and the Ghostly Duellists have all been seen and heard in recent years.

If you enter Wiltshire from Hungerford and, on the outskirts of Froxfield, turn right, in a little over a mile you will come to one of the most famous haunted houses in England: **Littlecote.** Three of the ghosts here may have their origin in the same horrifying story. One rainy November night in 1575 Mrs Barnes, midwife of Great Shefford (see Berkshire), was blindfolded and taken to a large house to attend a woman in labour – a woman in a mask. No sooner was the child born, than a man 'of haughty and ferocious looks', seized the baby from the midwife's arms and, in spite of the mother's piteous cries, ground it into the red-hot embers of the fire with his boot. The midwife surreptitiously cut a piece of cloth from the bedhangings, and it was this evidence that brought 'Wild William Darrell' of Littlecote to trial. Some say that by bribing the judge, Sir John Popham (see Park Farm, Somerset) – whose family subsequently became owners of the house – Darrell evaded punishment. (As Darrell died in 1589, and Popham became a judge only in 1592, this suggestion is probably unfounded.) However, Darrell came to a violent end when his horse shied – possibly frightened by the ghost of the Burning Babe – at a place known as Darrell's Style, now frequented by his ghost and his phantom hounds, at which horses still shy. The room where the infant was murdered is haunted by the spectre of a pathetic-looking woman carrying a baby in her arms. The mother may have been Darrell's own sister, or, according to a letter written by Sir John Thynne of Longleat, a Miss Bonham; or yet again the wife of Sir Henry Knyvett. But although versions differ as to the identity of the mother, all are sure that the father was Wild Darrell.

Other ghosts in this strange house include a woman in the garden, who Tom Corbett is sure is Mrs Leybourne Popham, another in the Chinese bedroom, and a lady with a rushlight. Some also believe that a tenant, Gerard Lee Bevin, who rented the place after World War I, and who subsequently served seven years for embezzlement, also haunts the Long Gallery.

The cellar of Athelhampton Hall is a likely haunt of the Phantom Cooper, one of six ghosts

From the Berkshire border travel south to the Hampshire border, to:

☺ **North Tidworth.** In the army camp here there is a well-authenticated apparition. Some say it is a Highlander in a kilt; others a Roman soldier (a Roman pavement, now in the British Museum, was found here in 1836).

☺ **South Tidworth,** just over the border, is the site of a famous haunting. The Demon Drummer of Tedworth (as it was formerly called) is an almost classic poltergeist manifestation. When an itinerant drummer was committed to Gloucester jail in 1661, and his drum sent to Magistrate Mompesson's house at Tedworth, strange things began to happen. Children's hair was pulled by invisible hands; clothes were snatched from beds; objects moved; knocking was heard and, of course, a ghostly tattoo from the drum. This went on for months. Charles II sent a Royal Commission to investigate, and the drummer admitted that he was the cause of the disturbances. He was promptly indicted for witchcraft and sentenced to transportation. Somehow he – or his ghost – managed to return, and the drumming continued.

Continue south across the 303 to:

✿☺ **Cholderton** where there is a sacred grove of yews, once used by the Druids, and now shunned by the villagers at night. A more recent ghost is thought to be that of a clergyman who died in the 1890s. He may have fallen or been pushed or jumped down the well. But why were his slippers put neatly together on the well-head wall?

&☺ **Wilbury House,** south of the village, is where a spectral dog – a friendly retriever rather than a fiendish hound – accompanies visitors up the drive.

The villagers of Newton Toney, nearby, talk of strange noises and the ghost of a parson.

☺ **Allington.** Many years ago the curate here, having dined well, is supposed to have fallen from his horse while mounting and broken his neck. Certainly he died in mysterious circumstances. His friends lost their heads and bundled his body into the well. Since then horses take fright at the spot. Years later, as she lay dying, his former hostess tried desperately, but in vain, to tell what really happened. It may have been murder, manslaughter or an accident; only his ghost can tell.

South again, across the A30, you will find:

☺ **Winterslow.** One hundred and fifty years ago Lyddie Shears, the Winterslow Witch, could always tell poachers and farmers where hares were to be found. The vicar of West Tytherley suggested to one farmer that he

The Demon Drummer terrifying a sailor on Salisbury Plain near South Tidworth

melt down a silver sixpence, make it into a bullet and use it on the next hare he shot. This he did; but he could not find the hare. Lyddie, however, lay dead in her cottage with a silver bullet in her heart.

The next site is:

&☺ **Salisbury.** White birds wheel round the cathedral spire before the death of the bishop – or sometimes minor-ranking clergy. Miss Moberly, the bishop's daughter, saw them in 1885, and Miss Olivier in 1911. Inside the cathedral strange phenomena have occurred at St Ormond's Tomb which mysteriously also holds the remains of a murderer, Lord Stourton, who was hanged with a silken noose on 16 March 1557, in the market place. See Kilmington. For 200 years a wire noose hung over the tomb. It was removed in 1780, yet its luminous outline has been seen within living memory by unimpeachable witnesses.

The 'Haunch of Venison' in Minster Street adjoins a graveyard in which a Grey Lady is to be seen.

The next site lies south-west in the Ebble valley:

✦☺& **Bower Chalke.** As you enter the village you cross Applespill Bridge, where gold is said to be buried. This legend is possibly connected with the rifling of a barrow on the downs, where they say a gold coffin was found. The ghosts of seven men carrying it are occasionally seen. So also is the spectre of a shepherd who became lost and died of exposure in a snowdrift. His voice is heard, plaintively crying, 'I want to go home'. At the far end of the village, at Patty's Bottom, above Woodminton, is the site of a battle between the Romans and the Britons, and 'on moonlit nights tramping feet can be heard and headless horses seen rushing madly about'. South of the village the counties of Dorset, Hampshire and Wiltshire meet. Here, at a crossroads, is Kit's Grave. The ghost of the poor girl, who committed suicide and was buried at this spot, still haunts the place. No birds sing in the avenue leading to it.

A mile to the east lies Vernditch Chase, where years ago a house stood in which a man was murdered. His ghost returns and the ghastly scene is re-enacted. People say that you can hear the three chops of the axe that it took to behead him.

To the north-west is:

☻⚔ **Wardour Castle** (O.P.). Here Blanche, Lady Arundel, with twenty-five able-bodied men, held out for five days against the Round-heads. Eventually she signed terms for an honourable surrender, which the Puritans – typically – broke. Either she, or one of the ladies of the house who loaded up the small arms during their gallant defence, still haunts the castle grounds, and is seen moving to-wards the lake at twilight. The last Arundel of Wardour died in 1944. Deaths in this family were presaged by the appearance of white owls.

You could now leave Wiltshire and take in three Dorset sites which are more easily reached from here or from Somerset.

⚑☻⚔ **Shaftesbury.** The abbey ruins still hide the treasure of the Convent of St Edward, buried before the Dissolution by a monk, on the instruction of Elizabeth Souche, the last abbess. Unfortunately he died before he could reveal the hiding place, and his ghost still tries to tell someone where it lies.

Up the steep cobbles of Gold Hill the ghosts of two men with pack-horses have been seen. They carry the body of Edward the Martyr Prince (who was murdered at Corfe in 979) to his last resting place.

☻ **Marnhull.** Two ghosts cross Sackmore Lane bearing a coffin, their faces hidden by the pall. They move towards Todber, the site of a legendary battlefield, where a large num-ber of bones were dug up in 1870. Rodney Legg, in his *Guide to Dorset Ghosts*, suggests that this 'indicates that there had been a battle'. But why take a coffin to a battlefield? I think it is more likely to have been a plague pit.

To the north, just south of Zeals, is:

☻ **Silton.** The church is haunted by a priest in full vestments, who moves towards the altar and then disappears into the vestry. A mural of angels above the Communion table is said to appear and disappear.

West of Mere, and south of the 303, is:

☻ **Zeals House.** Here the ghost of a young woman dressed in grey comes down the stairs and walks out of the house, over the ha-ha and on into the woods beyond the lake. She was a daughter of the house who eloped with a servant and was never seen again. How-ever a century ago a female skeleton was dug up in those woods, and a stone now marks the spot. Was she murdered almost on her door-step?

North again, but back in Wiltshire, is:

☻⚔ **Kilmington.** The churchyard was originally haunted by the ghosts of a band of thugs led by the eighth Baron Stourton, who was hanged at Salisbury (q.v.) for the murder of his father's steward William Hartgill, whose ghost has been seen in the church. Recent reports tell of a headless horse which appears in Bull Lane. (For the full horrorsome story see *Adventures with Phantoms* by R. Thurston Hopkins.)

There is a mystery about the Hartgills' house. The building to the south of the church, now called Hartgills, was known a century ago as the Malt House. The Hartgill house stood north-west of the church; farm buildings have been erected on the site.

To the east, where the 303 is crossed by the 350, is:

⚔ **Two Mile Down** which is haunted by a coach drawn by four grey horses.

North-west, near the Somerset border, you will find:

☻ **Longleat** (O.P.). The Green Lady's Walk is haunted by Lady Louise Carteret, who married the second Viscount Weymouth. He discovered that she had a lover and killed him in a duel, then buried him beneath the cellar floor. When central heating was being installed the remains of a young man were found under the flagstones. The Red Library is also haunted, and there are other ghosts as well, including one who knocks at bedroom doors.

From Longleat you go north-east through Westbury towards Bratton. Shortly, on your right, you will see:

✿ **The Westbury White Horse** (D.E.). Alas he was recut by an odious steward of Lord Abingdon, and a fine stallion with a crescent at the end of his tail, a decorated saddle and a wild eye was turned into a lifeless gelding. Or was he? T. C. Lethbridge thinks that the original Iron Age horse is still there, a little to the rear of Mr Gee's pathetic nag, but covered with grass.

The Westbury White Horse as it is now and as it used to be

North-east on the 361 is:

👁 **Seend** where a phantom cortege has been seen in the streets.

North-west is:

👣 **Corsham.** One day Lady Winifred Pennoyer (see Cold Ashton, Gloucestershire) and two other young women were sitting on a tombstone in Corsham churchyard when two of them saw an elemental. One fainted and had to be carried home, the second was profoundly affected, and the third saw nothing. The elemental was described as an intensely malevolent little man, about two feet six inches high. Psychic investigators believe it to have taken the form of a very evil monk who once lived there.

To the west at:

👁 **Ditteridge,** Cheney Court, where Queen Henrietta once lived, is haunted.

North at:

👁 **Yatton Keynell** the rectory is 'mildly haunted', according to a local guide.

Away to the east, between Calne and Marlborough is:

👁 **Avebury Manor** (O.P.). The ghost wears a White Hood, and there are reports of strange happenings in cottages whose walls contain some of the stones which originally formed the stone circle.

North of the 361 and ½ mile west of Beckhampton is:

🔪 **The Highwayman's Grave.** He was shot dead by the guard of the London to Bath stagecoach, and buried face down, so M. Chetwynd-Stapylton reports, with his head to the west. Gypsies believe he was a bona fide traveller, not a highwayman, and used to see that flowers were placed on his grave.

HAMPSHIRE AND
THE ISLE OF WIGHT

Hampshire provides a good circular tour so no centre is suggested. You can stay anywhere *en route*. Coming from London on the main road (A30) you turn right in Hartley Wintney for:

🔪 **Bramshill,** one of the places reputed to be the original site of the 'Mistletoe Bough' (see Marwell Hall; and Minster Lovell, Oxfordshire). In this famous legend the bride, at her wedding celebrations (or a Christmas party), hides in a chest which cannot be opened from the inside. She is not discovered till too late. Previous owners found that the 'Flower-de-Luce' room was haunted by a girl in a bridal dress. It is now a police college.

Further along the main road is:

👁 **Hook** where the ghost of a Cavalier has been seen in the streets, and the 'White Hart' is reputedly haunted.

South of Basingstoke is:

👁 **Winslade.** Near Hackwood House is Spring Wood, in which Polly Peachum's Garden is haunted by a woman in grey.

To the west you will find:

👁 **Oakley** where a female apparition wanders about peering anxiously at travellers, in the hope that she will find someone she has lost.

👁 **Winchester.** No. 45 Quarry Road has three ghosts – a nun, a lady in white and a tall man in a black cloak with brass buttons who stands and smiles – which have often been seen by Mrs Bowles. Curtains have been drawn by unseen hands and one can smell both ladies' scent and something dead. Two attempts at exorcism have not made much difference.

North-east of Romsey is:

👁 **Braishfield** where the lanes and footpaths are haunted by an Edwardian lady who is believed to be searching for her money and jewels, which she buried before she died.

To the south-west is:

👁 **East Wellow,** haunted by Colonel William Morton, a regicide.

South-west again lies:

👁 **The Rufus Stone.** William Rufus haunts this place on the anniversary of his death on 2 August 1100; and his ghost follows the route of the cart which carried his body to Winchester. But, as John Harries points out, the Gregorian change in the calendar may make the night of July 22 a more auspicious date for a vigil. The site of Castle Malwood, to the south-east, which Rufus used as a hunting lodge, can be distinguished. This is haunted; and the water of Ocknell Pond, to the west of the stone, is said to be red because the murderer stopped here to wash his hands. Margaret Murray expounds an interesting theory that Rufus's death was a sacrificial killing in a witchcraft ceremony.

North of Ringwood is:

🕯 **Moyles Court** (O.P.A.), said to be haunted by Dame Alice Lisle, who was 'allowed' to be beheaded instead of suffering Judge Jeffreys' sentence of being burned at the stake. She had been tricked into harbouring a Monmouth partisan, although her son fought for James II at Sedgemoor.

Almost on the outskirts of Southampton, north of Totton, is:

🕯 **Testwood House.** The drive is said to be haunted by a man in an ulster, and the house by a face at a window. There are also stories of a coach and four, and the ghost of a woman in the attic. Locals believe that a manservant murdered the cook and dragged her body down the drive.

South lies:

🕯 **Beaulieu** (O.P.). At Palace House, originally the abbey gatehouse, the chanting of monks is often heard and many people have seen their ghostly forms in the abbey ruins, and caught a whiff of incense. There is no dearth of witnesses who will testify to their presence, from Lord Montague to the Gypsies of the New Forest. An interesting point is that all find these ghosts benevolent and not at all frightening.

🕯 **Hurst Castle** (D.E.) on the other side of Lymington was the temporary prison of Charles I but is haunted by a monk.

Now go back to Lymington and take the ferry to the Isle of Wight.

☆ **Mottistone** is on the 3399. Here there is a standing stone, thirteen feet high, where Druids used to sacrifice a white bull (see Loch Maree, Scotland). There was also a logan, or rocking stone, which moved with the wind, but could not be rocked by the hand of a man with a guilty conscience.

South of Newport and west of Godshill is:

🕯 **Billingham.** Sir Shane and Lady Leslie found it 'very haunted' when they rented the place. A ghost and the smell of Madonna lilies can be traced back to a duel between a French and an English suitor, or a French lover and an English husband. The cause was a Miss Legh who married a Worsley. There is also a phantom monk.

Top You may meet the spectre of an Edwardian lady along the lanes of Braishfield

Above The Rufus Stone

On the outskirts of Ventnor is:

☆ **St Boniface Down** where there is a wishing well. You must climb up to it without looking back, and drink. Three wishes will be granted.

Inland from Bembridge you will come to:

☆ 🐎 **Brading.** Here there was once a sacred grove of oaks where the Druids sacrificed a man every year, by burning him in a wicker cage (see Castleton, Derbyshire). On the banks of the Yar, near Woolverton, is the site of a lost village, burned when a holy man was killed at a well. This story fills forty-seven pages of Elder's *Tales and Legends of the Isle of Wight*.

Just east of Ryde is:

🐎 **Puckpool** where Puck teased Father Martin of St Helen's and led him into the middle of the marsh by pretending to be a girl who cried out to be saved.

West of Ryde, just past Binstead, are the ruins of:

◉ **Old Quarr Abbey.** Here the Feast of Fools took place on New Year's Day. Under the direction of the 'Abbot of Misrule' the monks dressed up as women and 'conducted themselves indecorously'. They ate puddings off the altar, sang bawdy songs, and burned old shoes for incense. In this way the pagan saturnalia and bacchanalia became Christianized.

A ferry from Fishbourne will take you across Spithead to:

◉ **Portsmouth.** Before the Blitz there were several haunted inns. The most famous, perhaps, was the 'Spotted Dog', where John Felton murdered the Duke of Buckingham in 1628. An obelisk on Clarence Pier marks the spot where the murderer hung in chains. King's Bastion is still believed to be haunted by ladies in grey and bewhiskered sailors.

On the eastern bank of Southampton water you will find:

✦◉ **Netley Abbey** (D.E.) which abounds with legends. There are stories of buried treasure and an underground passage which contains so awful a secret that a man called Slown literally died of fright. His last words were screamed instructions to a labourer to 'Block it up! In the name of God!' The Military Chapel here was haunted, some say, by Florence Nightingale; but most of the quarter-mile long building was pulled down in 1966 during which time the ghost was frequently seen. The chapel remains, however, and so may the spectral nurse.

Now travel north on to the 3051 towards Winchester. At Fisher's Pond go east to:

The ruins of Netley Abbey by moonlight

🦌💀☠ **Marwell Hall,** another 'original site' of the Mistletoe Bough legend (see Bramshill). It is also haunted by Jane Seymour, who followed Anne Boleyn to Henry VIII's bed and died after giving birth to Edward VI.

Now go north-east to:

🦌💀 **Tichborne.** On her deathbed in 1150, Lady Maybell Tichborne requested her husband, Sir Roger, who seems to have been a curmudgeonly sort of fellow, to grant her the means of providing an annual dole of bread for the needy. He agreed, providing that she herself would mark out the land while a brand remained burning. Although she had been bedridden for years, she managed to carry the brand and encompass twenty-three acres on her hands and knees – an area still known as The Crawls. When she got back to her bed she uttered a curse on anyone who should let the dole lapse, saying that the house would fall and the line become extinct. Furthermore this would be heralded by a generation of seven sons, followed by a generation of seven daughters and no son. The dole was maintained until 1796, when the local magistrates said that it attracted undesirable characters to the neighbourhood, and

Jane Seymour haunts Marwell Hall

persuaded the seventh baronet, Sir Henry Tichborne, to break the tradition. The eldest of his seven sons had seven daughters and the property went to the third son who had changed his name to Doughty. This seems to have broken part of the curse, for although he left no heir the property went to the fourth brother. In the meantime the dole had been restored.

Those twenty-three acres covered by the dying Lady Maybell are said to have once provided 1400 twenty-six-ounce loaves which were distributed to the villagers of Tichborne and Cheriton, together with a purse containing tuppence for those most in need. Today thirty hundredweights of flour are distributed. After World War II, when bread was rationed, coupons flowed in from all over the country so that this dole could be continued.

To the south-east is:

👻 **Hinton Ampner.** The manor here marks the site of another classic and well-documented haunting. It started in the middle of the eighteenth century and became so obnoxious that the house was pulled down and rebuilt fifty yards away. Some of the phenomena, however, continued. The manifestations included a man in a drab coat, a woman in rustling silk, knocks, slamming doors and terrifying screams. The ghosts were probably those of the fourth Lord Stawell and his sister-in-law, with whom he consorted after his wife's death. When the old house was pulled down, a small skull, said to be that of a monkey, was found under the floorboards.

South of Petersfield is:

👻 **Buriton Manor,** haunted by a kindly ghost, whose presence nevertheless enabled the rateable value to be reduced in 1957. The mother of the owner, Algernon Bonham Carter, was the daughter of the rector of Buriton, and an underground passage is said to join the manor to the church which was, until 1886, the manor chapel.

The A3 leads through Petersfield to:

👻 **Liphook.** In the lanes north of the town, leading to Bramshott, a fairhaired boy, playing his pipes, leads lost travellers to safety.

North-west of Farnham, but south of the 287 is:

🐑👻 **Crondall.** In the village a ghostly flock of sheep is periodically seen and heard; Cromwellian troops ride up to the church; and in Alma Lane near the Alma Inn and Beam Cottage the sound of heavy-booted running is often heard. This is the ghost of an orderly who, while bringing news of the victory at Waterloo to Aldershot, was murdered by footpads.

65

If you enter the county from Hampshire you can cover West Sussex with comparative ease and then continue, if you wish, to the more numerous eastern sites. Cross the county boundary south of Haslemere. To the south-east near Blackdown Hill are the scanty ruins of:

⚐ **Verdley Castle.** A very rare animal ghost has been seen here: that of the last bear to be killed in England.

Make your way south-east, through country lanes to Ball's Cross and on to:

☆ **Kirdford,** where there is said to be a patch of earth where no grass will grow because a poacher's blood was spilled there.

The next site lies almost due south:

☺ **Amberley.** Noel Streatfeild, whose father was parson here, tells the story of two ghosts in the rectory, a little girl and an old man. In 1904 two skeletons were found under the floor in a dining-room cupboard; one was a little girl, but the other was an adult woman. Joseph Braddock classes this as an 'evil haunting'.

Just north-east of Bognor Regis is:

☺ **Flansham.** When the manor was turned into a guest-house, many visitors heard ghostly footsteps and the sound of something being dragged across the floor.

South-west is:

☺ **Nyetimber,** where the Lion Hotel and Country Club is reported by the B.T.A. to be haunted.

Between the sea and the A27, to the east, lies:

☺ **Poling.** At a house built on the site of St John's Priory, the sound of chanting is heard. Some people have had frightening experiences. A famous novelist, while staying there, is said to have sent herself a telegram demanding her immediate return to London, because she was too terrified to spend another night there.

☺ **Arundel Castle** (O.P.) lies to the north-west. At least three ghosts are reputed to be found here: a young girl who, crossed in love, threw herself from Hiorne's Tower; a scullion in the kitchen; and a Cavalier, known as the Blue Man, in the library.

North of Shoreham, to the east, you will find:

☺ **Bramber Castle.** For 800 years the ghosts of William de Breone's children – starved to death at Windsor as hostages of King John – have been seen piteously begging for bread in the streets near their old home.

North again, west of the A24, is:

⚐ **Knepp Castle,** and should you see a white doe here, it could be the ghost of a girl bewitched in the thirteenth century.

East of Horsham lies:

⚐☺ **St Leonard's Forest,** a place full of mysteries. At Faygate, on the main road, there was once a fabulous beast, perhaps a dragon, described in 1614 as being nine feet long, with a black back and red underbelly. In the forest the Devil himself is said to appear and also the ghost of Squire Paulet, who jumps up on a horse's back, behind the rider. Furthermore here:

> The adders never styng
> Nor ye nightingales syng.

🐎☺⚐ **Cuckfield.** At Cuckfield Park a gigantic lime tree shed a branch before the death of one of the family. Originally the house belonged to the Warennes, Earls of Surrey; then to the Fitzalans, Earls of Derby; and from 1654 to the Sergisons who, I believe, kept it in either direct or collateral line for three centuries. I think this is the park to which Henderson alludes in his *Folklore of the Northern Counties*. He says that in 1830 the avenue was haunted by the spirit of a Madam S(———), who objected to her daughter's

The ruin of Bramber Castle

marriage. Attempts were made by the local vicar to exorcise the apparition.

At Butler's Green House, which also once belonged to the Sergisons, a phantom coach and horses appear, connected in some way with a girl who drowned herself in a pond. She was either the daughter or wife of the owner, and waited for her lover to come and carry her off. He was unfortunately delayed. The pond has now been filled in.

The Brighton road leads south to:

Pyecombe, the scene of good-natured junketing on November 23 when the exorcism of a smithy once haunted by witches is celebrated.

Brighton. The Lanes are haunted by the ghost of a pre-Reformation nun in a grey habit.

Lewes. On November 5 the bonfires are the biggest in Britain. The guy here is of religious as well as political significance. One night in 1557 six men and four women were burned alive in the Market Place, because they were Protestants. One of the six bonfire societies, Cliffe, still uses a 'No Popery' banner, and burns an effigy of the pope as well as that of Guy Fawkes. So pagan fires, which were given a political excuse for their preservation, have become Christianized by a most unchristian act.

East, and just north of the A27, at Selmeston, is:

Sherrington Manor, haunted by a benign brown-clad figure.

East again, and you come to Wilmington. On Windover Hill you will find:

☆ **The Long Man,** a chalk figure cut in the downs. He is not as ostentatiously virile as the Cerne Giant in Dorset, but impressive because of his stance and size: 231 feet high. The purpose and origin of this figure remain a mystery. Is he opening the doors of heaven? Is he connected with the eastern god Varuna? Are there other figures, grown over, as they are on Gog Magog Hill in Cambridgeshire (q.v.)?

South of Wilmington lies:

Alfriston where the Priest's House (N.T.) is said to be haunted.

Willingdon is on the outskirts of Eastbourne. The main road is haunted by a woman dressed in the dustcoat and veil of an Edwardian motorist. At dusk she is seen waving down travellers to avoid a car in which she and two men were killed some sixty years ago.

If you are interested in more modern ghosts, just east of Eastbourne, off the 2197, lie:

The Crumbles where the ghosts of Irene

Top An Edwardian ghost warns travellers of a bygone crash at Willingdon

Above Herstmonceux Castle reverberates with phantom drumming

Munro, murdered in 1920, and Emily Kaye, killed and mutilated four years later, have been seen.

Or you can go north along the A22 and turn west to:

Michelham Priory (O.P.). The gatehouse has been haunted for many years by a Grey Lady, but only recently has it been noticed that in the Tudor Room there are two ghosts, one a Blue Lady, the other a monk.

Almost due east is:

Herstmonceux Castle. The phantom drummer heard here may have been a soldier killed at Agincourt. Alternatively it could have been Lord Dacre, an elderly recluse, who drummed to keep lovers away from his beautiful young wife. She locked him up and let him die; but the drumming still continued and the lovers stayed away.

Another apparition is the ghost of an heiress, killed by her governess to prevent her inheriting a fortune. She is seen near the moat. There is also the ghost of a sleepwalking man. (See *The Story of My Life* by Augustus Harris.) Unfortunately the opening hours are not very auspicious for ghost-hunters.

Continue north-east and you will come to: **Battle Abbey** (O.P.). Sir Anthony Browne, 'Esquire to the Body of Henry VIII, Master of the Horse and Justice in Eyre', was given Battle Abbey in 1538. During the feast held to celebrate his ownership, one of the dispossessed monks cursed him and his family for taking ecclesiastical land (see Sherborne, Somerset), condemning them to die by fire or water. Sir Anthony inherited Cowdray Park from his half-brother, the Earl of Southampton, and this property was burned down in 1793, rather than Battle, which had passed into the hands of the Websters in 1699. While staying there as a child I was told that a friar haunted the Monk's Wall; but the present owner (who was *not* drowned with her mother in 1907, as reported by Charles Harper) says that it is thought to be the Duchess of Cleveland, to whom the abbey was let for a time, making her way to church.

Hastings. Ghostly music, rattling chains and groans have been heard in the castle. Thomas à Becket's spectre has been seen on autumn evenings.

North is:

Brede Place. Once the home of the Oxenbridge family who produced Sir Goddard, a giant, said to have eaten the flesh of babies. However, the house is not haunted by this ogre, but by the ghosts of: a benign priest called Father John; a sixteenth-century servant called Martha, who was hanged in the dell for stealing; a headless man whose presence has been recorded photographically; and a lady in a ruff. There have also been other manifestations. As a forbidding notice declares, 'Brede Place is no longer open to the public'.

So on to:

Winchelsea. The Queen's Head Hotel, once a farmhouse, is haunted. The ghost is either that of a tenant farmer who once lived there, or of a landlord who died at the turn of the century, and was laid out in an open coffin on the bar, so that his patrons could speed him on his way. This ghost has been seen frequently in the last two decades, and,

unlike phantoms at some inns, is not a publicity stunt.

The ghost of a Negro in a red uniform has been seen in the churchyard, and also those of two brothers called Weston, who were highwaymen and were hanged at Tyburn in 1782. **Rye.** Here a number of phantom monks have been seen, some say seven at a time. Monastery Hall was originally an Augustan Friary. Watch-bell Street is another place where a monk's ghost is often seen.

Now travel to:

Burwash. Although Rudyard Kipling's house, Bateman's (N.T.), is said to be haunted, the most mysterious site in the neighbourhood is described by Kipling as being

full of a sense of ancient ferocity and evil. I have sometimes . . . felt a secretive and menacing feeling all round me, holding me expectant and

Gladwish Wood, near Burwash

thing that plucked at its neck, coughed and choked and moaned, is one of the most frightening passages I have ever read. This is the ghost of David Leary, a farm labourer, who lodged with a couple called Russell. One night in 1825 the two men set out to steal some corn. Russell, unfortunately, fell down dead with the corn, and his body was hidden in Gladwish Wood until the next day, to cover up the theft and allay suspicion. Local gossip suggested that Leary and Mrs Russell were having an affair and had poisoned the husband. A blundering old doctor miscalculated the amount of arsenic in the corpse, and Leary was sentenced to death and Mrs Russell to imprisonment. Leary's last words to the chaplain were: 'I beg of you believe me when I say I am innocent, and to prove it I shall return to haunt those people who have hounded me to my death.' It was subsequently proved that Russell died from a heart-attack. Mrs Russell was set free; but it was too late to save Leary from being hanged, or those who visit Gladwish Wood from the venom and vengeance of his spirit. Land development may soon spread a genteel veneer over the ancient ferocity and evil.

South-east of Tunbridge Wells, the road from:

Hook Green to Bell's Yew Green is haunted by a phantom limousine which disappears when approaching cars are about 100 yards away. This road skirts:

Bayham (on the Kent border), which is haunted by more orthodox ghosts: monks have been seen, chanting heard and incense smelled.

To the south is:

Best Beech. At Beggar's Bush a ghost with a sack on its back, appears in the garden at dusk when the fruit is ripe.

South-west lies:

Mayfield. According to local inhabitants, it was here that St Dunstan, while shoeing a horse, noticed that the rider's feet were cloven, and seized the Devil's nose in his hot tongs.

The Middle House features in the B.T.A.'s list of reputedly haunted houses.

South again is:

Warbleton, the site of a well-known skull legend, but now of little more than academic interest. Priory Farm was once famous for its two skulls, one of which was that of an idiot. Both are said to have come from Hastings Priory. If they were removed, it was believed, the cattle would die and crops fail. One of them was advertised for sale at ten guineas in *The Times* in 1963.

always on guard. Yes, and in this evil wood everything is evil . . .

R. Thurston Hopkins identified this place as Gladwish Wood, which is marked on the o.s. map to the south of Burwash and a mile from Bateman's. He first came across the place on a walk which he had organized, and members of the party decided to explore it. In his book *Adventures with Phantoms* he admits that in writing about ghosts he has often used 'rather extravagant expressions, like "blood running cold" and "paralysed with fear". . . . But,' he goes on, 'both these sensations had not been fully appreciated by me [until] that long-drawn half-throttled cry came out of the wood. . . .'

The description of the ghost which his friend met in Gladwish Wood, the ragged

St Dunstan seized his opportunity and the Devil's nose in his tongs at Mayfield

North-west of Mayfield is:

☺ **Rotherfield,** near Crowborough, where the 'King's Arms' is haunted in late June by footsteps hurrying along passages and up and down stairs.

South-west, just short of Uckfield, is:

☺ **Buxted** which, I suspect, was the scene of a lynching. Nan Tuck ,a simple girl, was accused of being a witch. She sought sanctuary in the church, but was refused by the priest. She suffered trial by water, and half-drowned, bedraggled and terrified once more managed to escape. Her tormentors, like hounds on her heels, took up the chase. She was found hanging from a tree in what is now known as Tuck's Wood – a suicide, the villagers said. In the Church of St Margaret the Queen there is a record of her burial in 1661. But would a suicide have been buried in consecrated ground? And would a girl who had managed by her own desperate efforts to escape sentence of death then take her own life? I think the village of Buxted had a murder on its conscience. That is why they did not like going up Nan Tuck's Lane, and kept well away from Tuck's Wood at night, and that is why these places are still haunted by the ghost of a poor frightened girl.

Up the A22 you come to:

☺ **Wych Cross** where the 'Roebuck' is another hotel which the B.T.A. considers haunted.

East of Forest Row where the Tunbridge Wells road curves, there is a turning to the north which was probably once the drive to:

☺ **Ashdown House** (O.P.A.). Why Lord Heathfield should haunt what is now a boy's boarding school when he neither lived nor died there, I do not know. But every July 6 his footsteps are supposed to be heard on the stairs. His daughter married the man who built this house, but there must be a closer connection.

KENT

For a ghost hunt in Kent, I suggest touring the county clockwise. Leave London by the A2 and before you reach the countryside you come to Bexley. The A2 is called Rochester Way here; the 223 which crosses it is Bourne Road. To the north-east of the intersection, on the right-hand side of Bourne Road, lies:

☺ **Hall Place** (O.P.). It is now a school but 700 years ago it was a manor house belonging to Sir Thomas atte Hall. He was killed by a stag in the courtyard, a scene which so upset his wife, Lady Constance, that she flung herself off the tower. Her ghost still walks. Another spectre is that of the Black Prince, and a third, in the attic, the spirit of a distraught maidservant.

Continue east and you come to:

☺ **Northfleet.** No. 16 Waterdales, a council house built in the 1930s, was the scene of poltergeist phenomena, and the ghosts of both a young girl with fair hair and a headless woman were seen between 1962 and 1966. The tenants were forced to leave.

☺ 🏛 **Southfleet.** In spite of exorcism the rectory remains haunted. There is over a century of evidence collected by a whole sequence of rectors, relating to the ghost of a nun or nurse. Her height – 4 ft 6 in.; shape – dumpy; dress – brown. She carries rustling papers. Legend says that a friary once stood on the site, and three nuns, who were seduced by the monks and their sin discovered, were bricked up in the walls.

The road south leads to:

☺ **Meopham.** During the Napoleonic wars, a soldier was followed home by a Mlle Pinard, who had become his mistress. Sad to relate, she was not well received and so she hanged herself. Her ghost, in orange silk, haunts Steel Lane. Three other ghosts have been reported: a servant girl at Dean Manor, a miller who committed suicide, and a headless man who walks from the inn to the church.

☺ **Rochester.** On Good Friday 1264 Ralph de Capo defended the castle (D.E.) against Simon de Montfort. In the battle his betrothed, Lady Blanche de Warenne, was killed (accounts of the circumstances vary). Her ghost, usually with an arrow in the heart, haunts the place on the anniversary of her death. At the

A procession at Lewes on Bonfire Night

old burial ground in the moat, the ghost of a white-bearded man has been seen; it is thought to be that of Charles Dickens, who expressed a wish to be buried here. The same spectre has also been seen under the Corn Exchange clock.

Chatham. St Mary's Barracks are haunted during the Middle Watch by the sound of limping footsteps and the tapping of a crutch or wooden leg. It has been reported that in Magpie Hall Road two adjoining houses have been haunted for twenty years.

South-east, across the M2 but just short of the M20, is:

Hollingbourne where a Wild Rider is frequently seen – but not heard – in daylight, and heard – but not seen – at night. John Harries sets out the theory that it is a foolhardy lord of the manor who set his horse to jump the wrought-iron gates of Hollingbourne House, north of the village, and was killed.

Across the A20 is:

Leeds Castle where the appearance of a phantom dog is an ill-omen to those who live there.

Next make for Faversham where it would be as well to ask the way to:

The Shipwright's Arms. It lies nearly a mile from any other house (except for the boatyard next door) in the lonely marshes north of the town, on the banks of the tidal creeks that flow into the Swale. It is a fine setting for the ghost of a sailor in a reefer jacket, with glaring eyes, who is accompanied by a strange smell not, it would seem, of the mixture of rum, tobacco and tar that one might expect.

Canterbury. A place of pilgrimage must be saturated with belief, and the atmosphere of the cathedral, particularly the north-west transept, site of Becket's murder, cannot fail to make itself felt. But perhaps the devotion of so many pilgrims has calmed Thomas's spirit, if indeed it was ever restless. Canterbury's ghost is that of Simon Sudbury, archbishop, murdered in 1381 by Wat Tyler, and he haunts the tower that bears his name. The reason is that his head and body have never been re-united, for while the latter lies in Canterbury, the former is buried at Sudbury in Suffolk (q.v.). Yet those who have seen it say that this is no headless phantom, but a dignified figure with a grey beard and a fair complexion.

One entrance into King's School bears the awesome name of the Dark Entry. If you have

Lady Blanche de Warrenne and Charles Dickens haunt the corroded remains of Rochester Castle

read *The Ingoldsby Legends*, you will hope *not* to see the ghost of Nell Cook. She caught the canon, on whom she waited, in profane and compromising circumstances with a lady he said was his niece. So she murdered them both, and the appearance of her spirit every Friday night brings death within the year to those who see it.

Wingham lies to the east. Here the 'Red Lion' is reputed to be haunted.

Margate. The Theatre Royal, now alas! a bingo hall, is haunted. One version says that the spectre is an actor who committed suicide in a stage box, and fell out onto the boards. Even after the building was altered and the box bricked up, mysterious lights appeared. The other version says the ghost is that of Sarah Thorne, who died aged 62 in 1899, having established a fine company and school here. She walks majestically down the aisle and up onto the stage. The stories are unreconcilable, so I think this must be the site of a double haunting.

The 256 crosses the 253 at:

Cliffsend where a gibbet once stood; suicides and criminals lie buried nearby. A glowing light has been seen which takes the

A phantom dog heralds bad luck at Leeds Castle

73

Canterbury's spectre is Simon Sudbury, a fourteenth-century archbishop

form of a ghostly figure. Accidents which occur here cannot always be explained.

Inland, near Acol, originally a sacred oak grove, is:

💀 **Cleve Court** where the ghost of an unhappy lady is to be seen pacing the room where she was incarcerated by a cruel husband.

North of Sandwich, near the southern shore of Pegwell Bay, lies:

💀 **Richborough Castle** (D.E.). It is not surprising that the fort which covered the landing of legionaries during the 500 years of Roman occupation – and their withdrawal – should be haunted by the ghosts of Roman soldiers.

You would have to take a boat to visit the next site, but you can see it across the water from Deal:

💀 **The Goodwin Sands** are four miles offshore now but were once part of King Harold's father's estates. On 13 February 1748 the ship

Lady Lovibund set sail with a party of fifty guests celebrating the wedding of Simon Peel. During the night a jealous rival, a man called Rivers from Deal, deliberately ran the boat aground. This event is re-enacted by the lost souls every fifty years. It was last reported in February 1898 and on the same date fifty years later.

After Ringwould on the 258 you come to:

💀 **Oxney Court,** haunted by the ghost of a lady in a dark grey cloak, who is frequently seen by many different people, including a bus driver who once stopped to pick her up. The conductor swears he saw her go up to the top deck, but when he went to collect her fare she had disappeared.

💀 **Dover Castle** (D.E.) is haunted by a headless drummer boy, murdered during the Napoleonic wars; and the Prince Louis Hotel is on the B.T.A. list of reputedly haunted inns.

West of Folkstone and north of Hythe is:

💀 **Saltwood.** From here the road leads to Sanding station, passing Slaybrook Farm. This stretch of road is haunted. Manifestations include a ball of fire which gradually becomes a man carrying a lantern. Another apparition is thought to be that of an eccentric Victorian landowner, or a Roman soldier, or both.

Just west of Hythe is:

💀 **Lympne Castle** (O.P.), haunted by the ghosts of six Saxons, butchered here by the Normans; also the ghost of a Roman soldier who fell to his death. It is now a private house, but it is often open to the public.

The other side of Ashford, southwest of Charing, lies:

💀👥 **Pluckley.** The most haunted village in Kent can boast of twelve ghosts in and around it. Surrenden Dering, the site of the manor house burned out in 1952, is still haunted by White Lady Dering, and is the scene of various poltergeist phenomena. There is a Red Lady Dering who haunts St Nicholas' Church and graveyard. The ghost of a monk has been seen at Greystones; he is sometimes accompanied by the spirit of a lady from Rose Court. In Dicky Buss's Lane, you may find the ghost of a schoolmaster who committed suicide. A miller's ghost haunts the ruined mill near the Pinnock, where an old Gypsy woman was burned to death, and her phantom too may be seen. Near Dering Wood, at Fright Corner, you may find a spectral highwayman. In Park Wood, between Pluckley Thorne and Chambers Green, is the ghost of a colonel. In Brick Walk – near the station – the ghost of a screaming man who fell to his death in a clay-pit has been seen. The road

SURREY

You can make a circular tour of the Surrey sites, leaving London by the A22. Just north of Lingfield and about 4½ miles east of the main road, you will see on your left two stone gateposts and a cottage with a pond in front. You have arrived at:

Ⓖ **Puttenden Manor** (O.P.) whose owner Brian Thompson also holds the deeds of Downe Court (see London). The manifestation here is in the form of scent such as women use, and the male smell of pipe tobacco. Mr Thompson has apparently left the furnishings of the house very much as they were when he bought it, so the couple who haunt it in this redolent way must feel quite at home.

West of Dorking lies:

Ⓖ **The Silent Pool,** haunted by the ghost of a Saxon maiden.

Between Guildford and Woking is:

Ⓖ **Send.** At Boughton Hall the ghost of an elderly man smoking a pipe walks upstairs, and one can smell the tobacco.

Ⓖ **Sutton Place** is nearby. Once owned by American millionaire William Randolph Hearst, it now belongs to American millionaire Paul Getty. It is haunted by a Lady in White.

Ⓖ **Loseley** (O.P.) lies just south of Guildford. This house is also haunted. But by what? One American tenant is said to have packed up overnight and left, overcome by the horror of 'it'. The present owner, I am told, is too busy producing really good foodstuffs to be bothered by such things.

ᶜᶜᵃ Ⓖ **Farnham** to the west has the Hop Bag Inn which is reputed to be haunted by the sound of a coach and horses. The Lion and Lamb Café in West Street is visited by a ghost lady in a grey habit and a large hat. 'Very irregularly,' commented a retired manageress; 'sometimes she'll come in several times in one day, then not be seen for months.'

Now go north-east to:

Ⓖ **Egham.** As you come down the hill (passing Holloway College on your right) you will see a Victorian villa on your left, now turned into flats, but still called Hillside. It was the subject of litigation in 1904, 1906 and 1907. The *Daily Express, Daily Mail* and the occult magazine *Light* were all involved because they published stories which said that ghostly manifestations had forced the tenant to leave be-

Puttenden Manor is spiritually inhabited by a couple who used to live there

fore his tenancy was up. It was rumoured that a farmer had strangled a child on the site some fifty years before. The case revolved around the question of whether the ghosts, real or imaginary, had lowered the value of the property. The *Daily Express* settled out of court, but the *Daily Mail* fought the action and lost, then appealed and won.

South-east, near Byfleet, is:

Ⓖ **Brooklands,** the famous old motor-racing circuit, haunted by a ghostly driver in goggles and a leather helmet. Peter Underwood thinks it may be the spectre of Percy Lambert, killed at the end of the railway straight; but John Harries suggests that it is the apparition of the first motorist to lose his life on the track, whose name was Herman.

Ⓖ **Cobham,** to the east, is where a pop group, the Peter B.s, saw a ghost on the A3. Peter Bardens who led the group is the son of Dennis Bardens, author of *Ghosts and Hauntings.* Peter and other members of the group described a strange and frightening figure.

On your way back to London you can pass through:

Ⓖ **Thames Ditton** where the Church of England House of Compassion is haunted by a presence seen and felt by a succession of Reverend Mothers. The ghost was photographed by the local historian, the late J. S. Mercer, in 1962.

There is little sense in giving directions in London. The changing system of traffic control and the construction of new roads would make most of them out of date in a year or two. I have therefore grouped the sites into types and listed them alphabetically within each section.

Palaces, Castles, Mansions and Houses

ⓖ 🔼 **50 Berkeley Square.** A number of reliable sources list this as a haunted house, including Lord Lyttelton in *Notes and Queries*. Stories are numerous and varied. One tells of two sailors who broke in because they had no lodging, and experienced something so horrible that one died of fright and the other jumped out of the window in terror. The causes too are varied: a Mr du Pre of Wilton Park kept a lunatic brother there; a young woman dived out of the window to escape her uncle's advances; a Scots girl was tortured to death. Although the inhabitants, both tangible and ethereal, may change, the house at least retains its original lamp-bracket and fanlight.

ⓖ **Bruce Castle, Lordship Lane** (now the Tottenham Museum) was once the home of Robert Bruce's father. Rebuilt in the seventeenth century, it is haunted by the ghost of Lady Coleraine who was incarcerated there by her husband until she flung herself from the balcony. She appears screaming on the night of November 3.

ⓖ **Cranford Park** (O.P.). Little more than the stableyard of Cranford House remains, except perhaps the ghosts of the man who haunted it and the woman who used to be seen in the kitchen. Both these spectres were seen by two generations of Berkeleys, who once lived here, and, as the car-park attendant will tell you, 'It's eerie in November when the mists are rising from the river'.

ⓖ **Downe Court** (O.P.A.), **near Orpington.** Library, hall, pantry and stairs are all haunted. One ghost is a girl, wet and bedraggled, who was drowned in the old moat, and sobs at a bedside. Other manifestations include a severed arm. An old man appears in the barn. The owner, Brian Thompson, has photographed seven ghosts. Do not mistake this place for Downe House which lies across the road from one entrance to the Court, and which

was Darwin's home and is now his museum.

ⓖ ♿ **Ham House** (N.T.), **Petersham,** built in 1610, came into the possession of the Earl of Dysart, whose daughter and heir married the Duke of Lauderdale. In the 1931 edition of *Haunted Houses*, Charles Harper quotes Augustus Hare's story of a butler's child who was woken at night and saw an old lady standing by the fireplace, where papers were subsequently found, proving that Lady Dysart had murdered her husband in order to marry the Duke of Lauderdale. Harper's MS correction for a later edition, however, read:

> It is one of his (Hare's) completely unfounded and ill-informed tales. The plain fact is that the husband died in Paris in 1669, Lady Dysart being then either at Ham or in London.

There are other ghosts to compensate for the possible loss of this one, the most popular being a King Charles spaniel, seen in broad daylight.

ⓖ **Hampton Court** (D.E.) is haunted by several ghosts. There are the spectres of Jane Seymour and Catherine Howard. The former can be seen coming from the Queen's Apartments, carrying a lighted taper and then walking round the Silver Stick Gallery. Catherine Howard is more often heard than seen, and her shrieks are full of terror. She used to be seen in the haunted gallery leading to the chapel. Mistress Penn – foster-mother to Jane Seymour's son Edward VI – haunted her old chambers in the south-west wing after her tomb in the old church at Hampton was disturbed in 1829. About 100 years ago a lady, enjoying the grace and favour of what has been called 'the finest almshouse in Europe', complained about the noise made by invisible beings. Nothing was done about it, but some time later, workmen unearthed two skeletons from a shallow grave opposite her front door. A group of ghosts was seen in February 1917, by Police Constable 2657, who was stationed at the main gate and looking towards Home Park. Two gentlemen and about eight ladies were within thirty feet of him before they turned aside and vanished.

ⓖ **Old Court House, Hampton Court,** has two ghosts. An eight-year-old boy with long hair, dressed as a seventeenth-century page; and that of Christopher Wren who spent the last five years of his life here, and is said to appear on the anniversary of his death, February 26.

ⓖ **Holland House.** There used to be a room here in which three spots of blood marked the recess from which Lord Holland's ghost would appear, holding his head in his hand.

Spot the ghosts in this photograph taken by a former employee at Downe Court Manor. According to the owner, eleven phantoms are visible: Charles Darwin, a blackamoor in a three-cornered hat, a Cavalier, a Miss Smith, half a dozen faces, and a girl with a long plait

But although the room disappeared in the Blitz, the bombs did not affect the ghost, for it has been seen as recently as 1965 by students staying in what is now a youth hostel. Here too, according to John Aubrey, Lady Diana Rich saw her own wraith a month before she died.

Kensington Palace (D.E.). Here, on 25 October 1760, George II died while waiting for news from Hanover. His ghost has been seen peering at the weather vane, hoping for a fair wind, asking in a thick German accent, 'Vy tont dey comp?'.

Richmond Palace. Although little of the original palace remains, Old Palace Yard, through the gateway facing Richmond Green, is enchanting. It was at the palace that the indomitable spirit of Queen Elizabeth I kept her poor ageing body alive, day after day. And during that time her ghost was seen purposefully striding through her apartments. After her death, her ghost haunted the gatehouse, which was where her ring was thrown to the rider who informed James VI of Scotland that he was also King of England.

St James's Palace. Here lived two French ladies, friends of Charles II, the Duchesse de Mazarin and Madame de Beauclair. They promised each other that, if possible, the one who died first should visit the other in spirit form. After some years, during which time Madame de Beauclair turned sceptic, her dead friend's ghost did appear – to warn her that she would be joining the Duchesse that night between midnight and 1 a.m. Although in perfect health, Madame de Beauclair died at 12.30.

The ghost of a small man with his throat cut is believed to be that of Sellis, valet to the Duke of Cumberland, who may have seduced his daughter. His attempt to kill the duke failed and he committed suicide.

Tower of London (D.E.). E. L. Swift, a former Keeper of the Crown Jewels, wrote a detailed account of the appearance of a cylindrical form, like a glass tube filled with intermingling blue and white fluid, which moved round his room in the Martin Tower. Its presence was felt and seen by his wife, but not by his son or sister-in-law. A few days later a sentry literally died of fright at what looked like a bear coming under the Jewel Room door. The Martin Tower is also believed to be haunted by a Lord Northumberland, probably the eighth earl, who, while imprisoned there for participating in a supposed plot in favour of Mary, Queen of Scots, died mysteriously from three bullet wounds. However, his brother the seventh earl was beheaded in the Tower, and his son,

79

George II has been seen staring at the Kensington Palace weather vane

was murdered. His ghost has been seen on many occasions – and quite recently – both here and at Covent Garden Underground station, where he usually caught a train home after the performance.

🐀 **Century Cinema, Cheam,** is haunted, possibly by a workman who mysteriously disappeared while the place was being built.

🐀 **Coronet Theatre, Notting Hill Gate,** is now a cinema. Recently, when the place was being redecorated, a pot of paint would find its way, night after night, to a little-used room, not scheduled for painting, but obviously one which an unknown ghost thought was in need of being brightened.

🐀 **Gargoyle Club.** Although a strip club is not exactly a theatre, it fits this category better than any other. Its past is a little less stark than its present. Sweet Nell of Old Drury once lived here, and there are many who have seen her ghost, and smelled not oranges but gardenias.

🐀 **Haymarket Theatre** is haunted by John Buckstone, the actor-manager who died in 1878. His ghost has been seen by many actors and actresses, and in 1964 appeared before a full house. His presence presages a long run.

🐀 **Lyceum Theatre.** In the 1880s a couple in a box looked down and saw a woman in the stalls with a man's head in her lap. They subsequently found a portrait of the same man in a Yorkshire manor, and discovered that he had owned the land on which the Lyceum was built. But was this just a phantom head, or was the woman a ghost as well?

🐀 **Theatre Royal, Drury Lane,** is haunted by the ghost of an eighteenth-century dandy. In life he could well have been the man whose skeleton was found with a knife between two ribs in a small bricked-up room some 100 years ago. A spectre who may once have been Charles Macklin has been seen in the pit. Stanley Lupino and his wife swear they have seen Dan Leno's ghost in the dressing-room he once used.

Cathedrals, Abbeys and Churches

🐀 **St Bartholomew the Great** is haunted by the ghost of Rahere, the monk who founded St Bartholomew's Hospital.

🐀 **St Dunstan's, East Acton.** This Victorian brick church is not the place you would expect to find ghosts, but it stands in Friar's Place Lane, which is perhaps the answer to the ghostly procession of monks which has been seen – by many people – moving into the church and up the aisle. It is thought that it may occur in four-yearly cycles.

the ninth earl was also incarcerated here, so one cannot be certain which one it is.

The Little Princes' spirits have been seen around the Bloody Tower; Anne Boleyn haunts the White Tower, Tower Green, the King's House and St Peter-ad-Vincula, where her remains still lie. Although sometimes headless, she has been recognized by her clothes. Lady Salisbury, beheaded – with much difficulty – by order of Henry VIII, and Sir Walter Raleigh are others whose ghosts have been seen. One of the most recent is that of Lady Jane Grey, who was seen on the 403rd anniversary of her execution.

Ill-fortune, even death, befalls anyone who kills one of the Tower ravens.

🐀 **Walpole House, Chiswick Mall,** is haunted by Barbara Villiers, Duchess of Cleveland, who died here in 1709.

Theatres

🐀 **Adelphi Theatre.** Outside the stage-door in December 1897 William Terriss the actor

☠ **St James's, Garlick Hill.** The ghost of Jimmy the Mummy (which can still be seen in the porch) has made frequent appearances in the church.

☠ **St Magnus the Martyr, London Bridge,** is haunted by a figure in cowl and cassock, possibly a former priest, or maybe Miles Coverdale, Bishop of Exeter, who is buried here.

☠ **St Mary's, Twickenham,** is still haunted by the ghost of Alexander Pope. Legend has it that this started in 1830 when his grave was disturbed and his skull bought by a phrenologist. His spectral body demands to be reunited.

☠ **West Drayton Church** has been haunted for years, both inside and out, by a huge black bird. Could it be a ghostly vulture? It pecks at tombs and appears quite real, even to dropping a wing when hit, but when cornered it simply disappears. One rather macabre theory is that it is the spirit of a murderer who was buried in consecrated ground instead of a lime pit in the prison yard or at Harmondsworth Cross with a stake through his heart.

☠ **Westminster Abbey.** There are at least three ghosts here. Father Benedictus may be seen in the cloisters between 5 and 6 p.m., some say on Christmas Eve, walking above the present floor level. In 1934 he informed a witness that he had been killed in the reign of Henry VIII. John Bradshaw, who tried and condemned Charles I, now haunts the deanery; and the ghost of the Unknown Warrior of the 1914 war has also been seen.

☠ **Westminster Cathedral.** Five years ago a sacristan on night watch saw a black-clad figure near the High Altar.

The Adelphi Theatre stage-door where Terriss was murdered

LONDON

Hospitals

☙ **St Thomas's.** A Grey Lady, possibly the ghost of Florence Nightingale, has been seen by members of the staff, including a Matron.

☙ **University College Hospital.** The ghost of a nurse, who accidentally killed her fiancé by giving him an overdose of morphia, is said to appear when this drug is being administered.

Inns

☙ **The Gatehouse, Hampstead Lane,** is haunted by the ghost of a white-haired smuggler who was murdered here.

☙ **The Grenadier, Knightsbridge,** is said to be haunted by the ghost of an officer who, caught cheating at cards, was beaten up and died in the cellar. This may be the explanation of the ghost seen on the stairs and in a bedroom by successive landlords and their families.

☙ **The Greyhound, Carshalton,** is on the B.T.A. list of reputedly haunted inns.

☙♿ **The Spaniards, Hampstead Heath,** is haunted by the ghost of Dick Turpin. Black Bess's hoofbeats are heard.

Museums, Famous Buildings and other places

☙ **Amen Corner, Ludgate Hill.** On the other side of the tall wall lay Dead Man's Walk, where those hanged at Newgate prison were buried in quicklime. This may have something to do with the Thing that crawls and creeps along the top of the wall at night.

☙ **Bank of England, Threadneedle Street.** Peter Underwood records an apparition known as the Black Nun, actually the sister of an employee who was condemned to death for forgery in 1811. She went mad and spent twenty-five years searching for her brother. When she died she was buried in an old churchyard on the bank's premises.

☙ **Barnes Common** is haunted by a man in convicts' clothes.

☙ **Biggin Hill.** At this famous airfield of World War II you may hear the sound of a single Spitfire coming home, the ghost perhaps of one of the many which did not return.

☙ **The Black Museum, New Scotland Yard,** was haunted by a nun who had no face beneath her veil.

☙ **Blackheath** is frequented by a female phantom in Victorian dress.

☙ **Broadcasting House, Portland Place,**

Oliver Cromwell, one ghost in Red Lion Square

is haunted by the ghost of a butler with a limp, most often seen on the fourth floor early in the morning.

☙ **Cambridge Gardens, Ladbroke Grove.** A phantom bus has been reported on several occasions and more than one accident has been caused by its appearance at night.

♿ **Cheyne Walk, Chelsea,** is reputed to be haunted by the ghost of a bear.

☙ **Cock Lane, Smithfield,** was the scene of a classic eighteenth-century haunting, centred round poltergeist manifestations and a ghost known as 'Scratching Fanny'.

☙ **Gower Street, Bloomsbury,** is the haunt of a man swathed in bandages.

☙ **Hampstead Heath.** Here there is supposed to be a stone which whistles at the place where a highwayman was killed.

☙ **Hanbury Street, Stepney,** is haunted by the earth-bound spirit of Ann Chapman, murdered and mutilated here by Jack the Ripper.

☙ **Hill Street, Mayfair.** According to Eric Russell's *Conspectus of Traditional Hauntings*, this street has an apparition – seen by Lord

Lyttelton in 1779 – which is supposed to give warning of revenge or death.

☻ **Honor Oak Park.** On One Tree Hill an ordinary couple saw, quite recently, what is believed to have been the ghost of a dancing girl. An account of this by Andrew Mackenzie, prepared for The Society for Psychical Research, will be found in *Frontiers of the Unknown*.

☻ **Hyde Park.** Between Marble Arch and Lancaster Gate, according to Elliott O'Donnell in *Haunted Houses of London*, there is, or was, a tree known as the Devil's Elm, which brings death to tramps who sleep under it, and 'even respectable people' have nightmares. A ghostly horse-bus was said to drive past it down the Bayswater Road. I think the tree has been cut down, but whether the spirit remains I do not know.

☻ **Ilford Fire Station.** Both old and new stations are said to be haunted by the ghost of Geoffrey Netherwood, an old fire-fighter who lived at the end of the last century and was interested in ghosts.

☻ **Lansdowne Passage, Mayfair,** ran between Berkeley Square and Curzon Street, and once divided the grounds of Lansdowne House and Devonshire House. It was closed in the 1930s and replaced by Lansdowne Row. It was considered a very haunted place, and was used as an escape route for highwaymen after holding up people in Piccadilly.

☻ **Lewisham.** At 3 a.m., mournful voices are sometimes heard coming out of the sky.

☻ **Pond Square, Highgate,** has the oddest apparition of all. This is the ghost of a chicken which Sir Francis Bacon stuffed with snow as an experiment. It is seen flapping its wings.

☻ **Red Lion Square, Holborn,** has the ghosts of Oliver Cromwell, John Bradshaw and General Ironside.

☻ **Tagg Island.** Fred Karno, the Music Hall comedian, whose troupe included many famous names, Charles Chaplin among them, tried to turn the island into a pleasure garden revolving round his 'Karsino'. In doing so, he expelled some Gypsies, who laid a curse on those who were to follow, condemning them and their affairs to failure. Since then nine successive owners have become insolvent. In 1971 an American developer invited some Gypsies to lift the curse.

☻ **Tavistock Place, Bloomsbury,** is haunted by two ghosts which have been seen over the past 100 years. A nurse approaches a man in mourning, peers into his face, then turns and dashes away.

☻ **Vanbrugh Hill, East Greenwich.** Lord Angosteen's coach and four collected

The lamp outside Vine Street Police Station

him from the Ship and Billet Inn, to drive him home up Vanbrugh Hill. They can still be seen, at 6 a.m. in November, but now the horses are headless. The ghost of Lord Angosteen in black velvet breeches and silk stockings has been seen wandering around here too. But who was Lord Angosteen?

☻ **Vine Street Police Station.** One of three famous West End police stations, this is haunted by the ghost of Station-Sergeant Goddard, who committed suicide by hanging himself in the cells. You will find it in Picadilly Place which, until the station was superseded by West Central in Savile Row in 1939, was called Vine Street. It has now been re-opened under its old name, the Metropolitan Police showing more imagination and sense of tradition than the Greater London Council.

☻ **Wash-house Court, Masters Court and Charterhouse,** in the City, are all haunted by a monk. I think it must be Rahere from St Bartholomew's (q.v.) nearby.

☻ **Wellington Barracks, Birdcage Walk,** is frequented by the ghost of a guardsman's wife who was murdered by her husband.

To the north and north-west there are many sites near the great radial roads leading out of London which fall into adjoining counties, so study the map before planning your own tour.

If you leave London by the old A40, at Tatling End, just beyond Denham, turn left for:

👁 **Fulmer** where many still hear the clop-clop of a trotting horse, sometimes accompanied by the crunch of wheels on gravel, but nothing is seen.

On the southern outskirts of Slough is:

👁 **Upton Court.** Friday night, according to Peter Underwood, is the most likely time to see the ghost of a woman in a blood-stained nightdress.

South-west of Marlow you will find:

👂 **Medmenham Abbey,** famous from 1755 to 1763 as the scene of the mysterious rites and wild orgies of the Hell Fire Club, founded by Sir Francis Dashwood in 1742. Here a baboon was used to impersonate Satan, and terrified Lord Sandwich so much that he ran from the chapel screaming, 'Spare me, gracious Devil!' What is generally regarded as the fullest description of what went on here is given in the novel *Chrysal* (1760–5) by Charles Johnstone.

Just north of High Wycombe the 4128 will lead you to:

👁 **Hughenden Manor** (N.T.) where Disraeli's ghost has been seen on a number of occasions at the foot of the cellar stairs and on the upper floors.

👂👁 **West Wycombe.** The church contains several strange things, among them Paul Whitehead's heart which was bequeathed to Sir Francis Dashwood and interred with full military honours, and the globe on top of the tower in which the Hell Fire Club (see Medmenham Abbey) are reputed to have played cards.

The caves are a tourist attraction. I have heard that the park (N.T.) was laid out with hillocks, dells, streams and thickets, to represent a gigantic female form. When Tom Corbett and Diana Norman visited the house, Corbett found a female ghost 'of the utmost charm and respectability' in the Music Room. The description he gave exactly fitted the present Francis Dashwood's grandmother.

The George and Dragon Inn is haunted by Sukie or Susan, who scorned three local suitors to marry a man of higher social standing. One of the three sent her a message instructing her to meet her new fiancé in the caves, dressed in her bridal gown. This she did, only to be met by the jeers of her ex-suitors. She fell, cracked her skull and died.

Now go north-west for:

👁 **Haddenham.** The side road which leads from here to the 418 is haunted by the ghost of a farmer who was murdered in 1848 as he returned from Thame market. His wife first saw her husband's ghost in a dream, clutching his chest which had been crushed with a hammer. This led to a search for the body, and the eventual hanging of the footpads.

Take the same route as the farmer. On the 418 turn right for:

☆ **Hartwell.** The church, sadly falling into ruins, has a very poignant atmosphere, maybe because Louis XVIII spent his exile at Hartwell House (O.P.) from 1808 to 1814. Here his queen died and so did at least two of the 180 men and women who shared his sojourn. They are buried in the tangled churchyard. Down a road marked with a dead-end sign you will find an alcove with Egyptian symbols on the lintel. Opposite is a spring which was once famous for curing weak eyes and rheumatism, but is now choked with debris. When Louis returned to France, a Dr Lee, who was interested in astronomy and Egyptian antiquities, inherited the place; hence the alcove by the spring.

Less than a mile north of Whitchurch, a turning to the right (with a 10 m.p.h. sign) leads to:

👁 **Creslow Manor,** a romantic place. Christ's Low was the name of the royal pastures on which the king's cattle were fattened. Harper illustrates the hamlet – little more than a large trim farm – and tells the story of the haunted chamber, women's footsteps and rustling silk. These were reported a century or so ago, which is not long in the life of a house that dates back to Edward III.

West of the main road lies:

☆ **North Marston.** Sir John Shorne's Well (or Town Well) is a spring with the power of curing 'scorbutic and cutaneous diseases, ague and gout'. It is kept locked but several villagers have the key and will be pleased to open it up.

> Sir John Shorne, Gentleman born,
> Conjured the Devil into a horn.

This is a rhyme in which the last word has somehow been changed into 'boot', in defiance of rhyme and reason. Shorne was rector here from 1290–1314; so the well has had nearly 700 years of healing. A glass of the water drunk at night is said to cure a cold by morning.

A staircase at Hughenden Manor

To the north-west you will find:

⊛ **Claydon House** (N.T.), transformed, according to Steel, in 1752 by the second Earl of Verney, and haunted by the ghost of Sir Edmund Verney, King's Standard Bearer at the Battle of Edgehill in 1642. He refused to surrender the colours, saying: 'My life is my own, my Standard the King's.' He was killed, but the Roundheads could not prize open his grasp even in death, so they hacked off his hand. Later the standard was recaptured; Sir Edmund's hand was recognized by the signet ring which bore the king's portrait, and sent to Claydon for burial, but the rest of his body was never found. His spirit haunts Claydon seeking the lost limb. This may be the ghost

seen on the Red Stairs. A Lady in Grey has also been seen in the Rose Room. Could this possibly have been Florence Nightingale, whose sister Parthenope became the second wife of Sir Harry Verney? Many of her relics are to be seen.

North-east just before the A5 is:

✩ **Shenley Church End** where a holy thorn tree blooms at midnight on Christmas Eve. The *Wolverton Express* reported in 1963, 'Some who made the journey for the first time were very sceptical until they actually saw the tree in bloom.' Unfortunately the tree appears to be dying and so not many of its branches produce flowers.

North-east across the A5 is:

⊛ **Woughton on the Green.** The ghost of Dick Turpin lurks around here, waiting to strike. Legend has it that at the Swan Inn he made the village blacksmith reverse the shoes on his horse's hooves.

You may now care to slip over the border to visit Cranfield and Aspley Guise in Bedfordshire (q.v.).

South-east of Aylesbury is:

⋘ **St Leonards.** Hereabouts, pin-pointed by John Harries as at Uphill, the sound of snorting, rampaging animals has been heard. On the occasions these have been seen, they appear to be black boars. Hang Hill was once a place of execution.

To the south at:

☠ **Great Missenden** the abbey is reputed to be haunted. This is not surprising for the Black Monks of Missenden were once notorious: in 1530 a monk should not have been seen coming out of a house in the village dressed in doublet and jerkin with a sword by his side; and what lay behind the pitiful story of the novice in 1297 who cut her throat for fear of discipline?

The Little Abbey Hotel features on the B.T.A.'s list of reputedly haunted hotels.

Towards London, north of the main road, is:

⊛ **Amersham Common.** Peter Underwood quotes Dirk Bogarde as saying that when he lived at Bendrose House, seven different people, on different occasions, experienced the same phenomenon at the same time of day, without knowing that anyone else had experienced it. The sensation was always that of an electric shock, which was felt for four minutes between 4 and 5 a.m. by those who slept in one particular room.

The last site on your tour lies east at:

⊛ **Chenies** where the manor house is haunted by an unidentified ghost, and possibly two.

This trip starts from London and leads you zig-zagging over the county to Oxford. First: ☻⚴ **Windsor.** The castle (O.P.) is full of ghosts. Elizabeth I haunts the library and has also been seen on the castle walls. Charles I is reputed to haunt the Canon's House. George III's restless spirit has been seen in the room where he was confined during the last years of his lunacy.

Herne the Hunter appears in the Park. Some will tell you that Herne was Warden of the Forest to Henry VIII (whose ghost haunts the deanery) and that he committed suicide when he was suspected of witchcraft; but Herne is much older than that. With his deer-skin clothes, his helmet made of a stag's skull, the antlers spreading like mantling in the breeze, riding a horse which breathes fire and accompanied by a pack of hounds, he is Master of the Wild Hunt, or Cain's Pack as it was called in the Middle Ages. He may have served as forester to Richard II, but his ancestry goes back to Odin, who rode the wind on his horse Sleipnir. In *The God of Witches* Margaret Murray writes, 'The earliest known representation of a deity is . . . the figure . . . of a man clothed in the skin of a stag, and wearing on his head the antlers. . . .' She dates it as palaeolithic. In the seventh century Theodore, Archbishop of Canterbury, in *Liber Poenitentialis*, condemned any man who

> . . . at the Kalends of January goes about as a stag or bull-calf, that is, making himself into a wild animal and dressing in the skins of herd animals and putting on the heads of beasts . . . this is devilish.

And thus the gods of yesterday become the devils of today. Although Herne's Oak was destroyed in 1863, it, as well as the spectral hunter and his pack, appeared quite recently in the Long Walk. Here, too, the ghost of a sentry who committed suicide has been seen.

Through the Great Park the 332 crosses the 329 which leads from Ascot to: ☻ **Bracknell.** Hereabouts at night you may see the ghost of a policeman with a face so dreadfully mutilated that people gasp in horrified sympathy.

North-west of Maidenhead is: ☻ **Bisham Abbey** (O.P.A.) where the ghost of Elizabeth Hoby is seen washing her hands in a basin which floats before her. She is trying

Herne the Hunter appearing to Henry VIII in Windsor Great Park, where he is still seen

to remove the bloodstains of her son, whom she is said to have beaten to death because he was careless and untidy at his lessons and blotted his exercise book. Strangely enough in the nineteenth century when repairs were being carried out a number of exercise books were found, and they were full of blots. According to Charles Harper the ghost is seen 'in negative', that is wearing a white dress but with a black face and hands. Edith Sitwell, in *English Eccentrics*, writes, 'During her lifetime, the appearance of Lady Hoby must have caused almost as much alarm as that of her ghost. She was, when living, a pest of outstanding quality.' The house now belongs to the Sports Council.

North-west of Reading you come to: ☻ **Tidmarsh.** On clear nights with a full moon in June, the ghost of a drowned boy has been seen rising from the stream about 100 yards from the rectory.

In a little pocket south-west of Newbury is: ☻ **Combe Manor,** originally a priory with a ghostly reputation. This is another place to which Charles II brought Nell Gwyn. Figures in Caroline dress have been seen in the garden. The chanting of nuns has been heard. Not so long ago, a mournfully small skeleton was discovered under the stairs.

Just west of Newbury you will find: ✫ **Speen.** Here, 200 yards above the church, is St Mary's or Lady's Well, remarkable for its healing properties, and also for its echo.

North-east, across the M4, you come to: ✫ **Yattendon.** On the Pangbourne road, near the site of a kiln, is the Miraculous Well, which is always full but never overflows. The Old Rectory was once haunted by the most charming ghost in England. She appeared dressed in grey or black watered silk, and loved parties. She would lead rectors' wives to undiscovered hens' nests when there were no eggs in the house, and apart from always being in a hurry, she seems to have been as useful as she was mysterious. In life she was the unmarried sister of an eighteenth-century rector. Exorcism may have temporarily banished this gentle soul.

Due west lie Leckhampstead, Hangman's Stone, and:

📍 **Great Shefford.** This is the village where the midwife lived who brought Wild Darrell to trial (see Littlecote, Wiltshire). To the south, lies Shefford Woodlands, where the Roman road crosses the 338. Here, Wild Darrell's ghost is seen, with his head horribly awry.

📍 **Hungerford.** Instead of a mayor, alderman and council, this town is still administered by a constable, portreeve, bailiff, feoffee and tythe or tutti-men (so called because they carry tall sticks decorated with nosegays or tutties). It is the only remaining place in England to celebrate Hocktide on the Tuesday after Easter. The feast is fully described in most guides, but it is worth mentioning here because it is probably the last vestige of what was originally a Roman saturnalia.

South of the town, on the 338, a female ghost appears riding a grey horse in the day time, but at night in a coach and four.

If you drive up the Lambourn Valley, just before you reach Ashbury you will cross the Ridgeway, and I would advise walking to the two next sites along this ancient road to the right. Otherwise, turn right in Ashbury and drive through Compton Beauchamp. On your right lie the White Horse (described below) and, 2 miles south-west:

🐎 **Wayland Smith's Cave.** This was originally a cromlech, but according to legend if you left your horse and a coin here, the animal would be shod in your absence by Wayland Smith, a mythical demigod; as Christina Hole points out, blacksmiths have a long tradition of magic: 'Being associated with those potent charms – fire, iron and horseshoes – he was a servant of the sacred horse.' (See Shervage Wood, Somerset.)

☆ **The Uffington White Horse** is the most splendid of all the figures cut through turf to show the downland chalk. He is probably 2000 years old, and is thought by some to be a dragon. Dragon Hill or Mound lies just below

The Uffington White Horse

and, they say, is the site of St George's triumph. A bare patch marks the place made sterile by the dragon's blood. Stand in the centre of the White Horse's 'eye' and wish.

📍 **Faringdon.** The headless ghost which walks by the north wall of the church is said to be Sir Robert Pye, the Parliamentarian, who besieged his father's home, Faringdon House, when it was held by the Royalists.

Strong poltergeist activities have been reported at Oriel Cottage, Wicklesham Road, within the last decade. Exorcism seems to have quietened things down.

South-east, on the 417, is:

📍 **West Hendred.** Beware of a strange figure in cap and overcoat which may dash out in front of your car.

Due east at:

📍 **Wallingford** the George Hotel is reputedly haunted.

South-east of Abingdon, west of the 423, is:

📍 **Long Wittenham** where the Co-op Stores have been the unlikely scene of poltergeist manifestations.

North-west across the A34 and 420 is:

📍 **Cumnor.** The site of Cumnor Hall is still haunted by the ghost of Amy Robsart, who was married to Robert Dudley, Earl of Leicester, and favourite of Elizabeth I. Amy died, you may remember, in a mysterious fall. Attempts were made to lay the ghost in Lady Dudley's Pond, and it was said that from that moment the pond never froze. Perhaps this is the reason that it still cannot hold her restless spirit.

The Oxfordshire tour starts in Oxford and leads round the county and back towards London. First then, in the city:

⊛ **St John's College** is haunted by the ghost of Archbishop Laud, who was beheaded in 1645. Some say he bowls his head across the library floor.

On the banks of the Thames is:

☆⊛🐎 **Binsey.** The Holy Well restored Algar's sight after he had been blinded by stoning for daring to seize the hand of St ffrediswyde, the girl he loved. She called on St Margaret to help and the well was the result. It is still visited by thousands of pilgrims every year, with remarkable results. As the parish magazine says, 'Prayers are answered and cures effected.' The last royal pilgrims were Henry VIII and Catherine of Aragon.

North-west is:

⊛☆ **Woodstock** where during the last decade there have been many reports of poltergeist phenomena occurring in Room 16 of the Bear Inn. Things have been moved, lights switched on and drawers opened by unseen hands. Footsteps have resounded in empty corridors.

In the grounds of Blenheim (O.P.) is Fair Rosamund's Well, a healing well, once held in great repute.

To the west of Witney on the A40 lies:

⊛🐎 **Minster Lovell Hall** (D.E.). The ruined home of the Lovells is haunted by the ghost of Lord Lovell, supporter of Lambert Simnel in 1487. After the Battle of Stoke he lived in hiding, looked after by one faithful servant, locked into a secret room. When this man died, his master starved to death. In 1718, when the house was being repaired, a vault was uncovered in which a skeleton was found, sitting at a table with a skeleton dog at its feet. Another legend is that of the Mistletoe Bough (see Bramshill, Hampshire) which is also said to have happened here. The road from here to:

⊛ **Burford** is haunted by a terrifying apparition. It takes the form of a black cloud. If you drive through it you experience a feeling of utter terror. Animals are driven frantic.

In the town itself there is a priory which, after being a private house, is now inhabited by Anglo-Catholic nuns. Their chaplain lives in the Old Rectory. Both houses have long established reputations for being 'very

haunted'. Telekinetic phenomena, unearthly screams, the sound of singing near the monks' old graveyard, and the tolling of a bell at 2 a.m. are reported. Apparitions include an old-fashioned gamekeeper as well as a little brown monk.

To the north-east lie the dark mysterious Wychwood Forest and:

⊛ **Shipton Court** which had a ghost who was exorcised and the haunted room sealed up. No-one now knows where this room is.

Near the Gloucestershire border-is:

⊛ **Bruern Abbey.** An underground passage, four miles long, is said to lead to Tangley Hall, and its path is traced over the heath by a ghostly monk.

⊛ **Kingham.** The Langstone Arms Hotel, according to Peter Underwood, was haunted by the spirit of an elderly woman in 1964. The ghost appeared every ten days or so. People in the village think it is still haunted.

North-east of Kingham are:

🗡🐎 **The Rollright Stones** (O.P., D.E.) This 3500-year-old site was once used as a meeting place for witches. There is a stone circle known as the King's Men, and a menhir, now surrounded by iron railings, called the King's Stone (actually sited over the Warwickshire border). Below the circle stands a group called the Whispering Knights. A farmer once tried to move one of these stones. A team of horses could barely drag it downhill, but one eager animal easily pulled it back up to its original position.

Due east on the 423 lies:

⊛ **Deddington** where the vicarage is reputed to be haunted by the spirit of Maurice Frost, the vicar. Strange phenomena have been witnessed by his cousin and by local people.

The next site lies a long way south, between Oxford and Thame. A mile out of Thame, a signpost will lead you to:

⊛ **Rycote Chapel** (D.E.), an enchanting place, beautifully kept and full of history. It is haunted by the ghost of a Tudor lady. Mr Clifford, the custodian, has seen her quite recently, moving round the outside of the chapel, under the giant yew tree. He will gladly tell you all about it.

South-west of Rycote you will find:

⊛ **Clifton Hampden.** Courtiers, a square Georgian house, has been haunted for years by Sarah Fletcher, whose distraught arrival only just prevented her husband, Captain

The Rollright Stones

88

Fletcher, R.N., from bigamously marrying an heiress. He immediately went off to sea, while poor Sarah went home and, on 7 June 1769, hanged herself from the curtain rails of her bed with a pocket handkerchief tied to a piece of cord. She was not yet thirty, and her blameless character is reflected in the inscription on her tombstone at Dorchester Abbey Church:

> The remains of a Young Lady whose artless beauty, innocence of Mind and gentle manner once obtained her the love and esteem of all who knew her. But when nerves were too delicately spun to bear the rude Shakes and Jostlings which we meet with in this transitory world, She sunk and died, a Martyr to Excessive Sensibility.

Her story has touched the heart of more than one man. There was a boy who first saw her ghost when he was seventeen, and loved her. Another man, who saw her in a black silk cloak, with a purple ribbon in her auburn hair, was so struck by the anguish in her eyes that he was overwhelmed with the desire to comfort and cherish her. But perhaps the strangest part of her story is how she appeared in a dream to a Bournemouth landscape gardener who knew nothing about her.

The whole of Sarah's sad but enthralling story is told in a booklet sold in aid of the Abbey Monastery Guest House.

South-east from here, on the other side of Wallingford, is:

Ipsden where you can see a monument inscribed:

> John Thurlow Reade
> Esquire
> Sehaarunpore
> November 24th A.D. 1827
> Alas! my poor brother

It was erected by his brother Edward of Ipsden House (another brother was Charles Reade the novelist). John's ghost appeared to his mother at Ipsden, although he died in India. Nearby is the Maharajah's Well, an Indian monument built in 1863, by His Highness Ishree, Maharajah of Benares, as a token of gratitude to his friend Edward Anderton Reade.

Near Ipsden is an oaktree called Watch Folly. Here some sheepstealers hanged a shepherd boy. The place is haunted.

Going east, just before you come to the

Old Clibbon's Post, where a gang of thieves and killers met their comeuppance in Hertfordshire

4009 at Highmoor Cross, you will find:

Witheridge Hill. A track leading through the woods here will take you past a stone wall which is said to be haunted by a ghostly woman, sitting and brooding.

About 5 miles to the north-east, you come to:

Stonor Park (O.P.). Lord Camoys told me of many strange things that have happened here. People have heard the sound of voices coming from empty rooms, and a man's footsteps walking across a floor and down the stairs into a room where a cupboard is mysteriously opened. You can feel someone touching your face as you lie in bed at night. In the garden at the back of the house, dogs see something which sets their hair on end, and they back away growling. Outside the chapel is the site of a prehistoric stone circle, and here there is a curious animal smell.

Henley-on-Thames lies south. At the Bull Inn, a strange scent of burned candles has been smelled, and a cowled figure has been seen in a bedroom. The Kenton Theatre and the Town Hall have been the scene of poltergeist manifestations and the appearance of a ghostly young woman, whenever scenes concerned with the life of Mary Bland are re-enacted (for example, at the theatre in 1969 when *The Hanging Wood* was performed). This tells the story of how Mary Bland was hanged in 1752 for poisoning her father. Joan Morgan, the author of the play, herself witnessed these occurrences.

The Maharajah's Well at Stoke Row, Ipsden

GLOUCESTERSHIRE

This tour leads north and east. You should start in Bristol (see North Somerset) and go first to the eastern suburb of:

☿ **Hanham Abbots.** In the grounds of Hanham Court is a church which is haunted by the ghost of a woman in white, believed to be a nun who regularly visited Hanham Abbots many centuries ago. There is also a report of a cold and clammy atmosphere at night, even when the weather is warm and dry. At Court Farm barn, a particularly fine building, there is evidence of a more recent haunting. In 1971 when she was checking the site for this book, my wife saw the figure of a man going into the barn, but when she followed him to ask the way there was no-one there and no other exit.

☿ **Cold Ashton** lies to the east. It was the site of a remarkable haunting when Lady Winifred Pennoyer (see Corsham, Wiltshire) lived at Charterhouse during the late 1930s. One winter weekend she invited Olive Snell, the portrait painter, to stay, begging her to arrive in time for tea as it was difficult to find the way in the dark. In fact, she did get lost and stopped at a house with stone pineapples on either side of a wrought-iron gate. This she opened and went up to the front door and rang the bell. A man she assumed to be the butler opened it, and when he had given her instructions for finding her hostess's house, she gave him half-a-crown. She told the story to Lady Winifred, who suggested motoring over there the next day for she knew the only house answering to that description in the vicinity was empty. Much to Olive Snell's surprise the gate was locked, and they had to go to the gardener's cottage for the key. They went up to the front door and there, lying on the step, was half-a-crown.

North of Bristol and south-east of Stroud is:

◉ **Minchinhampton** where you will find the Long Stone; not on the golf-course as we were told, but on the Avening road, just past Hollybush Farm, in a field on the left. It is supposed to walk round the field at midnight. More credible is the story that children were passed through the hole in one end, to be cured of measles and other diseases.

The site which lies farthest east of the general line of the tour can be visited from Minchinhampton. It is on the far side of Cirencester, at the crossroads due east of Ampney St Mary and marked on the o.s. map as:

☆ **Betty's Grave.** Elizabeth Bastre who was buried here in 1786 has an uncertain identity. She was a witch who was hanged or burned at the stake; or a woman who committed

A building at Hanham Court once used as an armoury

suicide or was poisoned by her master; or a girl who died of exposure after challenging a man to hoe a field of turnips (or mow a meadow) faster than she; or a thief hanged for sheepstealing. Can anyone say which?

☙ **Cheltenham.** Here is what Andrew MacKenzie called 'the most famous case of haunting since the Society of Psychical Research was formed'. Between 1882 and 1889 the ghost of a tall woman was frequently seen at Garden Reach – now called St Anne's – a large house in Pittville Circus Road. At least ten people are known to have seen it and it was heard by double that number in those seven years. The ghost, holding a handkerchief to her face, has recently been seen again near St Anne's but in a different house. Mr Thorne, who lived in a flat there between 1957 and 1962, his brother and nephew, all saw and heard this apparition. The ghost is believed to be that of Imogen, second wife of Henry Swinhoe.

Captain Thomas Hardy's house in Victoria Walk is also reputed to be haunted.

North-east of the town is:

☙ **Prestbury** where the race-course is situated. There are, according to J. Hallam, four ghosts. The Black Abbot may be seen at the priory, in the High Street and in St Mary's church. A Cavalier, bearing news of the Battle of Worcester, gallops round the lanes. A girl plays the spinet in the garden of Sundial Cottage. Cleeve Corner is the haunt of the Phantom Strangler, and one may also see the spectre of Old Moses, of Walnut Cottage.

North and east again is the historic town of:

☙ **Winchcombe** which boasted an abbey in 797. From the ruins, which contain the shrine of the Martyr King Kenelm, come the sound of music and the chanting of monks at midnight. On the road from the railway station, in a hollow near the cemetery, a tall dark apparition, rather like a monk, is seen walking two feet above the present ground level. A ghostly monk is also seen at Pyke Bank. At Margrett's Hollow a cyclist, finding his machine bewitched, had to dismount and drag it along, although it was in perfect working order.

East, across the Cotswolds, you come to:

☙ **Stow-on-the-Wold.** In Chapen Street the house of Mr and Mrs Pethrick was the site of poltergeist disturbances in 1963/4, including the appearance of water which the plumber was unable to trace, and a baby's fist which grew into an old man's hand. Telekinesis and rapping also occurred, and a voice was heard saying that he was the builder who had died twenty years before.

HEREFORDSHIRE

Like the bulls and cider it produces, Hereford is a strong heady county with a pronounced character of its own. As you will see, one Black Vaughan is worth a dozen Grey Ladies. I suggest you start in the south. Just east of the A40 on the banks of the Wye is:

☙ **Goodrich Castle** (D.E.), haunted by Alice and Clifford. She was with her sweetheart in the castle in 1646 when it was besieged by her Roundhead uncle, Colonel Birch. They tried to escape but the Wye was in spate and they were both drowned.

A mile or so to the north is:

☙ **Pencraig** where the Mount Craig Hotel is reputedly haunted.

☙ **Hereford.** The ghost of a White Monk appeared to many visitors at the Three Choirs Festival some years ago. He was seen at midnight, north-east of the cathedral near Lady Chapel, and is supposed to have been killed by a Welshman in 1055. In the High Street there is a seventeenth-century haunted house which was moved to a new site 100 yards away in 1966. The ghost is – or was – an apothecary who poisoned his apprentice by mistake and then committed suicide. I cannot establish if this is 'Old Taylor', whose ghost still walks about White Cross and Morning Pit.

South-west, near the Welsh border, is:

⚔ **Longtown Castle.** According to tradition, '1000 guineas in a coffin be buried here'.

To the north-east, around Weobley, there is a clutch of sites. First at:

☙ **Weobley** itself. If you walk round the preaching cross in the churchyard, seven times at midnight reciting the Lord's Prayer backwards, you can conjure up the Devil.

☙ **Wormsley Grange** is haunted at midnight by a lady in silk and a man in black. They can be seen only by those born between 11 p.m. and 1 a.m.

🐾 **Garnstone.** Here there is a pond, and on the muddy bottom is a snuff box containing the spirit of a farmer who committed suicide at Field's End. His spirit returned in the form of a calf. At an exorcism it was conjured into the box and thrown into the pond.

☙ **Dunwood Farm** lies towards Weobley Marsh. It is haunted by the ghost of 'Old Gregg', who was poisoned by being given stewed toad for supper.

☙ **Devereux Wooten Farm,** on the 4230

before it joins the 480, is haunted by Lady Berrington.

North-west again, almost to the Welsh border, you will find:

Hergest Court. Although now a farm, it was for centuries the seat of the Vaughans. Sir Thomas, known as Black Vaughan, was taken prisoner and beheaded in 1483. As his head fell, it was seized by his faithful black bloodhound. It is sometimes seen hovering above the waters of the moat. He and the dog, in spectral form, either separately or together, haunt the roads to Kington Church, 2 miles away, and back to the Welsh border near Black Vaughan tree. Attempts to exorcise Hergest by twelve clergymen have apparently failed.

Near Kington are:

Stanmore Rocks where there is a piece of barren land where nothing will grow, known as the 'Devil's Garden'.

Almost due east of Kington, across the A49, is:

Hampton Court. Hanging on the wall is a painting of a dog – the Coningsbury Hound. Tragedy will come to the owner of the house if the picture is ever taken down. The painting was not among the items put up for auction by Lord Hereford in June 1972. It remained on the wall to preserve Captain Smith, who bought the place, from misfortune.

East again, south of Bromyard, are the ruins of:

Avenbury Church, haunted by ghostly music.

South-east, near the borders of Gloucester and Worcester is:

Bronsil Castle where hidden treasure is guarded by a raven. It will remain undiscovered until the rightful owner comes along, and even he, before he can claim the gold, must first find the bones of Baron Beauchamp, the former owner, whose skeleton was brought back from Italy.

The Coningsbury Hound protects Hampton Court from disaster

WORCESTERSHIRE

Worcestershire sites are rather scattered, but you could not do better than start with one of the most famous English villages:

Broadway. The bells of Broadway were hidden in Middle Hill beech wood during the Reformation. They are still occasionally heard ringing at night and even sounded during World War II, when bell-ringing was prohibited.

North-west on the 435 lie:

Lenchwick and Norton. Between these two places a ghostly coach, connected in some way with the Dench family, has been seen.

West of Pershore on the A44 is:

Besford Court which is reputed to be haunted by the ghost of either a nun or a Grey Lady, or both. An upstairs bedroom is where the latter is most likely to be seen. The place is now a boarding school for boys.

West again, you come to:

Great Malvern. The ghost and legend of Raggedstone Hill are concerned with human failing. A monk at Little Malvern Priory yielded to 'human passion'; tortured mentally by remorse he confessed to his prior, who although guilty of the same offence himself, nevertheless ordered the monk to crawl on hands and knees up the rough side of Raggedstone Hill from the bottom to the twin peaks at the top, every day. How many times he accomplished this is not recorded, but eventually he went mad, so some say, although others think he merely realized the gross injustice of his sentence. Be that as it may, one day, having crawled to the peaks, he stood up and cursed first the prior, then the Church and finally those on whom the shadow of the two peaks should fall. He then stretched out his arms and fell down dead. His curse is said to have claimed as victims Thomas à Becket, the Duke of Clarence, Richard III, the two little Princes of York, Prince Edward and Henry VI, Cardinal Wolsey, Anne Boleyn and a number of people who stayed at Castle Hanley and Birtsmorten.

North-east is:

Callow End. At Prior's Court, which lies, black-and-white timbered, at the south-east end of the village, there are reputed to be three ghosts: a lady who was murdered while sheltering from a storm; a Cavalier whose skeleton was found up a chimney; and a love-lorn girl who wanders from the courtyard to the orchard. There is also a ghostly shape which may be one of these, which appears in a bedroom. Books on black magic were discovered in the attic, and human bones have been dug up in the garden.

North on the 448 is:

🦉 **Harvington Hall** (O.P.). Outside the park, where the 450 crosses the 448, the ghost of Mistress Hicks is seen. She was hanged at these crossroads for being a witch.

Below The twin peaks of Raggedstone Hill, Great Malvern

Bottom A hoard of black-magic books was found in the attic at Prior's Court, Callow End

The great conglomeration of the industrial Midlands has its ghosts, but is less likely to draw tourists than the surrounding countryside, so I propose to start in the southernmost corner of the county. It links in well with the Oxfordshire tour.

🐎👻 **Long Compton.** A ghostly coach and four has been seen at Harrow Hill. The Close Field, which contains early earthworks, was used for making pacts with the Devil.

Almost due north lie:

🦉👻 **Honington and Tredington.** Halfway between these places you may see the ghost of a witch, sitting on a wall.

To the west you will come to:

🐎🦉 **Ilmington.** A ghostly carriage and six black headless horses haunt the hills above the village, usually at Pig Lane, now a bridle path. When I asked for information, a local inhabitant told me, 'Us aren't seen 'em lately, but doubtless us shall'. Although the apparition is known as the Night Coach, it has been seen in daylight. The spirit of Ed Golding, parish clerk, has been seen in the church.

North up the Stour valley is:

🦉 **Atherstone.** Here the ghost of a farmer, who had a wager on the time it would take to ride from Atherstone to Alderminster in the dark, appears along what is now the A34. He was unseated by a low overhanging bough and killed. If you see him once, you will see him three times.

To the west, a little south of Alcester lies:

🦉 **Ragley Hall** (O.P.), haunted by a Lady in White.

🦉 **Stratford-upon-Avon.** The only ghost I have been able to unearth is in a reference by the B.T.A. to the Red House Hotel.

The other side of Stratford you will find:

🦉 **Charlecote Park** (N.T.). Here the apparition of a young girl re-enacts her tragic suicide by drowning. Who is she? Why did she do it?

🐎 **Warwick Castle** (O.P.) lies north-east. Here you may see a ghostly Black Dog. Local tradition says that it is the transmogrified spirit of Nell Bloxham, who was forbidden by the earl to sell milk and butter from her cottage at the foot of the castle walls.

The 428 from:

💀 **Coventry to Rugby** is haunted by a ghost lorry with dim sidelights. It approaches one's car on the wrong side of the road, but disappears when a crash is imminent.

In the north-western suburbs of Rugby, down Little Lawford Lane, is:

👁☠🐎 **Little Lawford Hall,** now a farm, where the Elizabethan ghost of One-handed Broughton haunts a room, and is also seen in a coach and six. Clergy were called to conjure the ghost into a phial, which was then thrown into a marl-pit opposite the house. Twelve clergymen, each with a candle, took part, as was the custom. During the exorcism eleven candles were mysteriously extinguished; Parson Hall's remained alight, so he laid the ghost, but allowed it a certain space of time each night to roam abroad.

South of the 425, near the Northamptonshire border, lies:

👁 **Shuckburgh Hall** where at the beginning of the last century Sir Stewkley Shuckburgh expressed disapproval of his daughter being courted by Lieut. Sharp of the Bedfordshire militia. This led to a double tragedy and subsequent haunting, for Sharp first shot the girl and then himself.

South-west you will find:

👁 **Edgehill** where the battle fought in 1642 is re-enacted by phantom armies in the sky above the battlefield. This manifestation first took place on the Christmas Eve following the combat, and a Royal Commission testified to seeing this mysterious apparition. There are many people who have witnessed it in recent years.

The stretch of water at Charlecote Park where a suicide re-enacts her drowning

NORTHAMPTONSHIRE

Most of the Northamptonshire sites follow a line from south-west to north-east, but there are three exceptions. You should start with:

🐎 **Passenham** near Stony Stratford. Here the legends centre round the wonderful old tithe barn, the manor house, the church and particularly the mill, where at night strange cries are heard coming from the wheel. Then there was an unbelieving lady 'who was buried with a gooseberry in the coffin and the promise that if there was a living God the gooseberry bush would spring from her tomb – and it did!' So writes a friend whose grandmother's companion regaled her with such tales as they walked through the water-meadows to Passenham, but although I have tried several sources I have not been able to get further details before this book goes to press. This then is a field for someone else to explore.

On the west side of the A43 at Silverstone you come to:

👁 **Abthorpe.** This ruined manor house is haunted by the ghost of a Franciscan friar, and the rustling silks of Jane Leeson have been heard on quiet nights. She is also commemorated in more solid terms on the school wall: '1642 Feare God, Honour ye King, Jane Leeson hath builded this house for a free school for ever.'

North-west of Northampton, across the M1, lie the great house and park of:

👁 **Althorp** (O.P.). Here the ghost of an old retainer enters the bedroom of any guest who has a light burning, just to check that he or she has not fallen asleep leaving a candle alight.

☆ **Northampton:** Becket's Well, which still has a medieval-style well housing, has been used in living memory to ease blindness.

👁 **Wellingborough.** The balcony row of the Lyric Cinema (now a bingo parlour) in Midland Road is haunted by the ghost of a man called Daniel, who died on this spot long before the Lyric was built.

☆ **Woodford** lies north-east, on the banks of the Nene. The church contains a human heart which you can see through a little window high up in the fourth pillar of the north aisle. Whom it belonged to and how it came to be there is a mystery. Some say it is the heart of Sir Walter Trayli (whose carved wooden effigy lies with that of his

The heart preserved in a pillar of Woodford Church may belong to this thirteenth-century knight

wife at the end of the chancel) and was sent home from the Levant where he may have died towards the end of the last Crusade (1290). But why bury the heart in a pillar and not in the tomb with his wife?

A few miles to the south-east you will find:

☠ **Ringstead** where years ago Lydia Atley is said to have been seduced, made pregnant and murdered by a local farmer. Where her body was hidden was never discovered, so her restless spirit haunts the gate to the church at midnight, and then moves east. Maybe she is trying to lead someone to where her poor bones lie, so that they can be re-interred in sanctified ground.

☆ **Oundle** lies to the north. Here is the Drumming Well, which is said to sound a tattoo before an important event. It is now protected by a cast-iron manhole cover, and can be seen in Drumming Well Lane, reached by the passage at the side of the Methodist chapel.

There is no need for a centre on which to base a tour of the Bedfordshire sites. Start off up the MI, and first visit:

👁 **Woburn Abbey** (O.P.). Ghosts are not among the listed tourist attractions, for the hauntings take place in areas not usually open to the public. In a room which has a door at each end, first one opens to allow an unseen presence to enter, then the other opens to allow it to leave. This was so frequent that the Duke of Bedford had to stop using it as a television room. In the private part of the park, there is a summerhouse which the Duke believes to be haunted by his grandmother the Flying Duchess, who one day in 1937 failed to pilot her plane home. In the Wood Library, and in his office, the Duke feels a *malaise*. Before the dissolution of the monasteries, Woburn was a Cistercian abbey. The abbot was beheaded; so was John Russell in 1683; and the ninth duke committed suicide.

North of Woburn lies:

🐎👁🏠 **Aspley Guise.** In a cellar cupboard of the old manor, Dick Turpin discovered the corpses of a girl and her lover, shot by her father, and so blackmailed him into providing refuge in the cellar, and access to the wine it contained, whenever he felt the need. Even today you may see the highwayman come riding down Weathercock Lane.

North across the MI you come to:

☆ **Cranfield** where a well at Hartwell Farm, near Cranfield Rectory, has a reputation for curing sore eyes.

👁 **Bedford.** No. 38 Mill Street once housed the offices of the magistrate's clerks, and in their words is 'quite definitely haunted'. Strange footsteps and knocks on doors were heard. In the Methodist chapel, Newnham Avenue, the figure of a man in black trousers and a light tweed coat is sometimes seen going through a wall, leaving a trail of white mist.

North-east of Bedford, a small road leads from:

👁 **Ravensden to Wilden** and is haunted by the ghost of a woman with a malevolent expression, trailing black garments. This witch-like figure has been seen in broad daylight. Wilden Manor Farm is said to be haunted. It certainly looked eerie, and when I was last there I heard that the farmer wanted to build a bungalow in its place. No reason was given.

North, near the Huntingdon border, you come to:

☆ **Pertenhall.** At Chadwell End, the southern part of the village, is Holy Spring (originally St Chad's Well) where only eighty years ago water was bottled and used for sore eyes. The spring lies off Chadwell Farm, 200 yards to the west, through the farmyard and over a wooden bridge. Miss Banks, the farmer's daughter, may not only give you permission to visit it, but also show the way. No building remains.

A harmless ghost wanders round Little Gaddesden manor and the village pond

The sites in Hertfordshire seem to lie more or less along the radial routes out of London, so I suggest that you go out by the A41, cut across country to return by the A5, and go out again on the A1, returning by the A10 and A11. We start with:

☻ **Watford.** Cassiobury, once the home of the Earls of Essex, is now a golf-course and public park. Lord Capel's ghost appears here on the anniversary of his execution on 9 March 1649. Lord Capel had been a Parliamentarian, but finding the Roundheads too bigoted for his taste, became a staunch Cavalier.

North-west of Watford you come to:

☠ **Sarratt.** Rose Hall is the haunt of a headless apparition, according to Peter Underwood, who produces some first-hand evidence, as his grandparents lived here.

North-east across the A41 is:

☻ **Abbots Langley** where the vicarage was haunted for years by the ghost of a servant girl, supposedly ill-treated by a vicar's wife many years ago. She also haunts the church and has been seen on several occasions on All Saint's Day. A local builder has been reported as believing that it is no use repairing the fireplace in the room where she died a horrible death because it would never stay mended; and he would appear to be right. Exorcism by a bishop has calmed her restless spirit, but not effectively quietened the noise she makes.

To the north-west at:

☻ **Kings Langley** phantom monks have been seen in Priory Orchard.

☆ **Boxmoor Common.** Fifty yards from the London/Berkhamsted road, close to some trees, is the grave of Robert Snooks. He was the last highwayman to be hanged in England, on 11 March 1802. A stone marks the place where he died and was buried.

The next town on the A41 is:

☻ **Hemel Hempstead** where the 'King's Arms' is reputed to be haunted.

☻ **Bovingdon** lies south-west. Here a gleaming presence haunts Box Lane. A part of the churchyard has been desecrated by bloodshed, and they say that people buried there cannot rest.

North-east of Berkhamsted lies:

⚔ **Frithsden.** At Rose's Hole, so legend runs, a chest of gold was half-discovered, then lost again because the finders broke the silence which seekers must maintain.

Continue west to:

🐾⛓ **Tring** where in 1751 an old woman was drowned, allegedly as a witch. The man who murdered her was hanged in chains near the spot – which was subsequently haunted by a Black Hound. This animal is said to be the disembodied spirit of Colley, who murdered an Osborne and was hanged here. Whether Osborne was the witch and Colley her killer, I have not yet found out.

East and north lies:

👻 **Little Gaddesden.** The manor house and the village pond are haunted by a friendly ghost, believed to have been a seventeenth-century suicide called Jarman who was spurned in love by the daughter of Lord Bridgewater at Ashridge Park. He is reputed to make the lights (candle, oil, gas or electric) grow dim on one night of the year, but this cannot be very effective as people have forgotten which night.

👻 **Gallow's Hill** has manifestations of groaning timber, clanking chains, and a man in grey.

Continue north-east to the A5, which is Watling Street. Just north of Markyate is:

👻🏹 **Markyate Cell.** This was the home of the 'wicked Lady Ferrers', a seventeenth-century highwaywoman, who used a secret stairway at night, and then rode out to waylay travellers. Sometimes she would climb into a tree with branches overhanging the road, and drop down on her victim. One night she was shot, and died as she reached home. Since then her ghost has frequently been seen – as recently as the last decade – riding wildly across country, in the branches of a tree, and in the garden of Markyate Cell. The fortune she amassed – or maybe other treasure – still awaits discovery, and clues are given in the following rhyme:

> Near the cell, there is a well,
> Near the well, there is a tree,
> And 'neath the tree the treasure be.

Down the A5 towards St Albans, you come to:

🦌 **Redbourn** where, they say, 'When the Womere Brook overflows, famine and calamity ensue.'

👻 **St Albans.** At Battlefield House, in Chequers Street, people have heard two very different sounds: the noise of combat and the chanting of monks. It was here that a bloody battle was fought in the Wars of the Roses. I believe that St Albans is also haunted by Mother Haggy.

Four miles to the south-east is:

🐾👻 **Salisbury Hall** (O.P.) which King Charles II bought for Nell Gwyn. She dangled her first child by the king over the moat, threatening to drop him in because he had no title, and Charles begged her to spare 'the Duke of St Albans'.

A latter-day celebrity to live here was Winston Churchill's mother, and one of the many people to have seen a ghost was her second husband, George Cornwallis-West. In his book *Victorian Hey-Days*, he describes seeing the ghost of a youngish woman wearing a blue fichu. Immediately he was strongly reminded of a former nursery-maid and rang up his mother to ask after her health. It was only when his sister came to stay and reminded him that people had often remarked on the nursery maid's resemblance to a picture of Nell Gwyn that he realized he had probably seen her ghost. Then he was persuaded to write a letter which was given to a medium. The medium said the writer had seen 'an apparition of Mistress Eleanor Gwyn, who came to warn him of impending danger'. 'I knew nothing of impending danger at the time' he writes; 'but within six months of my having seen the apparition, a solicitor . . . absconded and let me in for over £10,000.'

Another ghost is that of a Cavalier who has been seen with a sword through his body. A friend of mine, who lived here as a child, told me that the family often saw one of the ghosts disappearing into a wall by the fireplace in the bedroom over the porch. Subsequent owners discovered a bricked-up door at this spot.

Across the A6, just south of Colney Heath, is:

👻 **Tyttenhanger House** where in the study Sir Henry Blount's ghost is said to appear. Which Blount is this? I like to think it is the Royalist and traveller who lived here from 1602 to 1682.

⛓👻 **Hatfield House** (O.P.) lies north-east. It is haunted by a coach and four which drive through the door and up the stairs; also by the ghost of a veiled woman concerned with passing a message to Charles II.

Now drive to the village of Essendon, where you will find:

👻🐾 **Camfield Place.** This was once the home of Beatrix Potter who one evening saw a dozen candles snuffed out one by one by an unseen hand. Barbara Cartland lives there now, and she, with other people, not to mention a number of dogs, sees the ghost of her brown-and-white spaniel, Jimmy.

99

Top Nell Gwyn dangled her son over the moat at Salisbury Hall to blackmail Charles II into giving him a title

Above Trees growing through a grave at Tewin, some say as proof of the Word of God

Due north you will find:

🦴👁 **Tewin.** A place remarkable for strange ladies. Lady Anne Grimston's grave in the eastern part of the churchyard, which lies outside the village, sprouted seven trees, because she denied the Resurrection – even, some say, the existence of God; and in November 1716, as she lay dying, she dismissed the priest with the words, 'If there is any truth in the Word of God, may seven trees grow from my grave.' You can see a large sycamore with several trunks, which has certainly forced open the stonework of the tomb and almost engulfed the original railings. Lady Catherine's ghost haunts a room at Tewin Water; and the phantom Lady Sabine has been seen at Tewin House.

North again the road runs from Bramfield to Datchworth. After passing the turning to Queen Hoo Hall on the west side of the road, you will find:

✪ **Old Clibbon's Post** which marks the spot where a mysterious band of wayside robbers and murderers met their end. They turned out to be a Jekyll-and-Hyde family, well known as itinerant pedlars who sold cakes in the local ale-houses by day, but who were secretly footpads at night.

North-west, across the A1, is:

👁 **Knebworth** (O.P.), once the home of the Lytton family, who were said to be warned of impending death by the sound, and maybe the sight, of a girl called Jenny spinning.

The next site northwards is:

🐾 **Stevenage.** The Phantom Hound is reported to have been seen at The Six Hills, Whomerley Wood, and in the avenue leading to the church; but the New Town may have disturbed his run.

About 3 miles south of Hitchin, on the 600, is an inn called the 'Royal Oak'. From here a path leads to:

👁 **Minsden Chapel,** a ruin in which a phantom monk was photographed in 1907 by T. W. Latchmore. It is reproduced on p. 39, Vol. II of *The History of Hitchin* by Reginald Hine, who says that he too will haunt these hallowed walls. There is no better description of this place than his, which starts: 'The very air . . . is tremulous with that *susurrus* – call it the under song of the Earth, the music of the spheres, the sigh of departed time, or what you will . . .' He knew at least four people who carried a flint from the chapel as a talisman, but I would not advise anyone to take a flint away today, for Hine is dead, and lies – I hope peacefully – buried there, so his spirit may well protect the place from vandals.

North of Minsden and east of Hitchin lies:

Little Wymondley where the priory is haunted by ghostly monks, and there is a chestnut tree supposedly planted by Julius Caesar.

Hitchin. The priory is haunted by the Grey Lady, and, on June 15, the ghost of a headless Cavalier is to be seen, who has ridden over from:

High Down, Pirton, which lies about 3 miles north-west. His name was Goring, but how, when, or where he lost his head, and why he rides to Hitchin, remain a mystery.

Now go north-east to:

Letchworth. At Scudamore, Letchworth Corner, some twenty-five years ago, thuds and footsteps were heard regularly every night at 10.30, in an empty room which a dog refused to enter.

Beyond Baldock is:

Bygrave House, haunted by the ghost of a pedlar who was murdered here; and also by those of a mother and child who were buried under the drawing-room floor.

A few miles to the north-west you will find:

Hinxworth Place where mysterious screams, thuds, and the crying of a baby have been heard on stormy autumn evenings. One explanation, quoted by Peter Underwood, is that years ago the son of the house frightened a nursemaid by dressing up as a ghost. She attacked the 'apparition' with a poker, and the boy fell downstairs and was killed.

At the nearby village of:

Ashwell, a headless phantom in black has been seen in St Mary's churchyard.

East at:

Royston, Banyers Hotel is reputedly haunted.

Barkway. I have a note that the ghost of a former mistress appeared to Sir Peter Saltonshall here.

South-east, near the Essex border, you will find:

Brent Pelham where Piers Shonks slew a dragon, which so annoyed the Devil that he demanded his soul. Piers promised he could have it, whether he was buried inside or outside the church; but he left instructions to be buried in the walls of the church, thus cheating the Devil. (See Tremeirchion, Wales; and Barn Hall, Essex.)

South-east again is:

Bishop's Stortford. The ghost of a volunteer officer who was accidentally shot in the grounds of Windmill House haunts the place.

Amwellbury House lies a mile south of Ware. The chanting of monks is heard, and their ghosts are seen marching past the house on land which once belonged to the Abbey of Westminster.

Jenningsbury Farm is south-west. Here a man drowned himself and his ghost haunts the place.

The last site is almost in the London suburbs. At:

Cheshunt the Great House (½ mile north-west of the church) is haunted by a Grey Lady, and there is reputed to be an indelible bloodstain upstairs. Old Palace House, in Theobald's Park, is said to be haunted by a number of ghosts.

The ghost in Minsden Chapel

Leave London by the A13 to Tilbury, and before you are over the G.L.C. boundary you will pass through:

@ **Rainham.** At the crossroads turn right and you will come to the Hall (N.T.), to which Colonel Mulliner, the Edwardian owner, became so attached that his spirit still cannot leave it. The ghost can be seen in daylight, and is friendly.

Continue along the A13 and after Pitsea turn right for:

@ **Canvey.** At the north-easternmost corner of the island the ghost of a Viking walks across the mudflats. This is probably one of the gang led by Halvdan that withdrew to Kent in 894. His main fleet gathered off Benfleet, but was routed by King Alfred's son, Edward, who showed as little mercy to the Vikings as they did to the English. The nails in some Essex church doors held scraps of Viking skin for years: evidence that those who were caught robbing churches were flayed alive.

@ **Southend.** In Prittlewell Park the remains of the Cluniac Priory are haunted.

@ **Rochford Hall** lies barely 3 miles north. It is haunted by Anne Boleyn's headless ghost, particularly on the twelve nights following Christmas.

Continue north-east to:

@ 🐾 **Canewdon** where the ghost of an old woman in a crinoline and poke-bonnet has been seen in the churchyard and surrounding lanes. She is thought to have been executed as a witch.

On the way west to Wickford Roundabout you will pass:

🚶 **Hockley,** a built-up sort of place, but the 1013 is said to be haunted by a Black Dog.

@ **Wickford Roundabout.** Here a girl was killed in a motorbike accident, and her ghost has been seen thumbing a lift. Anne Boleyn's ghost is also seen hereabouts in a coach.

North of Billericay is:

@ **Stock** where the Bear Inn is haunted by the ghost of an ostler, whose body, it is believed by some, may still be up the chimney in a bacon-curing chamber.

The road from:

@ **Stock to Ingatestone,** via Buttsbury, is haunted by the ghost of a Cavalier at White Tyrells.

@ **Springfield** is now a north-east suburb

The remains of the Cluniac Priory, Southend

of Chelmsford. Springfield Place, near the church, is periodically haunted by a phantom described as a 'hideous little dwarf', possibly an elemental. One small child called it 'Funny Man'. The local paper reported its return in 1946.

Down the 130 to the south-east lies:

@ 🚶 **Rettendon.** Turn left for East Hanningfield and along the road you may see the apparition of a farmer with his pony and trap.

Turn right cross country till you reach the 1418, then turn right again for:

@ **Woodham Ferrers.** Edwin's Hall is a mile to the east. It was the home of Edwin Sandys, Archbishop of York in 1619. There are two or possibly three ghosts here: a Cavalier, a girl who was drowned in the lake, and 'something' in the orchard.

Continue south to the 1012 and turn left for:

@ **Cold Norton.** In a house called De Laches is a bedroom which no animal will enter. At 2 a.m. appears a small woman in Victorian dress, whom the owners describe as the epitome of evil.

Continue east and you come to:

🚶 **Latchingdon and Snoreham,** haunted by a headless calf.

Fork left here for:

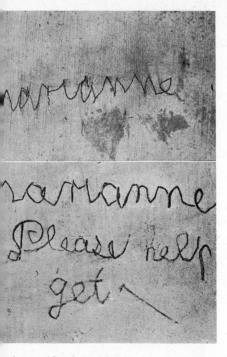

An appeal from beyond the grave in spirit-writing on the wall at Borley rectory

Borley rectory after the fire that destroyed it and, apparently, some of its ghosts

Bradwell - juxta - Mare. Continue through the village to St Peter-ad-Muram, a seventh-century church on the site of St Cedd's, astride the wall of a third-century fort. For years it was used as a barn. The nearby coastguard cottage is said to be haunted, and there is also a galloping ghost who rides through locked gates from the village to the church. He may be the same spectre who appears to be a centurion and who rides from Weymarks Farm to the north-west, down to the church.

Now go back to Latchingdon and take the 1018 through Maldon to:

Beeleigh Abbey, haunted by the headless ghost of Sir John Gates, which appears on the anniversary of his death on 22 August 1553, when he was executed for supporting Lady Jane Grey.

From Maldon take the 1026 to:

Tolleshunt D'Arcy. At the beginning of the village, a road on the right goes to Tollesbury. Halfway there, a drive on the right leads to Gorwell Hall. Here a phantom dog has often been seen.

North of Tolleshunt D'Arcy, and north of the Virley/Tiptree road is:

Barn Hall. The Devil, so the legend runs, destroyed the house as fast as it was built, until a certain knight made a pact with the Evil One that if he left the building alone he could have his soul, 'whether he was buried inside the church or out'. The Devil agreed, but was cheated of his reward because the knight was buried in the wall of the church. (See Brent Pelham, Hertfordshire; and Tremeirchion, Wales.)

Now go to Tolleshunt Knights and turn right for:

Layer Marney (O.P.). The tower is haunted by the ghost of Lord Marney who died in 1523 before he had finished building it.

If you drive round the north of Abberton reservoir, you come to:

Langenhoe. Both the church, demolished in 1962, and the manor house were the scenes of strange hauntings for many years. From 1937 onwards the vicar experienced various poltergeist phenomena, ghostly apparitions and the smell of violets in September. Peter Underwood lists them all; but by far the strangest happened when the vicar was in a bedroom at the manor and found himself in the soft embrace of a naked female ghost.

Continue along the 1025 to:

Mersea Island which is joined to the mainland by a causeway called the Strood. Between here and the Peldon Rose Inn, the ghost of a Roman centurion has been seen by many people, and as recently as 1970. Sabine Baring-Gould was rector here and heard legionaries fighting. A twenty-foot-high tumulus at The Mount was found to hold a Romano-British lead coffin and a glass bowl of human ashes.

Across the water, between Brightlingsea and Clacton is:

☠ **St Osyth** where there is a haunted well.

If you like you can now take in Sudbury (see Suffolk). A few miles to the north-west, you are back in Essex and at:

☠ **Borley** the rectory, now demolished, was the most famous haunted house in England. Not all the manifestations were concerned with the hideous Victorian house – for instance the ghost of a nun – so it is still worth a visit (you may prefer to take it in on the Suffolk tour). Arguments will rage about this *cause célèbre* for many years, simply because there is so much evidence on both sides (see Preface).

☠ **Coggeshall** lies about 13 miles due south, and is one of the most haunted little towns in Essex. The abbey and gatehouse (Cistercian, 1140) are both places where people have 'seen things'. No. 47 Church Street has been plagued by poltergeists. At Guild House, Market End, mysterious lights appear in an attic window and the ghost of a little old man is seen at the foot of the bed. Finally, at Cradle House, a mile or so north of the town near Markshall Old Rectory, a ghostly procession of monks is sometimes seen.

South-west lies:

☠ **Faulkbourne.** From here to Witham the road is haunted, particularly near Faulkbourne Hall, which lies on the left. The ghost is a gentleman in a billy-cock hat on an old-fashioned bicycle, and he rides straight towards you at dusk.

The next site lies almost due west on the 131:

☠☝ **Great Leighs.** Although St Anne's Castle Inn is definitely haunted, opinions differ about whose ghost is to be seen: a witch who was burned at the stake or a little girl murdered before her mother's eyes.

South-east of Cheshunt in the Lea Valley is:

☠ **Waltham Abbey.** A curious luminous light has been seen in the Church of the Holy Cross, and those who witness this are filled with a sense of evil.

On the eastern side of the A11 is:

☠🐎 **Loughton.** On Trap's Hill, Dick Turpin's ghost may be seen dragging a woman behind his horse, trying to force her to tell him where she has hidden her jewels – as he once did when they were both alive.

SUFFOLK

The centre for Suffolk must be Ipswich. One can work round the southern part of the county, then do a north-and-east coast tour, and finally visit the central sites on the way to Cambridge. First take the 137 south to Cattawade. To the east lies:

☝☠ **Seafield Bay** opposite Mistley, which is in Essex. Here the screams of witches are heard at night. They are not yells of devilish delight, but shrieks of agony as the women were tortured by Matthew Hopkins, Witch-Finder General. The loudest and most agonizing are those from the spirit of Elizabeth Clarke, a cripple.

☠ **East Bergholt** lies to the west. (This is rather muddling because West Bergholt is nearly 10 miles away in Essex.) The friary is reputed to be haunted. It was originally a Benedictine convent. Some years ago a door opened by itself regularly at 10.50 p.m., accompanied by a lowering of the temperature. A soldier stationed here during the last war felt cold hands placed on his face, and his hair turned white overnight.

West again is:

☠ **Thorington Hall** which is haunted by the ghost of a girl in a brown dress who walks the upstairs passage, but her footsteps

Matthew Hopkins with two of his witch victims and their familiars

must surely be lighter than the heavy tread which is also heard.

West and north is:

🏵 **Sudbury.** St Gregory's Church is haunted by Archbishop Simon Sudbury. No wonder: ghosts often seek some dismembered limb, and while his body lies at Canterbury, Kent (q.v.), his head remains in the vestry here.

A few miles north you come to:

🏵 **Long Melford** where the Bull Hotel has been the scene of poltergeist manifestations, footsteps, telekinesis and terrified dogs.

East and north is:

🏵 **Bildeston.** The fifteenth-century Crown Inn is haunted. Poltergeist phenomena have been experienced and the ghost of a man in a long overcoat and 'old-fashioned' hat has been seen.

South-east, between Hadleigh and Ipswich, you will find:

🏵 **Hintlesham Hall.** This Elizabethan manor, with a Queen Anne façade, was gambled away by the Timperleys and in 1747 came into the possession of the Lloyds, who kept it for nearly 200 years. The second wife of Richard Savage Lloyd starved her stepson to death, and, perhaps through remorse, her ghost is still seen on the stairs, in the library and about the south wing. For years a dummy figure representing the boy was known as the Luck of Hintlesham. If the figure became damaged or left the house, the property would pass from the inhabitant's family and disaster would follow.

For the second tour go north to:

🗡 **Hoxne.** St Edmund, King of East Anglia, pursued by the Danes, hid under a bridge, subsequently known as Gold Bridge. A newly-married couple saw his gold spurs glinting and denounced him. He put a curse on all who cross the bridge on their way to get married. People will still go a long way round to evade the curse.

North-east just over the Norfolk border is:

🗡 **Harleston.** On the river Waveney here you will find the Witches' Pool, presumably used for ducking.

Between Harleston and Redenhall is the site of:

🌳 **Lush's Bush** where a tree once stood which grew from a stake driven through the body of a suicide, buried here in 1813. Lush was a woman who poisoned herself because she was thought to have killed her child.

🗡🐎 **Bungay** lies further along this same road. St Mary's Priory churchyard contains the Druid's Stone. Like Stonehenge it may have been used by the Druids, but is probably

Dance twelve times round the Druid's Stone at Bungay and they say the Devil will appear

much older. To conjure the Devil, children danced round it twelve times. The ruins of Bigod's Castle are haunted by the Black Shuck. This phantom hound is the transmogrified spirit of the wicked Hugh Bigod.

Now go east to:

🐎💀🗡 **Beccles.** At Roos Hall (O.P.A.) on Christmas Eve, a coach and four arrives with a headless groom on the box. In the park there is an oak tree which was once a gibbet and is haunted by some of those who were hanged there. To conjure the Devil you must walk round it six times. Inside the house there is a haunted bedroom and the Devil's footmarks can be seen inside the wardrobe.

Just inland from Lowestoft, on the 1117, you will find:

🐎🏵🗡 **Oulton,** where the Wild Hunt has been seen at midnight, and in that ghostly company is a lady bearing a poison cup. During the reign of George II, the squire, returning to Oulton House after a day's hunting, found his wife *in flagrante delicto* with an officer, who killed the husband. The guilty couple fled, leaving behind the squire's daughter. She became engaged to a local farmer, but on the eve of the wedding a black carriage, drawn by black horses and with servants in sable livery, drew up at the house, apparently bringing the mother with

The grim shell of Westwood Lodge,
Blythborough

a poison cup to prevent her daughter telling
what had happened.

👁 **Oulton Broad,** nearby, is haunted by a
ghost ship. A wherry called *Mayfly* once set
off for Yarmouth with a chest containing
£4000 and a pretty young passenger. Both
proved too much temptation for the skipper,
who decided to make for foreign parts. His
voyage ended in death for himself, his
passenger and all the crew except the cabin
boy, who escaped in the dinghy.

Now go south down the coast, first
stopping at:

👁 **Covehithe** where the churchyard is
hunted by a faceless lady.

A few miles to the south, a road leads
from:

👣👁 **Wangford to Reydon.** Along this
stretch of road, near Reydon Hall, opposite
the turning to Frostenham, a phantom coach
and headless four have been seen, bearing the
ghost of a wicked squire. Horses hate the
place, and at the beginning of the century a
horse shied at nothing visible to the human
eye, and killed his rider.

👁 **Southwold.** The building which now
houses shops, offices and a club was once the
Old Vicarage, haunted by a ghost whose
presence was accompanied by deep sighs,
heavy footsteps and, in the attic, clanking
chains.

Inland, on the A12, lies:

👁👣 **Blythburgh.** The White Hart Inn is
said to be haunted by a little old man, whom
the landlord and his wife look upon as a
monk. In 1967 three misfortunes occurred:
a lorry smashed into the end wall, killing the
driver; the place was burgled; and a fire

broke out. Since then the ghost has been
quieter. Whether the Old Court House was
an inn in 1750 I do not know; but in that
year a Negro drummer, Tobias Gill, got
drunk, then raped and murdered Anne
Blakemore from Walberswick. He was
sentenced to death and his body hung in
chains at the crossroads. His ghost haunts
the heath on the box of a black hearse pulled
by four black horses; he has also been seen
in the church.

Westwood Lodge, once a manor house, but
sad and a little sinister since the last occupier
died ten years ago, is haunted by a lady in a
long silver dress. Three policemen sat in
wait for her one night in October 1972.
Their traps were sprung by unseen feet, they
recorded strange sounds, they experienced a
sudden chill – but the ghost did not appear.
Yet a retired gamekeeper has seen her on
several occasions and refused to go near the
Lodge at night, while the son of the present
keeper saw her just a few days before the
policemen's vigil.

Back at the coast, to the south, you come
to:

👁🏇👣 **Dunwich,** once a thriving town
with nine churches, but now a handful of
houses and the eerie ruins of the priory and
leper hospital. In 1552 the Lord Mayor of
London, Sir George Barne, came to live
here; two of his descendants haunt the place
yet. South of the village is Grey Friars, a
shooting-box in Victorian days, when the
Barne family lived at Sotterly Hall, 6 miles
to the north. According to legend, a young
brother of the lord of the manor fell in love
with a maid at Grey Friars. They were
forbidden to meet, and he died of a broken
heart. His ghost wanders disconsolately along
the paths that lead through the woods.
Another ghost is that of the Victorian squire
himself on a fine Arab thoroughbred. They
are the sole survivors, for the Barne family
sold the estate in 1947.

The headland north of Dunwich is
another haunt of the Galley Trot, Black
Shuck or Phantom Hound.

South-west and slightly inland is:

👁🐕 **Westleton.** Westleton Walks are said
to be haunted and there are reputed to be
smugglers' vaults at Scott's Hall. Perhaps the
smugglers themselves exaggerated the ghost
story to keep people away. J. Wentworth
Day says that in the graveyard there is a

Do not cross the Gold Bridge at Hoxne on your
wedding day for there is a curse on bridal couples

Witch's Stone over which no grass will grow. At the back of this thatched church I found a bare patch, but at the inn opposite no-one I spoke to knew of the Witch's Stone.

South of Westleton you will find:

Leiston where the Galley Trot is to be seen in the churchyard.

The next site on this coastal tour is past the Woodbridge turning, right of the main road north-east of Ipswich. It is of historical interest only, and will be found at:

Great Bealings. Between 2 February and 27 March 1834, all the bells in Bealings House rang frequently and without human aid. Peter Underwood says that the bells are now disconnected, but one wonders if that would necessarily prevent another outbreak.

☆ **Kesgrave** lies to the south. Here you will find Dobb's Lane leading to Dobb's Grave. He was a shepherd who hanged himself in a barn at Kesgrave Hall Farm. He was buried in unconsecrated ground, where four paths meet near the Pumping Station. His grave is marked by concrete head and foot stones.

The last part of your Suffolk tour will take you towards Cambridge from Ipswich. The sites lie on or near the A45. The first, west of Stowmarket and south of the road, is:

Woolpit, originally Wolfpit, so John Harries says. Here, when the snow lies thick, a ghostly wolf is seen and heard. Harries calls it a 'rare and infrequent' ghost, but the village has atmosphere.

Before you reach Bury St Edmunds, south of the road is:

Rougham Green. The path here to Bradfield St George across the fields was the route taken by Miss Ruth Wynn and her fourteen-year-old pupil, Miss Allington, in 1926. They came to a park wall, and looking through the wrought-iron gates, saw a large Georgian house. Both wrote a description of what they had seen but when months later they covered the same route, there was no wall, no gates, no house. And there is no record of a house ever having stood in that spot.

Rushbrooke is close by. The Hall, in danger of demolition, is haunted by the White Lady who is thought to be Agnes de Rushbrooke, and, according to Eric Russell, her purpose is either remorse or revenge.

Bury St Edmunds. Just inside the door of the museum in Moyses Hall, to the left on

Fred Archer still rides the course at Newmarket nearly 100 years after his death

entering, are the gruesome relics of William Corder, murderer of Maria Martin in the Red Barn, Polstead. The dagger and sheath, a brace of pistols, his scalp, and a book bound in his skin are exhibited. Seven thousand people attended his execution at Bury. His head was afterwards removed from his body, but it brought such bad luck to those who kept it that it was subsequently buried.

The gateway of the abbey is haunted by monks and has an impressively mysterious atmosphere.

Just beyond Kentford, where the Chippenham/Moulton road crosses the main Newmarket highway, is:

☆ **The Boy's or Gypsy's Grave.** This is 3½ miles from Newmarket. Some say it is the grave of a shepherd boy who hanged himself when accused of stealing sheep; others that a Gypsy lies buried there. Gypsies are thought to keep it well tended and it is certainly always decked with fresh flowers. Strange stories are told of cyclists who are forced to dismount at this spot.

Newmarket. Hamilton Stud Lane, on the Exening road, is the haunt of Fred Archer, the great jockey, who died in 1886 aged 29. He is also thought to ride on the race-course, and to have caused several horses to shy or stumble during a race. The heath is another place where the Black Shuck may be seen.

From here the A45 will take you to Cambridge.

The Boy's or Gypsy's Grave

I suggest three tours for Cambridgeshire: the town itself, the southern half of the county, and the north. First Cambridge:

Christ's College. The ghost of Christopher Round haunts the mulberry tree in the Fellows' Garden (O.P.). His bent head, stooping figure and slow step epitomize his remorse for killing another Fellow.

St John's College. A staircase is said to be haunted by the ghost of Dr James Wood (1760–1839).

Jesus College. This is the site of a ghost story concerning the Everlasting Club and Charles Bellassis. Many still believe it, but it has no place here, for it was the brilliantly worked-out invention of Arthur Gray, Master of the College in 1922.

Trinity College. A ghost in hunting kit has been seen in New Court.

Corpus Christi. An upper room in old court is haunted by either the ghost of Dr Butts, Master from 1626 to 1632, or by the suitor of Dr Spencer's daughter. The kitchen is also said to be haunted by the latter ghost. This is where he hid in the cupboard from Dr Spencer (another seventeenth-century Master) and suffocated.

The Old Abbey House, Barnwell. The Grey or White Lady seen here is probably the spectre of a nun from St Radegund's Convent, who came by underground passage to meet her lover, an Austin friar who lived here. But there have been other strange manifestations. As recently as 1959 bedclothes were torn off and other poltergeist activities experienced.

25 Montague Road. A woman in a hammock near the summerhouse appeared to a young boy in the 1920s. He later found out that this was apparently his aunt who had died at this spot in her youth.

Trumpington Street. In the 1890s a house here was for sale. A potential purchaser was shown by the maid into a room where over the chimney-piece hung a portrait of a lady with an odd expression on her face, and wearing a vivid green dress and a hat with a red feather. After being shown over the rest of the house the buyer was told that the house was haunted. Although the owner had never seen the ghost, several visitors had seen a woman in green with a red feather in her hat. 'Oh!' said the buyer,

Top Dr Butts, one-time Master of Corpus Christi, now its ghost

Above Bloody Mary is one of several phantoms at Sawston Hall

'the woman in the portrait which hangs in the first room I saw.' The owner was amazed for no such portrait hung in that room.

Addenbrookes Hospital. A ghost appears when morphia is being administered.

Just south-east of Cambridge are:

Gog Magog Hill and Wandlebury. Wandlebury was the home of a ghostly knight who could be challenged at dead of night, when the moon was shining, by these words: 'Knight, tonight come forth!' Robert, son of Hugh, according to Gervase of Tilbury in the twelfth century, overcame the ghostly giant. The custodian who has been at Wandlebury for the past seven years has not seen it. T. C. Lethbridge investigated the legend and found that there were giant figures cut in the chalk. His fascinating results are described in his book, *Gogmagog, the Buried Gods*. His linking of this with other hill figures, the cult of the horse, the Sun God, and the Great Earth Mother, is brilliant and a little breathtaking.

Of the great mansion which once stood here, ironically, only the stable block remains. And the horse myth may still live in fact, as Lord Godolphin's famous Arab stallion is buried in the archway under the cupola.

South-east across the A11, the 1052 runs between:

Balsham and Wratting. Before the hedges were cut down this must have been a frightening place to meet the White Lady who haunts it; but even more terrifying to encounter the Shuck-monkey: the phantom hound here has the face of an ape. One authority gives the favourite haunt of the White Lady as Spanney's Gate to West Wratting House.

South of Wratting is:

Horseheath. Money Lane is haunted by one who hid his gold here. On nights when there is a full moon a voice has been heard saying, 'Pick up your spade and follow me'. But no-one has ever dared. Might they not be going to dig their own grave?

To the west, just off the 130, is:

Sawston Hall. For more than 400 years the Huddlestones have lived here and entertained many famous people, including Bloody Mary. Her ghost haunts the house she helped to have built in the place of the one that was burned when she eluded capture by the Duke of Northumberland in 1553. Other mysterious happenings include the sound of a spinet, a lady in grey in the Tapestry Room, peculiar noises in the Panelled Room, and the lifting of the door latch by invisible hands in the room in which Mary Tudor slept.

West again on the A10 you come to:

Harston. Here there are records of another White Lady. The ghost has been seen throwing herself into the river from a bridge on the road to Haslingfield, but more often she walks from the 'Queen's Head' to Mill Road.

To the south-west is:

Steeple Morden. The ruins of Moco Farm are haunted by the ghost of a woman crying out in pain. Here, in 1750, a pedlar disappeared and a well was filled in. When a nineteen-year-old servant, Elizabeth Pateman, was heard to tell her lover that she had a secret to reveal, her guilty master thought

Sawston Hall by moonlight

she must refer to the man who had vanished, so killed her too. Her original tombstone was carved with the instruments of her murder: a peahook, a knife and a coulter; but the present stone is plain.

If you return to Cambridge by the 603 you will pass through:

Grantchester where the rectory is haunted by a ghost on the top floor, who apparently walks about moving books. It has been suggested that this may well be the spirit of Rupert Brooke.

For the northern tour first travel west to:

Madingley Hall where, from the higher terrace, the ghost of a young man with a greenish-white face, looks with loathing on mortals. As Rupert Brooke wrote:

And things go on you'd ne'er believe
At Madingley – on Christmas Eve.

Twenty miles or so to the north is:

☆ **Ely.** St Audrey's Well, half a mile from the town, is now only a muddy pond in a clump of elms on Barton Farm. St Audrey has given us the word 'tawdry', from the laces or ribbons that were sold at the fair held on her saint's day. Until recently the cathedral choir wore 'tawdries' or bunches of ribbons in their surplices on St Ethelreda's Day.

North again, a longish drive will take you to:

☠ **Elm,** just south of Wisbech. Here the vicarage is haunted by the ghost of Brother Ignatius who failed to ring the bell to warn the monks of impending flood, and so caused several to be drowned. Now he tolls a phantom bell which heralds death in the village. Peter Underwood tells a fascinating story of how Brother Ignatius' ghost saved a vicar's wife from being strangled by an evil spirit.

☠ **Hannath Hall,** 4 miles north of Wisbech, is the home of Derek Page, M.P. for King's Lynn. The society for Psychical Research visited this very haunted house twelve times between August 1957 and January 1960. There is a legend that 100 years ago the owner kept his wife's corpse in the haunted room for six weeks after her death, sending food up every day.

Now go back south of Ely, across Soham Mere to Wicken; a mile outside the village, on the Stretham road, is:

☠ **Spinney Abbey,** now a farm but in 1217 it was a monastery for Austin friars, founded by Mary de Bassingbourne and Beatrix Malebise. Today phantom monks are heard singing, and one has been seen walking in the garden. Mr Fuller (the farm owner), his parents and the maid all heard the singing on one occasion. Mrs Fuller says that a tunnel once linked Spinney with Waterbeach Abbey. Mysterious lights also appear, and according to Peter Underwood, who carried out experiments here, the temperature drops seven degrees where the ghost walks – but nowhere else – at 2.10 a.m., and at that moment the horses in the stable get very restless.

Upware is the next village to the west. From here southwards and particularly around Devil's Ditch, is the haunt of the Black Shuck, Odin's Dog of War.

South of Upware, near Swaffham Prior, the road from:

☠ **Beck Row to Holywell Row** passes Whitings Farm which is haunted. Beck Hall is haunted by a lady in a long black cloak who passes through a bricked-up gateway, while at Aspal Farm one dark night a huge figure appeared and was heard by villagers to say, 'Don't fear me, fear what follows me.' The figure then disappeared and a great gust of wind rushed by.

NORFOLK

Norfolk is the home of the Black Shuck; you may see him anywhere but he is particularly fond of the coastal areas. There are other more interesting ghosts than this phantom hound, but he is the most persistent. Some fascinating stories are to be found on the Broads. Here legends and hauntings are interwoven, so the ghost-hunter must accept some with a larger grain of salt than usual.

Although most of the sites can be reached by road it is often more direct – and more amusing – to travel by water for a change. Starting from Norwich go north-east and sail first down the Bure and then up the Thurne. Not all the sites will be covered but you can make further excursions later.

Coltishall is one of the places where the Black Shuck is to be seen.

The next stop is at:

☠ **Wroxham.** Two hundred yards from the northern entrance to the broad, you may see the ghost of a Roman who will order you away. He is clearing a passage-way for a ghostly procession of prancing horses and chariots, gladiators and lions, centurions and their prisoners, who make their way from Brancaster to the arena which once stood here. C. Sampson, quoting a source published in 1825, states, 'the apparition is said to occur several times between the Ides of March and the Nones of October'. April 13 and 16, May 7 and 21, June 1, 4 and 11, August 5, 13 and 19, September 13, 15, 22 and 26, and October 7 and 9 are particularly auspicious.

☠ **Salhouse.** On the night of May 12 or the third Tuesday in the month you may hear, or even see, a spectral midnight mass, originally solemnized soon after the Conquest on the shores of Salhouse Pool. It was reported in 1899, 1900, 1903, 1923 and 1926.

☠ **Horning.** On July 21, every five years, so the legend runs, the spirit of the Lord Abbot of St Benet's re-enacts the crowning of Ella, said to have been an early king of the Angles. He was known as the Swan of Peace. Stand 100 yards downstream from the Swan Inn on the opposite side of the river, in the hopes of witnessing this event.

☠ **Ranworth** is haunted by the ghost of Brother Pacificus who is seen on the broad in a boat with his dog. On December 31 the phantom of Colonel Thomas Sidney is seen.

🐾 **Swaffham.** Signs in the market place, the north aisle of the church and a prayer desk, commemorate the dream which came true – of a local fifteenth-century tinker called John Chapman. He dreamed three times that he would stand on London Bridge where he would meet a man who would make him rich. People thought him crazy, but he set out and reached London penniless. After waiting all day on the bridge he began to lose heart, but then a stranger asked him what he was doing, hanging around, peering at passers-by. John Chapman told his story and the stranger laughed and said he should not believe in dreams. 'Why,' he said, 'I had one the other night in which I was told to go to some place in Norfolk called Swaffham and find a tinker called John Chapman because under the only tree in his garden there is supposed to be a crock of gold. Catch me going on a wild-goose chase like that!' The tinker managed to hide his excitement and hurried home where he found a crock of gold on which was written, 'Dig deeper, under me doth lie one richer than I'. He did so and found a second larger treasure. (A similar legend is told about Upsall, Yorkshire.)

Drive through Norwich, keeping to the A47, and you will come to:

👻 **Acle** where the bridge is haunted by the ghost of a man who revenged the death of his sister by killing her murderer – her husband – who was called Josiah Burge. He slit Burge's throat, but a year later had his own throat cut by a ghostly skeleton. They say that on April 7 fresh blood appears on the bridge as well as the ghost.

South-east, actually in Suffolk, is:

👻 **Burgh Castle** (D.E.). On July 3 a ghostly body with a white flag wrapped round it appears to be flung from the ruins onto the foreshore.

Further south, just inland from Lowestoft, you will find:

👻 **Burgh St Peter** where the churchyard is haunted by a ghostly skeleton.

Now return to Norwich and skirting round the south of the city you will come to:

👻 **Great Melton** on the 1108. This place is haunted by the ghosts of four bridesmaids riding in a phantom coach. In life they were returning from a wedding one dark night, but disappeared, never to be seen again. Hallam reports an original twist to the story: if you see their pretty faces, all is well; but sometimes they are headless, and this foretells disaster.

Continue towards Attleborough and 5

miles west of the town is:

👻 **Breckles Hall,** originally haunted by a ghostly coach, bringing phantom guests to a party in an empty house. Doors open and shut mysteriously, strange noises and footsteps have been heard – not to mention a voice screaming in fear for mercy, and ending in a death rattle.

Continue south-west to:

👻 **Thetford.** Warren House or Warren Lodge (D.E.), a mile out of the town on the Brandon road, was once a Lepers' House. In *Adventures with Phantoms*, R. Thurston Hopkins tells of how he constantly dreamed of the place and its inhabitants before he even knew it existed. Even in this century the 700-year-old tower still contained the wooden platters, the begging bowls and the leper's bells. The local people continue to believe that the house is haunted by one of the former inmates. One person who has seen it said, 'It had a flat white face and burning eyes, and there was a sound like a running stream. It passed through me making a filthy gust of hot air.'

On the banks of the river Thet there is a barrow known as Thet Hill. It is very haunted. A ghostly red-haired chieftain has been seen, and is thought to be benevolent.

Queen Isabella's crazy cackles can be heard in the ruins of Castle Rising

Huntingdon has four sites so close to the Bedfordshire border that they could easily be included in a tour of that county. The other four lie in or near St Ives, and towards the northern border. From the last site in Bedfordshire – Pertenhall – cross the boundary to the north and you will come to:

☉ **Kimbolton** (O.P.). Catherine of Aragon was kept captive here in the castle for the last two years of her life, and her ghost is said to haunt the place. Although a large portion of the south wing fell down in 1707, the Queen's Chamber remained intact. This was the only room she used for she was a very frightened woman and feared poisoning so dreadfully that all her food had to be cooked in her presence.

A few miles to the south-east is:

☉ **Great Staughton,** where the Crown Inn has a most mysterious ghost. Clothes disappear and reappear in a different place. Footsteps are heard going upstairs and crossing a room. Mr and Mrs Green knew nothing of this when they became landlords in October 1970, but they soon found that the previous innkeeper had had exactly the same experiences. Local people believe it is 'Old Pork-and-Lard', a former publican who was also a butcher. He married a very young girl when he was in his seventies, but died while she was pregnant. Perhaps he so desperately wanted to see his child that his spirit cannot rest. Maybe he tries to help his wife by tidying things away; or perhaps he hid some money and died before he could reveal the hiding-place. The owner of the cottage next door has also experienced similar phenomena. Some Irish labourers witnessed a strange manifestation when Mrs Green told them she did not believe in ghosts. The electric clock above the bar jumped off the wall to hang by its wires.

On the moor nearby there is a farm where the doors had no locks because they were useless. The White Lady opened doors that were locked, bolted and barred. She was seen by workmen who were mending the roof, and another builder had to be called in to finish the job.

South-east again lies:

☉ **Waresley.** At Vicarage Farm the ghost of a small boy, who died most pathetically in 1921, has been seen as recently as 1965.

Top Kimbolton, Catherine of Aragon's last home and prison, still incarcerates her ghost

Above The girl buried under the flagstones in the Ferry Boat Inn haunts the bar

Opposite The tower at Woodcroft Castle from which Charles I's chaplain fell to his death

The Society for Psychical Research has published details. In *Frontiers of the Unknown,* Andrew Muir states that the haunting 'will rank high in the literature of psychical research because verification . . . was possible'. Vicarage Farm lies near the site of the old church which was destroyed by lightning. On the grey Sunday that I visited the place, it looked very forlorn. I hope the poor boy's spirit has now found rest.

East of Huntingdon you will find:

☺ **St Ives** where Room 14 at the 'Golden Lion' is said to be haunted by a ghostly Green Lady. She is thought to have been – strangely enough – the mistress of Oliver Cromwell. Poltergeist manifestations are said to have taken place here in 1970, though publicans who claim older-established ghosts are inclined to raise their eyebrows.

East again lies:

✿☺ **Holywell.** The spring which gave it its name is below the church on the south side. According to the typescript notes in the church, another well in a neighbourhood cellar 'has even more peculiar qualities'. But today most seekers of mystery go to the Ferry Boat Inn on March 17. This is Juliet's Eve when the ghost of a girl may appear at midnight. Spurned by her lover she hanged herself by the river and was buried where the inn now stands. The grave is under a stone in the floor of the bar. The innkeeper has heard but not seen her. Once, however, a boatload of visitors arrived on March 16 and asked when Juliet was due to appear. 'Tomorrow,' said the landlord, 'she'll not make herself known tonight.' At that moment a tankard appeared to be wrenched from its hook by unseen hands, and flung violently to the floor.

Now go north, and 2 miles south of Etton is:

☺ **Woodcroft Castle** where the ghost of Dr Michael Hudson has been seen. He was chaplain to Charles I, and was either beheaded or thrown from the tower by the Roundheads, who slashed off his hands as he clung to the battlements. Some say that he jumped rather than surrender. The *Shell Guide* quotes from an unknown source: 'His tongue was cut out by a low-bred shopkeeper from Stamford, and sent round the country as a trophy.'

To the west near the county border is:

☺ **Barnack.** The Old Rectory is now called Kingsley House and, according to Henry Kingsley, was haunted when he was rector by a fairly benign presence known as Button Cap, who did little more than scratch, breathe heavily and stroke the heads of the children. Charles Kingsley was more sceptical about these poltergeist activities. The ghost is listed by Eric Russell as 'Circa 1825; Purpose: frivolous.'

RUTLAND

Rutland has two sites, one in the north and one in the south. The latter, near the Eye Brook reservoir, is at:

Stoke Dry where a rector once imprisoned a witch in the parvis above the church porch and starved her to death. Her spirit haunts the place which is still accessible.

Just off the Great North Road near the Lincolnshire border is:

Stretton. On the outskirts of the village is Stocken Hall. Here you may see the ghost of a girl who was strangled in the attic; the ghost of a White Lady whose presence has also been felt; and the phantom of a hanged man, swinging from the branches of an oak tree. Underwood reports that the latter was seen at 2.45 p.m. on December 22 one year, although subsequent visits on this date in succeeding years proved fruitless. It may be difficult to carry out research here as it is now an open prison farm.

LEICESTERSHIRE

One would have expected Leicestershire to abound in Phantom Riders and Wild Hunts, but if they ever existed they have gone to ground. I have so far found only three sites.

South-west of Market Harborough is:

Husbands Bosworth. Bosworth Hall is the site of hauntings and an indelible red stain, which unlike most such stains is said to remain damp. This may be Communion wine, or the blood of the priest who had to make a dash for his secret room when surprised by the Roundheads. The ghost is that of a Protestant lady who married into the Catholic family of the house. She refused to allow a priest to visit a dying servant, and now haunts the place in remorse.

☆ **Leicester** itself has a mysterious site at Dane Hills. There is a cave here which was blocked up about 100 years ago because of its horrific reputation. Known as Anne's Bower, it may possibly have been a place of worship – and sacrifice – dedicated to the Celtic goddess Anu or Black Annis who, according to T. C. Lethbridge, is the earth-mother in her old-woman stage. Naturally she came to be considered a fearsome blood-sucking witch, with whom naughty children were threatened.

West of Leicester is:

Market Bosworth where the lanes leading south are haunted by a headless phantom soldier.

Left The spirit of the witch starved to death over the porch at Stoke Dry Church still permeates the place

Right The Hall at Husbands Bosworth is the scene of hauntings and a damp stain

The Trent passes through many counties, and the old sacrifice that the river god demanded could presumably be paid in any of them. People still believe that he demands – and gets – three lives a year. Just before the river is crossed by the A57, west of Lincoln, it runs past:

Clifton Hall. A carp, forcing its way upstream, is reputed to have been a harbinger of death for the Clifton family, who lived here for 600 years.

Between Clifton and Mansfield you will find:

Rufford Abbey which now belongs to the Nottinghamshire County Council. It is haunted by a monk. One witness, who saw the ghost in a mirror and described how he was dressed, was told that this was not the habit of the Order which lived here before the Dissolution. However it was subsequently discovered that a monk, whose dress was exactly as described, had once visited Rufford and, what is more, had died there.

South of Mansfield lies:

Newstead Abbey (O.P.), ancestral home of the Byrons, but now owned by Nottingham Corporation. As C. G. Harper states, the history of the Byron family after they had acquired Newstead confirms the belief that ill-luck comes to those who put religious houses to secular uses. From 1540, when Sir John Byron bought it, the family suffered misfortune. Several generations lost money until the 'Wicked Lord' was forced to live in the scullery, as it was the only room that remained watertight, and the poet's mother was too poor to live there at all. On the eve of his wedding to Anne Milbanke, he saw the ghost, known as the Goblin Friar, which brings bad tidings, and he described his marriage as the most unhappy event in his life. When the poet sold this place in 1818 for £95,000, more than that amount had to be spent on repairs, and the ill-luck continued with successive owners. Byron is said to have buried his dog, Boatswain, on the site of the Black Canon's high altar, and the animal re-appears as a Phantom Hound. The poet also asked to be buried near his dog, but this request was not carried out.

Nottingham Castle has a ghost which is believed to be that of Queen Isabella (see Castle Rising, Norfolk). She is searching for her lover, Mortimer, who was confined in a dungeon here before being executed in London.

Below, left Byron buried his dog on the site of the Black Canon's High Altar

Below The crowning of the Garland King at Castleton

DERBYSHIRE

Derbyshire is famous for its well-dressing. I think this ceremony originated in the Christianization of a pagan custom. Wells were sacred long before Christ was born. Offerings, often sacrifices, were made to the deities who were bountiful enough to provide water, and the ritual which accompanied such thanksgivings included decorating the well. If the first Christian missionaries were unable to persuade the people to abandon their customs, they could try to deflect interest to the new god, a subterfuge which has resulted in biblical scenes being the main subject of the decorated panels with which wells are now dressed. If you want to check the dates of well-dressing ceremonies consult the 'Come to Derbyshire Association'.

I suggest you start the tour at:
◉ **Derby** where Pace-egging (Pace meaning Pascal or Easter) takes place at Bunkers Hill. Eggs are rolled at Easter symbolizing, some say, the rolling away of the stone from Christ's tomb, but the egg was a symbol of fertility in pagan days. (See Preston, Lancashire.)

Take the road through Ashbourne to:
◉ **Tissington.** The well-dressing ceremony takes place on Ascension Day, the Thursday

next but one before Whitsunday. Six wells are dressed.

There is great rivalry among the various villages which still dress their wells, but there is no space to describe the differences here:
◉ **Ashford-in-the-water, Belper, Bonsall, Bradwell, Eyam, Stony Middleton, Tideswell, Wirksworth** and **Youlgreave** are all places which can be visited on the appropriate days.
☆ **Matlock** has the Lumsdale Wishing Stone which is still steadfastly believed in, and there are petrifying wells at Matlock Bath.

North-east, near the county border, you will find:
☺ **Renishaw,** the home of the Sitwells. Two ghosts are reported: a woman in her fifties – apparently a servant – with grey hair in a bun under a white cap; and another woman with dark hair and clothes. Before alterations were made to the staircase, people sleeping in one bedroom received three cold kisses during the night. When the reconstruction was being carried out, a mysterious empty coffin was found under the floor of this room.

The next important site is back in the Peak District:
◉ **Castleton.** Apart from Peveril Castle (D.E.), immortalized by Sir Walter Scott, and the remarkable caves with names like Roger's Rain House and Devil's Cavern, which have their own legends, you can also watch the survival of a very ancient rite. On May 29 – Royal or Oak Apple Day – the Garland King and his Queen ride out, the manes of their horses traditionally plaited with lilac and oak leaves, and the tails with bluebells. The king is covered with a cage of greenery topped with a bunch of flowers. This is removed at 6.30 p.m. and hoisted up to the top of the church tower. Here we have a symbol of an ascent into heaven. As Christina Hole points out, in similar rituals in Germany the cage is broken up and bits of it placed in every field to make the crops grow, a 'clear relic of the primitive custom by which the king himself would have been sacrificed and his blood scattered on the fields.' (See Brading, Isle of Wight.) So, although the king is now said to represent Charles II, he is really pagan in origin.

South, from:
🐾 **Miller's Dale to Peak Dale,** in the north-west, is the haunt of a werewolf.
☆ **Buxton** lies south-west. Here St Anne's

Hoisting the cage of flowers up Castleton church tower

Well reminds us once again of how early Christians sanctified pagan sites, for this was originally a shrine to the Roman nymph Arnemeza, goddess of wells.

The final site in Derbyshire near Chapel-en-le-Frith is:

🕯 **Tunstead Milton.** Dickie's Farm is haunted, some say, by the ghost of Ned Dixon who was murdered by his cousin when he returned from the wars. Other sources state it is the spectre of a co-heiress who was murdered and swore her bones would never leave the place. In any case when the skull was removed from the house, according to Harper, it prevented the London and North Western Railway to Manchester being built on its original course, as well as causing cattle to go dry and sheeprot in the flock.

Below The Lumsdale Wishing Stone at Matlock

Bottom St Anne's Well, Buxton, in Stuart times

STAFFORDSHIRE

A tour of the sites in Staffordshire leads one north from Walsall where at:

🕯 **Caldmore Green** the White Hart Inn was the site of a macabre discovery and mysterious manifestations. The mummified arm of a baby was found in an attic, and the imprint of its hand appeared on a dust-covered table. A female phantom has been seen and heard. It is thought that she may have been a servant who committed suicide at the beginning of the century.

East across the A5 you will find:

🦁🕯 **Tamworth** where King Alfred's granddaughter Editha founded a convent. The nuns were evicted by Robert de Marmion, who was given the castle (O.P.) by William the Conqueror. The ghost of Editha rebuked him and struck him with her crozier, causing a wound which would not stop bleeding till he vowed to make amends. The Haunted Staircase, leading to the Tower Room where the ghost still appears, echoes to the sound of sighs and groans which have been recorded on tape. There is also a White Lady who, in Saxon days, saw her lover killed by Sir Launcelot below the castle walls. Her spirit still haunts Lady's Meadow.

Just east of Blithfield reservoir is: *T Pine*

◉🕯 **Abbots Bromley.** The Horn Dance takes place on the first Monday following the first Sunday after September 4. Twelve men take part: six in Tudor dress, with reindeer antlers on their heads, accompanied by Robin Hood, a transvestite Maid Marion, an archer carrying a cross-bow, a Fool and two musicians. As reindeer disappeared from Britain at the time of the Conquest, the custom goes back for more than 1000 years, and probably originated as a pagan fertility rite (see Windsor, Berkshire, and Herne the Hunter). The dance continues all day. The Revd A. R. Ladell, Vicar of Abbots Bromley from 1928–60, has written an excellent booklet about the dance, attributing its origins to 'wife-hunger', and quoting Albert Babeau's *Vie Rurale*, which describes an old pagan marriage ritual in which young men wore the horns of cattle and pursued the village girls, who fled in all directions, screaming with laughter. The dance was once performed at Christmas, New Year and Twelfth Night, and the horns bore the coats of arms of the Bagots, Pagets and Welles, once chief landowners in the neighbourhood.

'Ye Olde Coach and Horses' is said to be haunted.

🐎 Chartley Castle's ruins are easily seen from the 518. Around it once grazed the famous herd of cattle bred by the Ferrers family. They were white with red ears, the traditional colouring of fairy cattle. When a black calf was born it presaged death for one of the Ferrers. This occurred when both the seventh and eighth earls and their near relatives died. Ill-fortune came to the herd too, for it languished and in 1900 there were only fifty-five beasts left. Chartley was sold by the tenth earl, who had no sons.

The Haunted Staircase at Tamworth Castle

SHROPSHIRE

Coming into the county from the south you will first arrive at:

ⓨ Ludlow. The churchyard and rectory are haunted by the ghost of a grey-haired lady in a dressing-gown; and at the Globe Hotel there is a ghost called Joe, a soldier who died in the castle in 1513.

The most compelling ghost, however, is at the castle. When on one occasion the castle was besieged, Marion de la Bruyere was a defender, but her lover was one of the attacking force. She lowered a rope from her room at night so that her sweetheart could

hold her in his arms. He purposely left the rope so that others could swarm in and capture the castle. Doubly betrayed, Marion killed her lover with his own sword and then threw herself from the battlements. The laboured breathing which is often heard comes from halfway up the Hanging Tower, where Marion's ghost has appeared.

To the north-east on the 458 at:

Morville the 'Acton Arms' is reputed to be haunted. The ghost is probably Richard Manners, Abbot of Shrewsbury and last Prior of Morville in the early sixteenth century.

Eight miles south of Shrewsbury along the A49 is:

Longnor. The White Lady of Longnor is the ghost of a pretty young girl who committed suicide by throwing herself into the stream.

Condover Hall (O.P.A.), now a school for deaf and dumb children, is said to have an indelible bloodstain where Lord Knevett was treacherously murdered by his son in the reign of Henry VIII.

Chester Wishing Steps

CHESTER

There is no better place to start a tour of Cheshire than:

Chester, which is on the Dee, a holy river that claimed no sacrifice and never keeps a drowned body. The Wishing Steps – seventy of them – lead up to the town walls. Girls should wish at the bottom, then run up and down without drawing breath. This ensures that the wish will be granted or that the outcome of a love affair will be happy.

South, on the borders of Wales, you will find:

Farndon where the bridge is haunted by the ghosts of two children who were entrusted to the care of Roger Mortimer by Prince Madoc. Mortimer dropped them into the stream, and their terrified screams may still be heard.

Further south is:

Shocklach. Here the ghosts of all the Breretons forgather once a year, and the lane leading to the isolated church is said to be jammed with spectral coaches. (Incidentally, the death of a Brereton heir has usually been presaged by the trunks of trees seen floating in Blackmere Lake.)

East, and near the Shropshire border, lies:

Combermere Abbey where the ghost of a little girl, frantically distraught, has been seen. She used to herald the death of a member of the Cotton family who lived here after the Dissolution, and held the abbey only as long as they remained as hospitable as were once the monks, whose ghosts have also been seen.

South-east of Crewe, near the M6, you will find:

Barthomley. The ghost of the Lady in White haunts the church field; and that of a dog the road nearby.

To the north, where the 357 crosses the 34, is:

Capesthorne Hall (O.P.), home of the Bromley Davenports, who have seen several ghostly apparitions, including a line of shadowy spectres descending into the vault beneath the chapel, a severed arm trying to open a bedroom window, and a Lady in

Hall Well, dressed at Tissington, Derbyshire

Grey, who was seen one night by – among others – Sir Charles Taylor, M.P.

North-east again, near the Derbyshire border, is:

🔮 **Lyme Park** (N.T.). Sir Piers Legh died in Paris in 1422, and his body was brought home for burial. The cortège still haunts the drive, though the ghostly Woman in White is seen more frequently, both inside and outside the house. She is thought to be Sir Piers' mistress, Blanche, who died of grief and whose body was found in a meadow known as Lady's Grave. The Ghost Room leads out of Long Gallery. Here a skeleton was discovered in a secret chamber.

Due north is:

🔮 **Marple Hall** where the ghost of Charles II has been seen. The river Goyt is haunted by the daughter of Henry Bradshaw, a Roundhead, who fell in love with a Cavalier and was murdered by drowning. Some consider this spectre to be of older origin, a river spirit who subsequently became identified with the Cavalier's sweetheart.

🔮 **Handforth** lies to the south-west. Here the Old Parsonage is haunted by the ghost of a woman, frightened to death by a visit from Prince Charles Stuart in 1745.

South again is:

🐎🐾 **Alderley Edge,** where King Arthur and his Knights sleep, together with their white horses, waiting to be called to Britain's aid. It is also believed that when a vast mere stretched from here to High Legh, a mermaid would appear each Easter.

To the south-west, just before you reach the M6, you come to:

🐎 **Lower Peover.** If a girl can lift the lid of the chest in the church with one hand, she is strong enough to become a farmer's wife.

🔮 **Knutsford** lies just to the north. There is a ghost on Higher Tower Common. An innkeeper murdered a rent-collector for his money. He was so haunted by his victim's spectre that he confessed on his deathbed.

North again is:

🐾 **Rostherne Mere,** all that remains of the great lake that is said to have stretched from Alderley Edge (q.v.) to High Legh. And again the mermaid legend is to be found. She is said to sing here still, and ring a bell.

South-west at:

☆ **Weaverham** there is a well which cures rheumatism, sprains and swellings.

South-west again lies:

☆ **Delamere Forest,** and here, 1½ miles from the Chamber of the Forest (now called The Old Pale), is a spring reputed to cure 'agues, sore eyes, acnes, blindness, rupture, issues of water, gout, wildfire (erysipelas), deafness and griefs of the joints'.

South of the forest and on the outskirts of Tarporley you will find:

🐝🔮 **Utkinton Hall** where the blackbirds in the walled garden are believed to be descendants of the bird in which a ghost was laid by a priest.

South of Tarporley there are three sites close together:

👢⊙🐾🔮 **Bunbury** where on the walls of the Image House you will see stone heads, carved – and cursed – by an eighteenth-century poacher. They represent the keepers, constables and magistrates who were concerned with his transportation. They are similar to the sheep's hearts and wax figures stuck with pins, more commonly used by witches.

Sir Hugh de Calverley's tomb in the church is badly damaged because the alabaster has been chipped away to be ground up and given as sheep medicine. A spectral hound has been seen near the school; and in College Lane a ghostly horseman crosses the road.

☆ **Spurstow.** Whitewater springs will cure the halt and the lame. Crutches were left here.

☆ **Horley's Bath,** near Beeston Castle, is reputed to cure rheumatism.

You can now visit the Wirral peninsula. In:

☆ **Bromborough** public park you will find St Gabriel's Well.

Just west of Wallasey is:

🔮 **Leasowe Castle,** originally the summer home of the fifth Earl of Derby (d.1594). It became known as Mockbeggar Hall and has been a private house, a hostel for sailors, a hotel and a convalescent home for railwaymen. It is haunted by the ghosts of a man and a young boy.

Down the coast at:

🔮 **Hoylake,** the Royal Hotel is said to be haunted by a ghost in a tweed norfolk jacket, knickerbockers and cap.

Round in the Dee estuary you will find

🔮 **Thurstaston Hall** where the ghost of an elderly lady is said to appear every night, wringing her hands.

A little further south is:

🔮 **Parkgate.** Quay House, which has served as a prison and an inn, is haunted by the spectre of a little old woman in a red cloak.

The spirit of the river Ribble will take a human life if not appeased by an animal sacrifice

I suggest that Lancashire is divided into four sections. There are sites in and around Liverpool, Manchester, the Ribble Valley and north along the M6. First, just north of Liverpool, is:

Maghull. South of the town the sound of galloping horses and the clash of accoutrements is heard at dusk; and sometimes, against a grey stone wall, the spectres of headless horsemen are seen. They may be the ghostly remnants of the Royalist army who fled south in 1648, or Jacobites who tried to escape when Preston was recaptured in 1715.

East of Liverpool lies:

Newton-le-Willows. The ghosts of the Royalists caught and hanged by Cromwell in 1648 can still be heard marching to their doom.

South of Warrington is:

Walton Hall where a locked and bolted door is reported to open, and after thirty seconds suddenly bang shut. This phenomenon is said usually to take place in June, and one story attributes the occurrence to the ghost of an elderly lady who, in the eighteenth century, died in her bath and still tries desperately to get back to her bedroom.

Manchester has its fair share of strange sites. An antique shop called the 'Rover's Return' is haunted by the ghost of a kilted Jacobite called James Stewart who came to Manchester with Bonnie Prince Charlie.

At Kersal Cell the ghost of a monk has been seen on Christmas Eve, and at Godley Green you may see a Phantom Hound whose coat is not black but yellow. It was once thought to be a lion from Bellevue. This apparition may be the same one which appears headless at the old bridge over the Irwell. Here, too, there is a farm haunted by Old Nanny; and there is a patch in the garden where nothing will grow.

West of Manchester at Worsley is:

Wardley Hall where, according to legend, the head of Roger Downes, a Restoration rake-hell, was delivered in a wooden

Left, top One of the effigies adorning Bunbury Image House

Left Wardley Hall houses a legendary skull

box. He had committed at least one murder and escaped justice through friends at Court before he had his head cut off in a drunken brawl with a waterman on London Bridge. His body was thrown into the Thames. The removal of his head from the Hall caused storms and dire reprisals. But when Downes' coffin was opened in 1779, his head was still attached to his body. The skull at Wardley is actually that of a priest called Father Ambrose, son of a neighbouring squire, Sir Alexander Barlow of Barlow Hall. He was hanged and quartered in 1641 for being a Roman Catholic.

North-west of Bolton is one of the oldest manor houses in the county:

Smithills Hall (O.P.). There is reputed to be a bloody footprint on the doorstep, which once a year becomes both wet and red. It is said to be that of George Marsh, whose ghost has also been seen.

North-east is:

Burnley Parish Church, haunted by a Phantom Hound, locally known as Trash or Skriker.

East of Colne, which is to the north-east of Burnley, is:

Wycoller Hall, now a ruin, but once the house on which Charlotte Brontë based Ferndean Manor in *Jane Eyre*. It is haunted by a spectral horseman who rides up to the house, dashes up what was once the staircase and enters a room. Screams are heard, turning to groans. This happens on wild tempestuous evenings, for it was on such a night that a Cunliffe of Billington murdered his wife here.

Now travel west to:

The Ribble, a river which was sacred to Minerva during and after the Roman occupation. This goddess became associated with Peg O'Nell, the spirit of the river who demands a life every seven years. She will now be appeased by the sacrifice of a small animal or bird, but if this is not done she will take a human life. Some say that Peg O'Nell was a servant at Wadden Hall, drowned as a witch – the gods of yesterday once again becoming the devils of today.

Just east of Preston is:

Samlesbury Hall (O.P.A.), haunted by the ghost of Dorothy, daughter of Sir John Southworth, a staunch Catholic who forbade her to marry a neighbouring squire who had forsaken the old faith. The couple planned to elope, but were overheard by the girl's brother who killed his sister's lover. Dorothy was sent abroad to a convent where she went mad and died, but her spirit still meets the

George Marsh left his footprint and his ghost at Smithills Hall

ghost of her betrothed and they walk in the grounds, sighing in despair before they embrace and disappear. It is said that she is also seen on the main road and buses have actually stopped to pick her up.

Preston has a spectral headless hound which presages tragic events. You will also find the remnant of an old springtime fertility rite in egg-rolling, symbol of new life (see Derby, Derbyshire).

Six miles north of Preston is Goosnargh and:

Chingle Hall which is full of secret hiding places, and where doors open of their own accord, mysterious footsteps have been heard, ghosts seen, and sudden and intense cold experienced.

South-east of Silverdale is:

Warton. On the crag is the Bride's Chair, in which a girl should sit on her wedding day to ensure having a baby.

WESTMORLAND

Westmorland has, I am sure, more sites than the following; but I have not yet discovered them. Coming in on the A6, halfway between the county border and Kendal, you will find: 👁🦌🐕 **Levens Hall** (O.P.), haunted by a Grey Lady, who appears to be a ghostly nanny. She only appears when children are about. A phantom dog has also been seen, but this is a pet, not a Gabriel's Ratchett. A curse on the owners of this fine Elizabethan house says that strangers will separate them from their lands, and no heir will succeed his father until a white doe is born in the park and the waters of the Kent, flowing by, are still. The estate has generally gone from father to nephew and brother to cousin. In 1913 a Bagot did succeed his father, and that year a white doe was born in the park and the Kent froze over. Unfortunately he died unmarried.

North-east of Kendal on the 685 there is a farm which marks the site of the 'Quaker's Curse':

🐕 **Grayrigg Hall** was owned in the seventeenth century by a magistrate called Duckett, who sentenced the Quaker Howgill to imprisonment in Appleby jail. Howgill told Duckett that his name would 'rot out of the earth, and his dwelling become derelict and a habitation of owls and jackdaws'. The Duckett children died childless and in penury. Grayrigg was dismantled and by 1777 little more than the foundations remained, the haunt of owls and jackdaws. But although that may have been true 200 years ago, it now appears to be a flourishing farmstead, with outbuildings older than the house.

To the west is Lake Windermere where, on the outskirts of Troutbeck Bridge, you will find:

🐕 **Calgarth,** a sixteenth-century manor, now a guest house, which has a legend very similar to that of Grayrigg Hall. It was once a small holding owned by Kraster Cook and his wife Dorothy. They were falsely accused of theft by a local magistrate called Myles Phillipson, who wanted their land. The Cooks were condemned to death, and from the dock Dorothy cursed the family of Phillipson and their enterprises, and she promised to haunt Calgarth day and night as long as the walls still stood. Myles Phillipson was indeed plagued by the apparitions of two skulls for ever after and his family sank into poverty and died out. But the place became prosperous and Dr Watson, the Bishop of Llandaff who only visited his diocese on one occasion, built the present house.

👁 **Thirlemere** is actually in Cumberland and now belongs to the Manchester Municipal authorities. It is difficult to find traces of its ghosts, although it looks a gloomy, dark enough place. For years the road above Dalehead was haunted by one of the Leathes family. Armboth Hall, just across the lake, belonged to the Jackson family and this too was haunted. The ghost was that of a girl who was married at midnight and then murdered. The empty house appears lit up as if for a great banquet, and according to A. G. Bradley in *Highways and Byways in the Lake District*, among the guests are – or were – the Calgarth skulls.

The last site lies off the A6, just south of the Cumberland border:

👁 **Lowther Castle** was the home of the Lowthers (who became Earls of Lonsdale) till 1936. It is haunted by an eccentric member of the family who drives about in a spectral coach.

A dwarf guards the treasure buried at Thirlwall Castle

CUMBERLAND

Cumberland is the county of talismans. You can start in the south-west pocket with:

🐾 **Muncaster Castle** (O.P.). For some 700 years it belonged to the Penningtons, and for the last 500 it has been under the protection of the Luck of Muncaster, a talisman given by Henry VI, who found refuge here in the 1460s. It is a bowl made of clear, greenish glass, decorated in purple, gold and white, six inches in diameter and probably of fifteenth-century Venetian manufacture. A traditional verse promises:

> It shall bless thy bed, it shall bless thy board,
> They shall prosper by this token,
> In Muncaster Castle good luck shall be
> Till this charmed cup is broken.

North on the 596 lies Aspatria, and here:

👁 **Gill House** was found to be terribly haunted when it was used by the Land Army during World War II. According to Peter Underwood, the manifestations which frightened the inhabitants included the sensation of being strangled.

East of Carlisle you will find:

🐾 **Corby Castle.** Those who see the 'Radiant Boy' rise to power but die a violent death.

North-east, by Hadrian's Wall, lies:

☆ **Gilsland Spa,** with its famous chalybeate springs. You can still take the waters. One account mentions thousands of visitors – 'unconscious adherents of heathen rites' – coming by rail, other vehicles or on foot on the Sunday following Old Midsummer Day.

Below the spa lies the village of:

👁 **Gilsland** where you will find the story of the 'cauld lad', a pathetic child ghost who, through chattering teeth, says:

> Cauld, cauld aye cauld,
> And ye'll be cauld for ever mair.

His small icy hand is sometimes felt. In earthly form he was a six-year-old orphan, deliberately left to freeze to death on Thirlwall Common by a wicked uncle, who wanted to gain his inheritance. I think the murderer may well have been a Thirlwall of:

👁🗡 **Thirlwall Castle,** over the border in Northumberland, which has not been occupied by human beings since the beginning of the seventeenth century. It was built in the thirteenth century and King Edward I stayed there. Now it is haunted by a ghostly dwarf who guards its buried treasure.

South-east of Corby Castle, below Geltsdale, is:

🐾👁 **Croglin Grange,** haunted by a ghost which Russell describes laconically as: 'Unidentified solid apparition, presumed to be a vampire; late 19th century.' The postmistress says that Croglin Grange is now called Lower Hall. It is a farm, set in superb unspoiled country, which, judging from a fine avenue of trees, may have once enjoyed greater importance.

🐾💀 **Penrith.** At Southerfield spectral horses and riders have been seen.

To the east on the river Eden is:

🐾 **Eden Hall,** home of the most famous of all the talismans. In the garden is St Cuthbert's Well and a butler of the Musgrave family, going to get water there, found a group of fairies dancing. In their midst was a cup made of painted glass which he seized and refused to return. So the leader marked him and warned him:

> If that cup should break or fall
> Farewell the Luck of Eden Hall.

The lucky goblet is probably of Syrian origin and may have been brought back from one of the Crusades. It is now in the Bank of England, and Eden Hall is a girls' school.

NORTHUMBERLAND

You should start this tour at Newcastle upon Tyne, take a sweep westwards and then come back east and north up the coast to end at Holy Isle. First, just east of Newcastle, is:

👁🐾 **Willington Gut** where Willington Mill was the scene of one of the most famous hauntings of the last century. W. T. Stead

A knight in armour haunts Bamburgh Castle

devotes no less than five pages to it in his *Real Ghost Stories*. The spectres included a Lady in Lavender, a Lady in Grey, and a woman with no eyes in her sockets; while among the animal apparitions were a cat, a rabbit and a sheep. Whether or not the ghosts are connected with the spectre which still haunts the road between North Shields and Willington, I do not know. Local legend says that this is the ghost of a woman who tried to confess to murder, but was refused confession by the priest and so committed suicide.

South-west of Newcastle, nearly on the Durham border, is:

🐾 **Hedley,** home of the Hedley Kow, a mischievous sprite that can take any form it

NORTHUMBERLAND

wishes – a pretty girl, a milch cow – and then plays practical jokes. It leads young men into bogs and old men on wild goose chases. Yet whatever its form, it always makes the same sound: a loud, braying laugh of derision.

South-west again, on the other side of the Derwent Reservoir, you will find:

ⓖ **Blanchland,** a charming village with stone roofs and walls and blue and white front doors. The 'Lord Crewe Arms', once a priory, then the home of the Radcliffes and Forsters, and now an inn, is haunted by the ghost of Dorothy Forster who at twenty-one married Nathaniel, Lord Crewe, Bishop of Durham, when he was seventy-one.

North-west is:

ⓖ **Haltwhistle.** Near Hadrian's Wall the Wild Hunt is sometimes seen. There are also those who have seen a bridal procession in medieval dress between here and Alston. One source says that this was the wedding of a girl called Abigail, hastily contrived by her father to prevent a love affair with a stranger who was really his illegitimate son.

Three miles away, in the South Tyne Valley, is:

ⓖ **Featherstone Castle.** The tower of this rambling, romantic building is where Sir Reginald FitzUrse was starved to death. He now haunts it. Even if you do not see him, you may still hear his groans and the clink of his armour.

ⓖ **Blenkinsop Castle** is nearby. It was partially burned down, but is still haunted by the ghost of a White Lady.

ⓖ **Bellister Castle,** another border strong-hold, is haunted by the Man in Grey.

Now turn east, and 1½ miles south-west of Corbridge you will find:

ⓖ **Dilston.** Here the ghost of Lady Derwent-water stalks the woods bemoaning the fact that she sent her husband to the scaffold by forcing him to side against the Hanoverians.

North of Stamfordham is:

ⓖ **Black Heddon,** the haunting ground of Silky, ghost of a woman in a silk dress who has often been seen walking among the trees. Sometimes she confronted belated travellers and demanded a lift. Once she prevented a carter from crossing a bridge nearby, till he cut a stick of rowan and broke the spell. Some say that since hidden treasure was found she has ceased her strange behaviour.

To the north-west lies:

ⓖ **Wallington Hall** (N.T.), originally a medieval castle, then an Elizabethan manor before the present house was built in 1688. It is haunted by the sounds of packing and unpacking. Wings are heard beating against

St Cuthbert's ghost makes beads from the pebbles on Lindisfarne beaches.

the windows, and an invisible 'thing' breathes on you as you lie in bed.

North-west again, but east of the main road, you will find:

ⓖ **Elsdon** where three horse skulls were uncovered – a protection against lightning, or maybe the remains of a sacrifice. A ghost here takes the form of a dwarf with red hair and a ferocious expression, known as the 'Brown Man of the Moors.'

North across the moors you come to:

ⓖ **Alwinton** where, according to Peter Underwood, in 1967 the Newcastle Institute of Psychic Research investigated a haunting by the ghost of a monk who had no face, hands or feet.

Now make for the coast. At:

ⓖ **Craster** poltergeist phenomena occur in the Tower (O.P.A.) before the death of the owner.

☆ **Wooler** lies inland. Here, near Kettle Camp, is a wishing well; bent pins should be offered.

ⓖ **Bamburgh.** The castle (O.P.) belonged to the Forster family (see Blanchland) and through Dorothy Forster came to Lord Crewe. Her ghost does not haunt the place. The spectre here is said to be a knight in armour.

And so to the northernmost site in England:

ⓖ **Lindisfarne or Holy Island,** a place one feels must have been old and sacred long before St Aidan came here in 635. The fishermen consider that pigs are harbingers of evil (as they are at Whitby) and touch silver if they see one or even hear the animal mentioned. St Cuthbert came here in 664 and his ghost is said to haunt the rocks, making St Cuthbert's Beads, which are pebbles with a hole running through them, and are good omens. Another island ghost is that of Constance de Beverley.

You can enter Co. Durham by the MI over the Tees. This river's goddess is Peg Powler, who lies in wait for victims at Piercebridge. She used to demand a sacrifice. Coming in by the MI you will arrive at:

🦌 **Blackwell** on the southern outskirts of Darlington. The legend of how the body of Christopher Simpson bled when his murderer was called upon to touch the corpse is told in the ballad 'The Baydale Banks Tragedy'.

👁 **Darlington.** The manor house, built by Bishop Pudsey at the turn of the twelfth century, is haunted by Lady Jarrett who was murdered here, and left her bloodstained finger and thumb prints on the wall. Her ghost appears with one arm; her real arm was cut off to obtain a valuable ring on one of her fingers.

West on the 688 is:

👁 **Raby Castle** (O.P.) which has enough history to teem with ghosts, yet it is not the Nevilles who haunt the place, but the wife of a former owner, Lady Barnard, known as 'Old Hell Cat'. She is seen on the ramparts, knitting with red-hot needles.

The old colliery at Littleburn is still worked by a phantom miner and pit pony

The countryside around is haunted by Maria Cotton and those she murdered in Durham in 1873, before she was caught and hanged. They chase one another over the surrounding fields in a kind of macabre blind-man's-buff.

👁👣🐎 **West Auckland** is a site haunted by a phantom rider on a grey horse. He rides towards Hamsterly Forest, to the north-west, his face a mask of blood.

👣🐎👁 **Littleburn Colliery** (now disused), just south of Durham, is haunted by a phantom pit pony and the ghost of a miner who was killed when the pony bolted.

🦌👁 **Durham.** In the Cathedral Library is the Conyers Falchion, a twelfth-century sword with a curved cutting edge, which was the tenure weapon of the Manor of Sockburn, and the 'Luck of the Conyers'. Whenever a new bishop was installed he was presented with the sword as token rent, but immediately returned it. According to legend, the Worm of Sockburn (a dragon) was slain with the weapon by Sir John de Conyers. The Pollards' lands at Bishop Auckland were also held 'of the bishop by a falchion', but after Dr Longley received it in 1856, the sword seems to have been lost.

A secret passage is said to lead from the cathedral to Finchale Abbey (see below), but it is so full of horrors that no man can stand it.

🦌👁 **Neville's Castle** is on the west side of Durham. If you walk round the walls nine times and put your ear to the ground, you may hear the sound of battle and the clash of armour. On 17 October 1346 the Scots were defeated and King David Bruce taken prisoner here. On St Thomas's Eve (December 20) the path from Neville's Cross to Cradlewell is said to be haunted by the ghost of a murdered woman with a child dangling by her side.

North-west, along the road leading to:

👣🐎👁 **Langley Hall,** a phantom hearse appears at midnight. Some say that it is a coach drawn by headless horses and with a headless coachman on the box.

North of Durham are :

☆ **Finchale Abbey** (D.E.) and **St Godric's Garth,** the retreat of a hermit who started life as a pedlar and became a pirate. He made a pilgrimage to Jerusalem barefoot; took his mother to Rome; foretold Thomas à Becket's murder; performed miracles; saw visions and re-appeared after death. The whole fascinating story is told in a booklet obtainable at Finchale Farm.

On the outskirts of Sunderland you will find:

Anne Griffith haunts Burton Agnes Hall as 'Awd Nance'. She insisted that her head be left at the Hall after her death and plagues the place if anyone tries to give it a decent burial

Yorkshire sites are widely scattered and remarkably varied. I suggest that you travel up the MI, then cut across to the east, returning to York as base. Next, cover the south-west part of the county, returning again to York, and finally visit the north-east and travel west to the borders of Lancashire. You will leave the motorway at Maltby, south of which lies:

☆ **Roche Abbey** (D.E.) where there is a wishing well. Pins should be offered.

North-east, between Doncaster and Bawtry, you will find:

◉ **Rossington Hall** which is haunted by the ghost of a previous owner, dressed in top hat and frock coat. He appears to be inspecting the stables.

North-east across the Humber is:

◉⛄ **Beverley** where the headless spectre of Sir Jocelyn Percy, driving a phantom coach and headless four, has been seen in the streets.

North-east again, on the Bridlington/Driffield road, you come to:

◉ **Burton Agnes Hall** (O.P.), haunted by a ghost familiarly known as 'Awd Nance'. She was Anne, youngest daughter of Sir Henry Griffith, who built the house at the end of the sixteenth century; Anne was an enthusiastic supporter of the project. After being attacked by a robber at Harpham (see below) and realizing that she was near death, she asked that her head should remain in the house she loved. This was promised, but not fulfilled. The hauntings became so frantic that the coffin was disinterred. The head was found to be severed from the body. Neither trunk nor limbs showed any sign of mortification, but the head was already a skull. It was taken to the house and since then all attempts to bury it in consecrated ground have led to dire trouble.

☆⛄ **Harpham.** Behind the church a drumming well foretells the death of a member of the St Quentin family. A drummer, Tom Hewson, was pushed down the well by a squire in the fourteenth century. Hewson's mother was a witch and decreed that her son would drum the squire's descendants to their deaths.

On the outskirts of the village a more reputable well, certainly better kept, is dedicated to St John of Beverley; its waters will subdue the fiercest animal.

⛄ **Hylton Castle** (D.E.), haunted by a mischievous naked sprite known as the 'Cauld Lad of Hylton'. He cleaned and tidied things away; and became destructive only when there was nothing else to do. One source says that he is the ghost of Roger Skelton (Eric Russell gives this a macabre twist by spelling the name 'Skeleton'), a stable boy killed in a fit of temper by Robert Hylton in 1609.

On the coast between South Shields and Sunderland is:

◉ **The Marsden Grotto.** The hotel was built in 1850 in front of caves used by smugglers, and is haunted by the ghost of a smuggler informer, who tipped off the coastguards about another smuggler's activities.

About 1½ miles south of Driffield is:

ⓖ **Sunderlandwick Hall.** Here the sound of wet feet slapping along a stone-flagged corridor is heard. Why it should be thought to be connected with the son of a previous owner who killed a Negro servant in Africa, I do not know.

Due south you come to:

ⓖ **Watton.** The meadows which run down from the ruined priory to Watton Beck are haunted by the ghost of a headless nun. She was seduced, and punished by execution.

You now go to:

ⓖⓔ **York.** Trinity Church, Micklegate, is haunted by a family of three ghosts. York Castle is the scene of a very curious manifestation reported by Sir John Reresby in 1717: a piece of paper blowing in the wind suddenly turned into a monkey, then a bear.

For the next tour take the Leeds road and turn off at Tadcaster to Boston Spa. Just south of the town is:

ⓔ **Bramham Park** (O.P.). Spectral horses are heard galloping in the dell near the cricket pitch. They are the ghostly echoes of those who fled from the Battle of Bramham Moor in 1408.

✡ **Thorp Arch** is nearby, and here you will find St Helen's Well and possibly tattered cloth fluttering from a bush close by, for the offering is a rag.

To the north of Bradford is:

ⓖ **Calverley Hall,** haunted by Master Walter Calverley.

Due north again past Otley and 3 miles north-east of Weston you will find:

🗡ⓔ **Dobb Park Castle.** Buried treasure is reputed to be under the stairs, but beware of the dog that guards it – it has three heads.

Only an honest man can move the Rocking Stone, one of Brimham Rocks

West, but north of the A59, is:

ⓖ **Bolton Abbey,** haunted by a monk.

North-west of Ripley are:

✡ **Brimham Rocks,** which include the Lover's Rock, the Wishing Stone (place the middle finger of the right hand in the hole and wish) and the Rocking Stone which moves only at the efforts of an honest man.

ⓖ **Ripley Castle** (O.P.) is haunted by a nun who knocks on bedroom doors, but only enters if the occupant says, 'Come in!'

ⓖ **Fountains Abbey** (D.E.), to the north, is where a ghostly choir has been heard chanting in the Chapel of the Nine Altars by numerous people on many occasions.

Between:

ⓖ **Boroughbridge and Scotch Corner** the Great North Road is haunted by the ghost of Tom Hoggett, the highwayman.

To the west of York is:

ⓖ **Marston Moor.** The roads around Long Marston are haunted by the Cavaliers put to flight by Cromwell on 2 July 1644.

The next tour takes you up the A64 from:

ⓖ **York to Norton.** This road is said to be haunted by the protective spirit of Nance, a girl who was born at Sheriff Hutton, betrothed to the driver of a mail coach, seduced and abandoned by a highwayman, and who, with her baby, died of exposure. She now guides travellers through fog and warns them of any danger.

ⓔ **Flixton,** south of Scarborough, is reputed to be the haunt of a werewolf.

ⓖ **Scarborough.** The magnificently sited castle ruins (D.E.) on the headland, 300 feet above sea, are haunted by the ghost of Piers Gaveston who was killed here in the fourteenth century.

ⓔ ⓖ ✡ **Whitby** is a ghost-hunter's paradise. Among the apparitions are: Hob, who makes motorists skid and changes signposts round; a coach which drives to church from Greenlane and then plunges over the cliff; a ghost with its head under its arm at Fitz-steps, on the fieldpath from Prospect Hill to Ruswarp; a ghost called Goosey who haunts between Ruswarp and Sleights (Goosey was a simple fellow who once accepted a challenge to eat a goose at a sitting; he was subsequently murdered); and Lady Hilda, probably the most famous ghost of them all. In summer spectators should stand on the west side of Whitby churchyard so that they can see the north side of the abbey past the north end of the church. They may then see Lady Hilda in one of the highest windows, in a shroud.

There is also a Wishing Chair at the end of

Love Lane, by the telephone box outside a laundry. Like many of these chairs, it was originally the base socket of a cross, one side of which has been broken away.

Bagdale Old Hall, facing Baxtergate, is said to be haunted, and remained empty for some considerable time because of its poltergeist phenomena. Aislaby Hall is haunted by a ghost in rustling silk and also by a spectral carriage.

At:

Esk Hall in Sleights the avenue and old drive are never used because it means death to a member of the owner's family or a visitor staying there.

Due west across the A19 and the MI you come to:

Melsonby where Lady Well is haunted by a headless woman, and fairies are still believed to be found nearby at Diddersley Hill on Gatherly Moor.

Richmond Castle (D.E.), due south, has its legends of buried treasure.

South again lies Wensleydale, where a line of sites leads westward:

Middleham Castle (D.E.), stronghold of Warwick the Kingmaker, is reputed to be the site of buried treasure, but the directions seem too simple: just run three times round the castle and dig where you stop.

Middleham Moor is haunted by the ghost of a woman in mourning. In life she had two suitors. Her plans to elope with one were discovered by the second, who murdered her on the moor. The skeleton of a woman, dressed in the remnants of black clothing, was found by peat-cutters.

West Witton. Why an effigy of St Bartholomew should be consigned to the flames of a bonfire at Grassgill in a ceremony known as 'Burning Old Bartle', I do not know. Nor has anyone satisfactorily explained the mysterious lights seen along the 684 on the far side of the village.

Woodhall is reputed to be the haunt of a lady dressed in black with white gloves, carrying a walking stick. She has been seen both at night and during the day and appears very natural.

Nappa Hall, a mile east of Askrigg, formerly the home of the Metcalfes, is haunted by the ghost of Mary, Queen of Scots.

The next site, across the moors to the north, is one source of that remarkable legend, the 'Hand of Glory', which is found in France, Belgium, Ireland and even Mexico, although it is not widespread in any of these countries. It is told about an inn on the Great

North Road, the 'Oak Tree', at Leeming Lane, as well as about the following Yorkshire site. Thieves believed that a candle held in the hand of someone who had been hanged for a crime would cause all those who slept to remain asleep as long as it stayed alight. Only milk could break its spell. Southey describes the Hand of Glory in 'Thalaba' in these words:

> . . . And from his wallet drew a human hand
> Shrivelled and dry and black.
> And fitting, as he spoke
> A taper in his hold,
> Pursued, 'A murderer on this stake had died;
> I drove the vultures from his limbs, and kept
> The hand that did the murder, and drew up
> The tendon-strings to close its grasp.
> And in the sun and wind
> Parched it, nine weeks exposed.
> The taper . . . but not here the place to impart,
> Nor hast thou undergone the rites
> That fit thee to partake the mystery.

Lady Hilda, wrapped in a shroud, appears in a window of Whitby Abbey

With this hand, Mohareb was to lull to sleep Zohak, the Keeper of the Caves of Babylon. The mysterious constituents of the candle are, according to Colin de Plancy's *Dictionnaire Infernal*, the fat of a hanged man, virgin wax and Lapland sesame. The most famous site where the Hand of Glory was used in England was:

The Old Spital Inn, on Bowes Moor, which lies roughly halfway between Barnard Castle and Brough. Between 1790 and 1800 a traveller dressed in woman's clothing appeared at the inn, asking to be allowed to sleep by

Below The Hand of Glory, used abortively at The Old Spital Inn

Bottom The stairway leading to Jeffrey Chamber at Epworth Rectory

the fire for a while before continuing on the way. The maidservant noticed men's trousers under the traveller's skirt and guessed something nefarious was afoot. She feigned sleep and watched him produce the Hand of Glory. He lit the candle saying, 'Let those who sleep, sleep on, and those who are awake, remain awake!' He then opened the door to let in his accomplices. The maid jumped up and slammed it, locking the man outside. She then rushed upstairs to rouse the landlord and his family, but could not waken them. Meanwhile the thieves were breaking down the door, safe in the conviction that those who were asleep could not be woken as long as the taper in the Hand of Glory continued to burn. The maid, in desperation, threw a bowl of 'blue' (skimmed milk) over the hand, whereupon the landlord and his family were immediately woken by the commotion. The thieves promised they would leave quickly if they could reclaim the Hand of Glory. The innkeeper's reply was a shot from his gun which successfully routed them.

This legend is believed to have been confirmed by Belle Parkin, daughter of the maid. One might assume that the Bowes Hotel, about 5 miles from Bowes, is the Old Spital Inn, but the gamekeeper who lives next door thinks the original site is now the farm about ¾ mile to the west. The hotel, he maintains, was built as a shooting lodge.

Now go south-west to Clapdale, which is north-west of Settle:

Clapdale Hall, passed by climbers on their way up from Clapham to Ingleborough, was once a castle, owned by John de Clapham. It is haunted by the ghost of his foster-mother, Dame Alice Kytell, who became a witch.

On the borders of Yorkshire and Lancashire, near Clitheroe, is:

Rainsber Scar. A bluff, seventy feet above the river, is Pudsey's Leap. It commemorates the escape of a Pudsey from Bolton Hall. Pudsey was suspected of coining – using the silver mined on his estate, which he discovered with the help of his elves, Lib and Michael. Legend says it was a magic silver piece, which the elves had given him, that enabled him to escape.

Up in the Forest of Bowland, is:

Bashall Eaves where John Dawson was murdered in 1934. Harries gives a fascinating account of this unsolved murder. Dawson, who had no known enemies, was shot with a home-made bullet, and after superhuman resistance to pain, died a most mysterious death. His ghost, which haunts the place, may one day provide the answer.

LINCOLNSHIRE

If you are travelling south down the east coast you will probably take the ferry from Kingston-upon-Hull in Yorkshire to New Holland. You can cover Lincolnshire in a sweeping 'S', starting with one of the oddest legends, found just south-east of New Holland near the coast at:

⊕ **East Halton.** Apparently Manor Farm used to be haunted by monks. At least the place-names round about substantiate the site of a religious house: Thornton Abbey and Priory Chapel Farm, for example. The ghosts were exorcised by being conjured into a large iron pot. Pins were placed on top to keep the lid down. As late as 1932 the pot was untouched for fear of freeing the spirits.

North of Broughton, on the west side of Ermine Street at:

⊕ **Santon,** is a depression known as Queen Maude Hole, where the spirit of Queen Maude – or maybe Queen Mab – walks.

To the south-west of Scunthorpe lies the Isle of Axholme, which teems with ghosts. The lower reaches of the river Trent at spring tides produce a tidal wave or bore known as the Eager, a survival of the Scandinavian god, Aegir, once worshipped here; and the river demands three lives a year. The first site, however, is:

⊕ **Epworth.** The Old Rectory (O.P.) was the birthplace of John Wesley in 1703. He was the fifteenth of nineteen children. The house was rebuilt in 1709 and seven years later a ghost, known to the family as Old Jeffrey, began his disturbances. These poltergeist phenomena were fully described by Wesley in an article originally written for the *American Magazine*. It is full of interesting facts, and it is worth noting that while the poltergeist phenomena were taking place, many of the Wesley children were still adolescent: John Wesley was thirteen and his sisters included Molly (twenty), Hetty (nineteen), Nancy (fifteen) and two more who were younger still. Wesley remarks:

> Kezzy [one of the younger sisters] desired no better diversion than to pursue Old Jeffrey from room to room. In fact, the dog was more afraid of the ghost than the children.

To the south-west is:

⊕ **Westwoodside** where a headless woman has been seen walking in the street.

East on the Trent is:

⊖ **Owston Ferry.** Between here and Wildsworth the river makes a sharp turn. This is known as Jean Yonde, or Jenny Hearn, and is haunted by a pygmy with long hair and the face of a seal.

⊕ **Thornholme's Farm,** nearby, is haunted by a woman in a black silk dress, thought to be connected with a religious order which once occupied the site (although silk seems unsuitable for a nun's habit).

A mile or so up the Trent is:

⊖ **Gunthorpe.** Three hundred yards from the riverside road leading to West Stockwith at the end of Commonpiece Lane, the ghost of a cat, nearly as big as a pig, has been seen. A human skeleton was found here and reburied.

North of Gainsborough at:

⊕ **Morton** the White Lady of Gymes appears near the riverside road. There is a pit here which, although reputedly bottomless, was originally dug to build up the banks of the Trent, and from this the ghost rises.

South of Gainsborough lies:

⊖ **Knaith** where the Black Dog legend – prevalent all over Lincolnshire – is given a new twist. A rich widow called Mrs Dog was murdered here for her money. Although her house was pulled down, the place is haunted by the Phantom Hound, which has a woman's face.

West of Lincoln is:

⊕ **Doddington Hall** (O.P.). The most famous story here is the ghost of a girl who, screaming, flings herself off the roof to escape the unwelcome attentions of the squire. But this tale, said Ralph Jarvis, whose son now lives there, was lifted straight out of a Victorian novel, and was probably kept as a practical joke when the Delavals lived there. He did, however, tell me of three unexplained incidents. His mother, 'idly tinkling away at the pianoforte' in the Gallery, suddenly felt compelled to play an eighteenth-century minuet, which she had never heard before and could not remember afterwards although it was most vivid at the time. Ralph Jarvis's wife, entering the house for the first time after their marriage, saw a benevolent-looking woman wearing a long stiff brown dress, peering down from the first landing, and she suddenly felt a deep feeling of welcome. The third story tells how a neighbour saw what appeared to be a proposal of marriage taking place in the drawing-room – a man on his knees imploring a girl – but the bottom six inches of the tableau were cut off.

Very few people, and certainly not this neighbour, knew that the floor was raised by that amount when the room below was heightened in the eighteenth century.

To these stories I can add the experience recounted by mutual cousins of the Jarvis family and my wife. As young girls staying there, they were in their room when they heard someone running down the stairs, walking sedately along the passage, then running down the next flight. Thinking it was their cousin, Ralph, they opened their door as the tread approached. No-one was there but the footseps continued along the landings and down the flights to the bottom of the staircase.

⊙ **Lincoln.** A house in Minster Close was certainly haunted when a friend of ours lived there. While doing some ironing one day she looked up and thought she saw her sister, who was a nun. She quickly realized this was impossible as her sister was dead, and she could see her son's cricket bat through the figure.

North of Lincoln is:

Below Legends and tales of ghosts abound at Doddington Hall

Below, right The photographer followed the ritual at Robert Cooke's tomb, Digby, but did not hear the cups and saucers

⊙🦴 **Fillingham Castle** (O.P.A.), haunted by a suicide who had been jilted. This may be either the man who rides through the park on a big white horse, or more probably the Green Lady who looks for her lover in the narrow plantation between the road and the lake.

Northwards the road leads from:

🦌 **Grayingham to Kirton.** 'Where Trafford murdered Copeman' no grass will grow on the spots marked by the victim's head and heels.

In the corner formed by the A18 and the A15 lie:

🏚️ **Sturton and Scawby.** Captain Lidgett, a Roundhead, was killed and buried here under an ash tree at the crossroads known as Lidgett's Gap. A boggard haunts the place – but it is more likely to be connected with the buried treasure found here than the Puritan.

On the road from:

🏚️⊙ **Scawby to Broughton,** north of the village, but before you reach the Brigg/Scunthorpe road, a phantom carriage and horses once lured a man into the lake where he drowned. Even those who do not follow the ghostly apparition, hear the coachman's mocking laughter.

East, just off the Caister road, is:

⊙ **Owmby** (not to be confused with the

place of that name near Normanby). Here there was once a haunted abbey which is now a row of cottages.

⊛ **Caistor.** In the church a ghostly monk plays the organ, and his music has been recorded on tape.

Just south of Grimsby is:

⊛ **Humberston Manor** where mysterious patches of light occur on a bedroom ceiling. Doors open and shut by themselves, furniture is moved violently about by unseen hands, and loud noises are heard. All this may well be connected with a skeleton found under the hearth.

⊛ **Thorpe Hall,** on the western side of Louth, is the haunt of a Green Lady. She was a Spanish woman taken prisoner by Sir John Bolle in 1596, and with whom she fell in love. Unfortunately Sir John was already married, but as a parting present she gave him a portrait of herself in a green dress, and after he had set sail for England she killed herself. Her spirit followed him home and still haunts the place.

South again is:

⊛ **Maidenwell.** In Ostler's Lane a phantom carriage and horses appear, drawn by a coachman who has his head on the box beside him.

South-east, 7 miles inland from Skegness is:

⊛ **Gunby Hall** (N.T.) which has a strong reputation for being haunted.

Go south-west now to the last three sites, north and east of Sleaford. First:

⊛ **Digby** where the churchyard is haunted by a man on a grey pony. They also say that if you run twelve times round the tomb of Robert Cooke backwards and then listen, you can hear the rattle of cups and saucers inside the grave.

Due south is:

⊛ **Dorrington.** Near Fen House a spectre is seen carrying his head.

Finally, to the north-east, near Ewerby, is:

⊛ **Haverholme Priory** (where in 1164 Thomas à Becket hid to escape Henry II). This Gilbertine establishment became a priest's house, and served as a model for Chesney Wold in Dickens' *Bleak House*. It was pulled down in 1927, and little remains; yet a ghost can still be heard walking on the gravel which once lay in front of the house. In the long avenue of elms, where a bridge crosses the Ruskington Beck, a whizzing sound, fierce and loud, is sometimes heard, and dogs become terrified at something they see. Tradition says that it is the ghost of a Gilbertine canoness.

ISLE OF MAN

The Isle of Man is full of magic and mystery. There are old legends and modern witches galore – but above all there are spell-binders. The notes I have are full of quite extraneous quotations, but they were given – and, under the Manx spell, accepted – as evidence. Take, for instance, the man who married a fairy; she disappeared but always managed to bring presents for the children ... '*and all grew up with blonde hair just like hers*'. This remark was delivered with such intensity that one almost considered it as proof of the mother's supernatural background.

On a small island, traditions become less diffused. Bessie the Bonnack's ghost is seen in many different parts of the island. In real life she was a poor soul who was murdered for money which she did not possess. Her spirit is sometimes seen as a skeleton on a farm cart; this warns the viewer of impending tragedy. The Phantom Hound is prevalent too; here it is called the Mauthe Dhoog, which like other Manx names has a peculiarly evocative look and sound – much more sinister than the Shuck of East Anglia or the Gwyllgi of Wales, and less sophisticated than the Gabriel Ratchetts. Also to be seen all over the island is a beautiful phantom dapple-grey horse, but its favourite haunt is:

⊛ **Earystane, Rushen.** It originally belonged to a young farmer, who once went to market and sold his flock of 200 sheep extremely profitably. He set off for home, but never arrived. Next day his body was found. The beaten bracken showed that he had put up a good fight, but his horse and money had disappeared and only the ghost of the horse returns, usually to do a good turn. For instance, between:

⊛ **Peel and Castletown,** people travelled by 'the conveyance'. One night a dapple grey phantom horse reared up and stopped the vehicle. On dismounting the driver found that had he not been prevented from going on, he would have run into a landslide with fatal results. Perhaps the grey horse's ancestry goes back to the days of the 'Horse People' (see Kilberry, Scotland).

⊛ **Peel Castle** is the chief lair of the Mauthe Dhoog, particularly a haunted corridor leading out of the Guard Room. One soldier became sufficiently drunk to search for the Phantom Hound. His blood-curdling shrieks

A Grey Lady is the apparition at Castle Rushen in Castletown

brought his companions to the rescue, and they pulled him back into the Guard Room by his heels. All he could jabber before he died was, 'The Black Dog . . . ghost dog!' They say a Methodist parson who saw it died within a week.

Castletown. Castle Rushen is haunted by a Grey Lady, possibly the ghost of the lady who was hanged for killing her son. It was discovered too late that he had died of natural causes. A guide, sitting in the garrison dining hall, once saw a woman in grey with a little boy on the drawbridge, but no-one of that description had passed the pay-box. One of the Boy's Brigade who camped here had to be given sedatives after seeing the Grey Lady. Those who served with the Home Guard in World War II can tell you all about it, and so can the cook.

Visit the Isle of Man Museum of Magic and Witchcraft which houses Gerald Gardner's necromantic collections.

Halfway along Castletown Bay, 1 mile south of Derbyhaven, is a ruined cottage. It lies on the landward side of the road. surrounded by the remains of a gravel path. Those who have lived there will tell you they have heard the crunch of a wheelbarrow on the gravel when nobody was there, and they have experienced the sensation of being choked.

Take 'the road to the mountains' and you will find a white boulder in the bank by a gate, this is:

☆ **The Fairy Stone** which has been christened the 'Wesley Stone'. It is near Ballabeg, which is on road 5. If you drive downhill 200 yards past this stone, switch off the engine and release the brake; your car will run back *uphill* to the Fairy Stone.

Spanish Head lies at the south-west end of the island, and here you will find The Chasms. In the reign of Olaf I, so the legend runs, when the moon was full and the wind in the west, Olaf's nephew sent twenty-four men to kill the king, so that he could take the throne. But the Manx rose and killed the raiders, and ever after their headless spectres have haunted the place. Not so long ago a shepherd, on returning from Douglas, was told by his wife that a sheep had fallen down The Chasms. He went to rescue it, but his dogs would not follow. He saw something glinting at his feet and found it was a dirk, the handle of which was covered in blood. Then the headless spectres appeared; as the blades of their dirks touched the shepherd's skin, he fainted. He was rescued two hours later, but carried a red mark on the back of his neck for the rest of his life.

Crosby is situated between Peel and Douglas. At the Highland Inn you will be told the story of Timothy the Tailor who tried to defy the Buggane, a witch who could not bear the church bells, and tore the roof off the church next door.

☆ **Glen Roy** is west of Laxey. The water of St Patrick's Well makes death easier, but you must invoke its aid in the Manx tongue.

Between Laxey and Ramsey is:

☆ **Ballig Wonder Well,** ½ mile from the sea. Offerings are left for 'themselves' in the niche alongside.

☆ **Maughold** is on the east coast, south of Ramsey. St Maughold's Well (called after a Norse pirate who became a bishop), is patronized by lovers. The offering of a bent pin is made by girls, but men must pay 2½p.

Up on Ardronan, Andreas:

☆ **Chibbyr Pherick or St Patrick's Well** is to be found. It cures rheumatism, but must be visited 'when the books are open' in church.

At West Nappin, between Jurby West and Jurby Head is another:

☆ **St Patrick's Well,** which cures bad eyes.

I have heard that above Lonan harbour is:

☆ **Chibbyr Niglus,** which stanches bleeding when its water is applied to a wound with these words:

Niglus as moirry bannit jeen yn vill as cur bioys da . . . [name] ayns ennym yn ayr as yr mac as in spyrrid noo.

The treasure of Castell Coch is guarded by eagles

Wales

If England is the country of Grey Ladies and Scotland the home of Green Jean, then Wales is the land of wells: wishing wells, cursing wells, healing wells, holy wells and haunted wells. There are probably more than 1000 to which some legend or belief is attached. I have had to be very selective: some are merely muddy pools, puddled by cattle; others are enclosed in, say, baptistries maintained by the Department of the Environment. Most are called Ffynnon, shortened in the text to Ff. Start your tour in South Wales in:

Glamorgan

Just north of Cardiff is:

⊛⚓ **Castell Coch** (D.E.), an utterly absurd but delightful thirteenth-century castle, built in 1870 for the Marquess of Bute by William Burges, architect of Tower House, Melbury Road, London, which was his home. The foundations of the castle go back 700 years, and the place is haunted by the ghost of a man who buried treasure in a subterranean passage. The treasure, according to one legend, is guarded by eagles.

Up the 470 is:

✰◉ **Taff's Well.** This should be the most famous well in Wales: since Roman times it has enjoyed a reputation for curing rheumatism. At one time it was surrounded by a screen to preserve the modesty of the bathers, who hung their clothes over it to reveal the sex of those who were using the pool. On the eighth Sunday after Easter young people sprinkled each other with the water and danced. Now it lies sadly neglected at one end of a derelict swimming pool, evocative of the kind of pubescent dreams which would have delighted Dylan Thomas. It is haunted by a Grey Lady.

West on the 473 between:

✰ **Llantrisant and Llanharan** is Ff. Garth Maelwg, which lies up in the woods north of the road. It cures piles, gravel, shortness of breath, blood troubles, skin diseases and other disorders. It is rich in sulphur, and I heard it called 'Rotten Egg Well'.

Paviland Caves, haunt of the Red Lady

South-west on the coast:

⊛✰ **St Donat's Castle,** once the home of William Randolph Hearst, and now the Outward Bound College, is haunted by the ghost of Lady Stradling, said to have been murdered here. The apparition, in a trailing dress and high-heeled shoes, comes to warn of impending mishaps. On the cliff below the castle there is, or was, a well capable of curing erysipelas.

Now travel down the Gower Peninsula for the last three sites in the county. On:

✰ **Cefn Bryn** there are, I believe, two wells. There is a curative well under the cromlech known as Arthur's Stone, and a holy well to be visited on Sunday evenings in summer. Pins are offered for cures.

On the coast east of Worms Head are the:

⊛ **Paviland Caves** where the 'Red Lady', a red-oxide-stained skeleton was found in 1823. She is said to have been a woman who was imprisoned here by a storm while seeking for treasure, and is believed to haunt the place. The skeleton, however, was found to be male.

At the most westerly point of the peninsula, near Worms Head, is:

⊛ **Rhossili.** On the moor behind the village, 600 feet above the sea, many people get a horrible feeling of timeless watching and menace. The air seems full of evil foreboding. It is thought by locals to emanate from the spirits of Stone Age men who once lived there.

Carmarthenshire

From the last site in Glamorgan it would be easiest to make your next site in Carmarthenshire:

⊛ **Llanelli.** Parc Howard, built by James Buckley in the 1870s, was first called Bryncaerau Castle, and the ghost which haunts the room above the porte-cochère is connected in some way with the Celtic Mound on which, as the original name implies, the house stands. The lovely Llanelli House, next to the library, is also haunted. I have heard that Stradey Castle, just outside the town, has a ghost, but this is not confirmed.

North at:

✰ **Llannon,** in a field opposite the isolation hospital, is Ff. Josi; it is overgrown now, but was once held in such high esteem for healing that an attempt was made to commercialize it.

✰⚔⊛ **Kidwelly.** In a marshy field 300 yards north of the castle and surrounded by a circle of stones is Ff. Fair where the Virgin Mary is said to have been killed. She came by

Kidwelly Castle

ship (perhaps to visit the places where Christ is said to have been as a young man, see Priddy, Somerset) and was murdered. Where she fell a spring rose.

Also in Kidwelly parish is Pistyll Teilo. Mr Kemmis Buckley, an authority on Welsh wells, says:

It is in a wild and exceptionally melancholy ravine below the site of the Old Chapel dedicated to St Teilo to the south of the road from Mynydd-y-Garreg to Four Roads and is well described in the words of a local historian – 'The path to the pistyll is extremely inaccessible and dangerous; one has to descend the rock face to reach it. Tradition persists from the past that one could get a draught fairer than wine here and that the stream had special powers. I remember twisting my feet as a young lad, and some surgical expert's advice to facilitate my recovery and free me from lameness was to hold my feet under the main torrent in the gully.'

Mr Ebenezer Jones of Bryn Forest, now aged eighty-six, remembers miners believing that the waters of the pistyll could remove bruises incurred in their work. They used to hold their limbs under the icy water until 'they were red hot'.

It is said that a ghost haunts this pistyll and cries in pitiful tones: 'Mae'n hir ac yn o'r i aros i orwyr Wil Wattar'. (It is long and cold and tiresome to wait for the descendants of Wil Wattar.)

To this day natives of the district prefer not to walk by night along the road which skirts this ravine; and one can only assume that this is because of the ghostly voice which is supposed to come from the bottom of the *cwm*. If only it were possible to discover the identity of Wil Wattar, a whole wealth of local legend might be uncovered.

At Pont-y-Gwendraeth the ghost of a White Lady can be seen. She was involved in a tragic love affair with a Norman knight, Sir Walter Mansel, and threw herself from the bridge, which used to be called the Ghost Bridge.

West of Kidwelly are:

☆ **St Ishmael and Llansaint.** Within the last two decades people in both these villages have firmly believed in the properties of Pistyll Giniwil for curing eye and stomach complaints, when the water is taken with brown sugar.

North at the county capital:

☆ **Carmarthen,** in Lower Franchise, is Job's Well. According to Lhuyd, it cured 'scabs, ulcers and rickets', and more recently sore eyes. But now a notice by the metal pipe warns, 'Unfit to drink'.

East on the A48 you will find:

☆ **Llanddarog.** In a wood here is Capel Begewdin, built over a well, probably in the twelfth century, and famous for curing sprains and spasms. It is now in ruins and again I cannot do better than quote Mr Kemmis Buckley:

. . . the interior is choked with mud and fallen masonry. Nevertheless, it remains a remarkably fine and romantic structure where it is still possible to determine the mason's marks on the trefoil window, a niche for the statue of a saint, and the site of the well. Seeing this ruin for the first time on a summer's day, one is irresistibly reminded of the paintings of the Pre-Raphaelite movement. Cows, eglantine, wild garlic and endless briars, bar one's way to this chapel in the wood; and the picture of *Sir Isambras at the Holy Well* comes vividly to mind. This is one of the great architectural and ecclesiastical relics of the County.

North-east at:

☆ **Llanarthney,** the fourteenth-century chapel well was excavated by the Carmarthen Antiquarian Society in 1970. There is no spring but a rill runs through the chapel and cistern, fed by a stream in which those suffering from spasms bathed. As is so often found, there is a niche for the statue of a saint.

The A40 is joined by the 483 at:

☆ **Llandeilo.** Carreg Cennen Castle (D.E.) about 2½ miles from the village, has an underground passage ending in a cave, where, in a small basin-like depression, there is a wishing well. Pins should be left, bent or otherwise, according to your wish.

North-west at:

☆ **Llanfynydd,** you will find Ff. Lygald, ¼ mile outside the village by the roadside. It cures sore eyes. On cold and frosty mornings a column of mist fifteen feet high is sometimes seen. It is in good condition and the water is still fit to drink.

Away to the west, near the Pembroke border is:

☆ **Trelech.** On Bronlas Farm is Ff. Fronslas, now overgrown. Its waters should be drunk before sunrise. Farmer Rees had not heard the legend, but the water served the farm till forty years ago.

South on the Tywi estuary is:

☆ **Llanstephan.** St Anthony's Well enjoyed a great reputation for healing, and is still used for wishing. Pins are the offering.

Across the river Cynin at:

🐾 **Laugharne,** Pant-y-Madog is haunted by a spectral mastiff with baleful breath and blazing red eyes – the Gwyllgi, Dog of Darkness – which runs from the castle to the town.

To the west, on the coast at:

🎻 **Pendine** is Green Bridge Cave where a fiddler went in and never came out, but his music is heard to this day.

To the north near Whitland is:

☆ **Llyn Ddewi.** Ff. Ddewi is situated beside it. St David is said to have sent people here to be cured, particularly of eye troubles. (This may be the well now known as Ff. Foidi, on the western side of the river Gronwy, but no longer used.)

Pembrokeshire

North-west of Whitland there is a little pocket of Pembrokeshire called:

☆ **Llangan West,** approached from Carmarthenshire. In a field to the east of the church is Canna's Well, much visited by those suffering from intestinal complaints and ague. The ritual demands that the sufferer should throw a pin into the water and then sleep in Canna's Chair, a stone which used to be in the middle of the field, but has now been moved to the hedge near the church. The cure could take up to fourteen days.

South-west on the coast is:

💀🐾 **Stackpole Elidor.** The main building

Failing sight, lameness and rheumatism were cured by St Govan's Well

of Stackpole Court, which belonged to the Earls of Cawdor, was recently demolished. I doubt if this has laid the ghosts of either the old woman or the headless coachman, driving headless horses which draw a coach carrying a headless lady. She is supposed to be Lady Matthias, whose ghost was exorcised by a parson from St Petrox, who doomed it to empty a pond with a cockleshell.

At the southern tip of Pembroke is:

☆ **St Govan's Well,** now filled in with small stones. It is next to St Govan's Chapel (thirteenth century) which is his tomb. It is reached by some fifty steps, but if you count them going down, it is said you will get a different total coming up. The well was particularly famous for curing failing sight, lameness and rheumatism. Red clay from nearby was made into a poultice and the sufferer lay in the sun. In Murray's *Handbook of South Wales*, it says that St Govan's attracted patients 'even of the upper class'. Water had to be lifted to the afflicted part in a limpet shell. It was also used for wishing, as, indeed, is the ritual of getting into St Govan's Bed or Coffin, a vertical interstice between two flat rocks, just big enough to hold a normal sized-person.

Across the estuary lies:

👁 **Milford Haven.** At certain phases of the moon, the shape of a dagger appears on a tombstone in the churchyard. My informant,

Mr Stanley Dove, landlord of the Grosvenor Hotel in Cardigan, remembers keeping a vigil as a boy, and seeing it appear. It is thought to be proof of a murder.

At the most westerly promontory:

☆🐾 **St David's** peninsula teems with interest. There were once twelve holy wells in the district, seven of them in the immediate vicinity of St David's. There is a prophetic stone, Llechllafar, bridging the river Alun, whose waters contained unusual fish. At Clegyr-Boia the family of Boia were staunch Druids and therefore anti-David. The wife of the head of the family persuaded her stepdaughter Dunawd to go with her into the wood of Glyn Hodnant to gather nuts. She then suggested that they rested and that Dunawd put her head in Mistress Boia's lap so that she could dress her hair. Dunawd complied and had her throat cut. As the blood flowed, a clear fountain sprang out of the ground. This is Ff. Dunawd. As Francis Jones writes in *The Holy Wells of Wales*, 'The primitive elements are all here, the woodlands with hazel trees, the ceremonial dressing of the hair, the sacrifice and a well.'

On the south side of Castell Clegyr Boia there is an ebb and flow well, good for the eyes, called Ff. Lygard. At Porthclais Creek is Ff. Ddewi, where St David was baptized and at the third immersion, the man who held the babe had his eyesight restored. The most famous well is St Non's, near the ruin of her chapel (D.E.) which was demolished in 1810. St Non was David's mother and her saint's day is March 2. When the well was restored in 1951 pins and pebbles were found – thank-offerings from those whose sight had been restored and from pregnant women who visited the well to gain strength.

East is:

☆ **Little Newcastle.** Hot Wells, once famous for healing, have been incorporated into the district water supply. Ff. Olden still exists on a farm near the Letterston road. It was once used for curing sick children.

Again to the east is:

☆ **Maenclochog** where Ff. Fair, by the roadside, cured rheumatism, but is not much used today.

To the south-east, but still in the same parish is:

☆🐾 **Llandilo.** Ff. Deilo, north-east of the ruined church, cured tuberculosis and whooping cough. During World War I people went to drink the water out of St Deilo's skull to bring peace. The head of the Melchior family was hereditary keeper of the saintly skull. The Melchiors came from Ireland, and this Welsh property was their reward for warning the original owner, who was collecting rents in Ireland, that plans were afoot to take his life and money. I heard locally that this family harboured a dozen or so Gypsies in their house, and one of these foretold that no Melchoir would die in his bed – a prophecy that came true with one exception. The well is bricked up, but a ram takes the water up to the house above the spring.

To the north-west near Fishguard is:

☆◉ **Llanllawer.** Outside the churchyard, in a little stone vault behind the adjacent cottage, is a holy well which effected miraculous eye cures. Coins and pins were given. If ill was wished, the pins were bent.

In the Gwain valley, New Year's Day is still celebrated on January 13, and old customs – children singing from farm to farm while their parents keep open house – still prevail.

East, in the Prescelly Hills is:

☆ **Cilgwyn.** At the foot of Carn Ingli, on the right of the road, is Carnwn Well, which cures warts and demands a pin in payment. It is also said to be a wishing well.

Cardiganshire

Continuing northwards, the first site in this county lies 2 miles from Synod Inn off the Llandysul road:

☆ **Ff. Blaengowan Fawr** cured cripples and sore legs.

◉ **Llandyssul.** In the valley joining Blaen Cwm and Faerdre Fawr is Ff. Feirad, haunted by the ghost of a parson; while in the river Teifi is the Pool of the Harper, haunted by the musician who was drowned there and whose harp can still be heard.

To the north-east lies:

☆ **Llangybi.** The postmaster here told me that Ff. Gybi is opposite the chapel, on his land. You go through a wicket gate above the bridge to reach it. It cured scrofula, scurvy and rheumatism. Lhuyd called it Ff. Wen, and wrote at the end of the seventeenth century:

On Ascension Eve, they resort to Ffynnon Wen; after they washed ymselves at ye well, they go to Llech Gybi, it is an arrow's flight from ye well. There they put ye sick under ye Llech, where if ye sick sleeps it is an infallable [sic] sign of recovery, if not, death.

North-east again, in Llanddewi Brefi parish, is:

☆🐾 **Gogoyan,** where you will find Ff.

Ddewi. St David's help was sought by a woman whose son had just died. He went into her cottage and raised her son from the dead, whereupon a spring gushed up from the kitchen floor. Just across the bridge over the river is a house called Ff. Ddewi, but I was told that the house opposite had a spring in the cellar floor. On my visit I found both houses empty, so I was unable to check.

To the north you will come to:

☆ **Tregaron.** Near Glanbrenig Farm is Ff. Garon, where children used to come and drink the sugared water at Easter.

Between Tregaron and Pontrhydfendigaid is a farm called:

☆ **Maes Elwad** where Ff. Elwad was visited by women with sore breasts.

North-west is:

☻ **Pont Llanafan,** haunted by the ghosts of pirates who hid treasure here, probably somewhere in Craig-y-Rogof, the Rock of the Cave.

The lowest level of Devil's Bridge was built by Satan himself

About two miles south of Devil's Bridge, on the Rhosygell, is:

☆ **Ff. Trisant,** which consists of three springs about a foot apart. The first one cures eye troubles, the second wounds and sores, the third general complaints. Crutches used to be left at Dolcoion Farm, which is now derelict, but Miss Humphreys at Dolgors could direct you to these springs, which are difficult to find.

🐾 **Devil's Bridge.** Many years ago, before there was a bridge here, a woman lost her cow and saw it on the other side of the river. The Devil told her he would build a bridge if the first to pass over it belonged to him. The woman agreed and the bridge was built. She then threw a crust of bread over it, her dog rushed after and she followed.

Just off the road to Aberystwyth, about 2½ miles before you reach the town, is the fine eighteenth-century house:

🐾☻ **Nanteos.** Until 1952 it belonged to the Powells, then the line died out and Major Merrilees bought it, but sold it again in 1967. He left the Powell possessions and portraits, but took to his new home in Herefordshire

According to legend, Christ used the Nanteos Cup at the Last Supper

the famous Nanteos Cup, a very old olive-wood bowl supposed to be the Holy Grail, the cup used at the Last Supper, or that which held the vinegar given to Christ on the Cross. It is said to have been taken to Glastonbury (see Somerset) by Joseph of Arimathea, and when a group of Glastonbury monks founded the monastery at Strata Florida, they took the Holy Grail with them. At the Dissolution, Strata Florida went to the Stedman family, and with it the Holy Grail, its true value being disguised by its appearance. The Powells and the Stedmans intermarried and thus the Cup came to Nanteos. Although that has gone, the ghosts remain. There are three: the Grey Lady, believed to be a Miss Corbett who married a Powell in the eighteenth century, and appears carrying a candelabra when the head of the family is about to die; the Jewel Lady, who left her deathbed to hide her jewels (which still remain concealed in spite of intensive searches); and the Phantom Huntsman who appears where a culvert opens into the shrubbery.

In the southern outskirts of Aberystwyth is:

⛧ **Pen-parcau** where a headless phantom dog is sometimes seen.

Four miles north-east of the town is Llanfihangel-Gebeu'r-Glyn, which the Great Western Railway shortened to:

☆ **Llandre.** Above the church, in the woods, is a well where, about fifty years ago, a crippled girl from Glamorgan threw down her crutches and walked away cured.

North, near the Merioneth border, is:

☆ **Lodge Park,** where Ff. Bushell has a sinister reputation. In the reign of Charles I Thomas Bushell murdered his wife and threw her down the well.

Merionethshire

The tour of Merioneth is circular, so it can be started at any point. I suggest, as a change from wells, that you begin in the north-east of the county at:

🐟 **Bala Lake** (Llyn Tegid) which is believed to cover an old town.

☆🐟 **Llyn Arennig-Fach** lies to the north-west. This is a fairy lake. A farmer found a bull-calf in the rushes and took it home where it sired a superb herd of red and white cattle; but one day a little old man came and enticed them all back into the lake.

Westward is:

☆ **Ffestiniog parish** where you will find Ff. Fihangel, which has cured rheumatism and fractured limbs within living memory.

Between Ffestiniog and Harlech, near the coast, is:

☆🐕 **Maes-y-Neuadd,** a Tudor house which Robert Graves describes as 'the most haunted I have ever been in'. Rappings were heard, doors opened and shut, and lampshades were knocked off by unseen forces. 'The visible ghost was a little yellow dog that would appear on the lawn in the early morning to announce death.' It is now a hotel.

South down the 496 you come to:

☆ **Llanenddwyn.** There are two wells here. To reach Ff. Enddwyn, you take the road to Cwm Nantcol till you reach the carpark. Go through a wooden gate on the left, past two stunted trees and you will find the well on the left, near the wall about 200 yards from the carpark. It consists of a two-level stone basin and is sadly overgrown. The waters, either applied direct or in a 'plaster' of moss, cured eye and glandular diseases as well as the King's Evil. St Enddwyn is said to have been cured of a 'sore disease' by bathing in the well.

☆ **Ff. Badrig** is not far away. Fifty yards below Caer Ffynnon is an iron gate fastened with a harness hook. Go through this and you will find the spring near the stream. It is fenced off because it supplies water to the district. This well is said to have magical but unspecified qualities for curing and protecting children from ill-health, and was used at christenings.

North-east of Dolgellau is:

☆ **Llanfachreth,** but before you reach the village, near Glasdir, is Ff.-y-Capel, which heals sore eyes.

☆🛡 **Dolgellau.** Ff. Fair is on the outskirts of the town. You reach it along Springfield Street. It cured rheumatism and must have been known to the Romans, as their coins have been found here.

One mile south of Dolgellau, in Brithdir parish, is Ff. Afridd Awr which cured rheumatism. Also near the town is Ff.-y-Gaer, used for cursing and bewitching. I believe this may be near a house called The Rock, on the way to Gwernan Lake, under Cader Idris. A pin was offered to effect a spell. I have heard that near Ty Blaenau, between Dolgellau and Garnedd-wen, Ff. Gwenhudw cured rheumatism.

Caernarvonshire

The Lleyn peninsula has fifteen or more sites, probably because it was on the pilgrim's route to Bardsey. I have chosen six. First I suggest you visit:

🐕 **Beddgelert.** Most people are familiar with the story (said to have originated here) of the boy who was killed by a wolf. His father, finding his favourite dog covered in blood, assumed that it had killed the child, and slaughtered it only to find the body of the wolf which the dog had killed while trying to save the child's life. (See Arisaig, Scotland.)

Less well known is:

☆🐉 **Dinas Emrys,** a mile north-east of the village. This was a fort from the Iron Age till the twelfth century. Here, to quote *The Shell Guide*, is 'the mysterious crag closely connected in legend with Vortigern and Ambrosius. Excavation shows the layout to be closely similar to that described in the earliest legends. The pool is the spring where the dragons prevented Vortigern building his palace.'

To the south-west is the delightful:

☆ **Cwm Pennant.** I have no qualms in recommending this site, although I did not find Ff.-y-Cythraul which cured sore eyes and warts in humans and animals. It is reputed to be at Llanfihangel-y-Pennant, and I am sure the people at the remote farm by the church would know. Unfortunately they

Right, above An old town lies under Bala Lake

Right The overgrown well at Llanenddwyn

were out when I visited the place, but this lovely valley alone was worth the trip.

On the coast at:

☆ **Criccieth** there is a well near the church, past the Memorial Hall, where, on Easter Sunday, pins and keys were thrown in to solace St Catherine.

☆ **Llangybi** lies inland. Follow the signpost through the churchyard gate to the well of the Cornish St Gybi. It is a small rectangular building containing a pool for immersion. In the eighteenth century the crutches and wheelbarrows of those cured were to be seen here, for it was famous for curing lameness and rheumatism, as well as warts, blindness, scurvy and the King's Evil. It was also used for divination of lovers' intentions if visited on the Eve of Gwylm-ab-Sant.

At the most south-westerly point of the peninsula is:

☆ **Braich y Pwll.** Below Mynydd Mawr is Ff. Fair, dangerous to reach, and covered at high tide. The remains of the chapel can be seen. Pilgrims walked the last mile barefoot. An apparition is said to give instructions on how to get one's wish. You have to go down the path to the well, get water (it is pure at low tide), ascend to the chapel, and walk round it, then your wish will be granted.

North-east on the 499 is:

☆ **Clynnog-fawr.** At the roadside is Ff. St Beuno. Feeble and epileptic children were immersed in the well, and then lay down on a 'tombstone' covered with rushes. If they slept a cure was certain. Scrapings from St Beuno's Stone (in his chapel alongside the church) were added to bottles of the water.

☻ **Caernarvon.** At the Black Boy Inn, Northgate Street, a ghost haunts the bar.

South-east of Llanfairfechan, on the A55, a Roman road runs through a pass in the mountains at:

☻ **Bwlch-y-Ddeufaen.** Some farmers prefer to leave their watches at home if passing this way, for they say it is haunted by the ghost of Jack Swan, who killed Jesse Roberts for his watch and chain, and was hanged for it.

Up in the mountains to the east is:

☆ **Llangelynin Church.** It can be reached by taking the Henryd road from Conway and continuing up 800 feet by Plastirion. In a corner of the graveyard is Ff. Gelynin. Sick children were immersed in the water in the

Left, above The remains of the ancient fort of Dinas Emrys

Left The peaceful Cwm Pennant

early morning, and carried in blankets to the farmhouse Cae Iol, where a bed was always kept ready. The child's clothes were placed on the surface of the water and if they floated the child would recover. The offering was bent pins. Either this well, or Ff. Gwynwy, said to be ½ mile away, also cured warts, but the bent pin had to be offered *before* immersing the afflicted part, or the sufferer would catch the warts of all the previous patients.

South at:

☆ **Llanbedr-y-cennin,** the well near the church is curative and especially efficacious for children. Ff. Armon is in the middle of a farmyard. It is overshadowed by a yew tree. A local man told me that he remembered its being used to cure warts, but nobody goes there now.

For a change from wells, the last four sites in Caernarvonshire are lakes. To the south-west, high in the mountains, is:

☆ **Lake Dulyn** which a century or so ago, was described as

> a dismal dingle, surrounded by high and dangerous rocks; the lake is exceedingly black and its fish are loathsome, having large heads and small bodies. No wild swan or duck or any kind of bird has ever been seen to light on it. . . . There is a row of stepping stones and if one steps onto these stones and throws water to reach the furthest stone, called the Red Altar, it is but chance that you do not get rain before nightfall even when it is hot weather.

🐾 **Llyn Cowlyd** is to the south-east. In its depths there lives a water-bull – a Welsh Loch Ness Monster.

To the west, on either side of the road, are: 🐾 **Llyn Idwal and Llyn Ogwen.** The former is another sinister birdless lake. The latter, according to one version, is where the pale arm rose out of the water to grasp King Arthur's sword Excalibur, cast away by Sir Bedevere on Merlin's instructions (see Dozmary Pool, Cornwall).

Anglesey

At:

☆ **Llanddaniel Fab,** Bryn Celli Ddu (D.E.) is a 1500-year-old site described as a burial place; but the phallic symbols suggest that fertility rites must have been performed there.

☆ **Llanddwyn Island,** a low rocky peninsula between two sandy bays, is the most south-westerly point of Anglesey. It is about 1½ miles from the carpark. Near the church is the site of a well, Ff. Ddwynwen, which

Llanddaniel Fab – a burial place or a site for fertility rituals?

foretold the outcome of a love affair. If it bubbled all would be successful. Pilgrims visited it carrying candles, and it cured the ravages of love, so presumably it was thought to possess aphrodisiac qualities, as is shown in the following poem by Ceirog, translated from the Welsh:

> I went to Llanddwynwen on a summer day,
> Melancholy and love-sick;
> I drank from the well and immediately
> I loved my sweetheart more than ever.
> I asked for advice and an old man
> Told me to bathe in the water.
> I leapt into the well and sank like a stone,
> But arose twice as much in love as ever before.

The bright little guidebook, *Hidden Haunts in Wales*, says a sacred eel was once kept here, and maybe still remains. If you sprinkled breadcrumbs on the surface of the water and spread your handkerchief on top, the eel came out to eat the crumbs. If the handkerchief was disturbed it denoted unfaithfulness.

On the north coast is:

☉ **Llanbadrig** where St Patrick is reputed to

Gwydir Castle, Llanrwst

have set sail for Ireland. It is now the site of Wylfa Nuclear Power Station. When this was being built in 1964 workmen, excavating a tunnel, saw the apparition of a woman in white who hummed. This happened so frequently that several workmen threw in their jobs. It is the site of Galan Ddu, the Black Bank, a house in which lived Rosina Buckman, the New Zealand opera singer. The casket containing her ashes is said to have been disturbed while the excavations were in progress.

Denbighshire

If you are travelling from Caernarvonshire, the first site is:

☙ **Llanrwst,** where Gwydir Castle (O.P.) is haunted.

North, almost on the coast, is:

✿☙ **Llanelian.** In a field behind the chapel, below a cottage called New York, is St Elian's Well, once considered the most awesome well in Wales. It was a cursing well of evil reputation. Inscribe a pebble with the name of the person you wish ill, with a pin, into the water.

North-west of Denbigh you will find:

☙ **Henllan** where the Llindir Inn is haunted by the ghost of Sylvia, who was murdered by her husband because she was unfaithful.

South-east of Denbigh is Ruthin where the:

☙ **Ruthin Castle Hotel** is haunted, and finds a place on the B.T.A. list.

South and east again is:

✿◉ **Llandegla.** Near the parish church is the site of Ff. Degla, Tegla or Tecla, said to be the second oldest healing well in Britain. Fowls, coins and quartz have been offered at various times for curing epilepsy, and I include this well because of the complicated magic ritual which had to be observed. A sufferer visited the well after sunset on Friday, washed his hands and feet and circled the well three times, carrying a cock in a basket. Each time he had to repeat the Lord's Prayer. Then the cock was pricked with a pin, which was thrown into the well, and a groat was given to the parish clerk. He next went into the church, repeated the Lord's Prayer three times and put a groat in the Poor Box. Then he lay under the Communion table, with a Bible for a pillow and a carpet for covering, where he remained till daybreak when he put the cock's head into his mouth and blew, thus transferring the disease to the bird. Silver was put in the Poor Box and the cock was left in the church. If it died the cure was certain. The sufferer had to return to the well and walk round it three times repeating the Lord's Prayer as before. Today an enterprising Parish Council has plans to restore the well. One member told me a slightly different version of the ritual: the cock was left at the well, and if it crowed in the morning then the cure would be effective.

Flintshire

Most people will approach Flintshire from Chester, so make straight for the most famous of all British wells at:

☆🐾 **Holywell.** St Winifred's Well (D.E.) had a splendid reputation for curing withered limbs, failing eyesight, dumbness, lunacy, fever, paralysis, epilepsy, stones, piles, gout, cancer, and skin diseases. It was patronized by Richard I, Edward IV and James II.

According to legend, the well's origin stems from a lecherous attack by Prince Caradoc on the virgin St Winifred. Scorned, he cut off her head; where it fell, water gushed out from the stones, which still retain the bloodstains. St Beuno, her uncle, restored her to life.

The well also detected thieves. A man who had stolen and eaten a goat was brought here and accused. The well pronounced him guilty. He protested his innocence, whereupon a goat's bleat was heard coming from his stomach. A contemporary chronicler wrote: 'What a dreadful thing, this, which is denied by a rational creature with an oath, is revealed by a brute, and, what is more, by one already eaten.'

The bath in the baptistry, built by Henry VII's mother, is now fed by a reservoir.

To the west is:

🐾☆ **Tremeirchion.** Near the banks of the Elwy, Daffyd Ddu, Vicar and Black Wizard of Hiradduec (1340), is buried in the wall of the church, 'neither within nor without' to cheat the Devil. (See Barn Hall, Essex; and Brent Pelham, Hertfordshire.)

St Beuno's Well is south of the village. The water gushed out through a gargoyle beside a cottage, but as there is evidence that the nearby caves were inhabited 2500 years ago, the well obviously pre-dates the Christian saint.

Montgomeryshire

The sites in this county are spread right across Wales, but start with:

☺🐾 **Machynlleth.** The road from here to Bala in Merioneth is said to be haunted by a holy apparition on a grey horse. A man, about to be set upon by brigands, prayed for help and a ghost rider appeared beside him. The brigands made off. The traveller said, 'Thank God', to which the rider replied, 'Amen', and disappeared.

North-east, near the borders of Denbigh and Merioneth, is Llangynog. Two miles from the village you will find a small valley which leads to:

🐾 **St Melangell's (Monacella's) Shrine.** The daughter of an Irish King, she vowed celibacy and fled here. Brochwel Yscythrog, Prince of Powys, hunted a hare which sought refuge under the saint's skirts. Some power prevented the hounds from coming near and the huntsman from blowing his horn. This so impressed the prince that he gave her the land, where she built a religious house.

North-west of Welshpool, on the borders of the parishes of Guilsfield and Meifod, is the:

☆ **Treferid** estate. Here, where the forest comes down in two points leaving a triangular wedge at the top of a field, is a spring called the Clawdd Llesg Spout. Sugared water was drunk on Trinity Sunday.

☺ **Welshpool.** At haunted Powys Castle (N.T.), one of the ghosts once showed a sewing woman (who had been allocated the haunted bedroom as a joke) where a box and key were hidden. The apparition also instructed her to send the box to the Earl of Powys in London. This was done. The contents were so valuable that Lord Powys invited the woman to stay in the castle for the rest of her life as a reward.

South is the county capital:

☆ **Montgomery.** The churchyard contains the grave of John Davies, wrongfully accused, tried and hanged for the theft of a watch and some money in 1821. He prayed that God would prevent grass from growing on his grave as a sign of his innocence. The bare earth is in the form of a cross. An excellent little book about John Davies will be found in the church.

Radnorshire

On the south-western outskirts of:

☆ **Knighton** there is a petrol station on the 488. The road passes within 40 yards of the river, on whose bank is Jacket's Well (formerly St Edward's), which eased sprains and rheumatism, and was used for this purpose by Ken Cadwallader, who showed me the site. Alas! you will now need a skeleton key to get the water, for it has been bricked up and the trapdoor padlocked by the local water authority.

South at:

☆ **Pilleth,** a well on the north side of the church tower is 'powerful good for the eyes'.

Brecknockshire

This is one county in Wales that I have failed, so far, to visit; but I have heard that at:

☆ **Brecon** there is St Michael's Well, near the saint's chapel, which cures whooping cough and nausea. When water is carried to the sick, it must on no account be placed on the ground.

Monmouthshire

My sites in this county would have been less than half the number had it not been for Mr Steve Clarke of the *Monmouthshire Beacon*. His two collections of *Ghosts and Legends of Monmouth* have proved invaluable. Chepstow is a good place to start; you can then work round the county and into Herefordshire. Between Chepstow and Monmouth, to the north, is:

☆☻⚰ **Trelleck.** Of the nine wells once to be found here, I believe only four remain. They are curative and wishing wells. Pebbles should be dropped in the water. If many bubbles rise your wish will be granted; if there are a few, your wish will be delayed; if none, your wish will not come true. A farmer is said once to have closed one of the wells, whereupon a 'little old man' appeared and told him no water would flow on his farm till he reopened it. Fairies are reputed to be seen here on Midsummer's Eve; and a phantom coach runs from Trelleck to 'somewhere in the Bigswear district'.

Way over to the west, on the other side of Ebbw Vale, on top of the mountains above Abercarn you will find:

⚰ **Trwyn,** a fascinating old farm haunted by Master Pisca, or Puck, who is obviously a link with the piskies and pixies of Devon and Cornwall.

But if this site is too far afield you can continue north to:

☻⚰ **Redbrook** where Swan Pool is haunted by the sound of a baby's screams, and by the sight of a mother and child. Here, too, there is talk of a ghostly coach, lurching and swaying as the coachman lashes the horses, with a beautiful lady peering out of the window as it dashes by.

On the way back from Trwyn you pass:

☻ **Raglan Castle** (D.E.) where a bard has been seen by visitors who did not know that this was the scene of great bardic activity 500 years ago.

If you visited Redbrook instead of Trwyn go to Penallt (see below, the penultimate site in this county) and work back. Otherwise, to the north lie:

⚰☻ **Tregare and Penrhos.** Here the Cwn Annwn – the Welsh Phantom Hound or Dog of Hell – has been seen. At Tregare, Mary George's spectre, dressed in Victorian clothes, has been seen opposite Old Park Road.

To the west, near Llanngatock, is:

☆ **Llanofer House.** In the grounds there is, I believe, Ff. Gofer which cured diseases of the limbs. Crutches were left here.

North-east at:

☆☻⚰ **Newcastle,** a well enjoyed a great reputation for healing and protection. The tumulus here is said to be haunted, as an atonement, by the ghosts of those who have done evil when alive. An oak tree here was for years believed to be the meeting place of elves and fairies.

South-east there is a cluster of sites around Monmouth. First:

🗡⚰ **Rockfield,** where the red stones of St Michael's Well are said to have been stained with the saint's blood when he was beheaded here.

On the Monmouth side of the town at Ancre Hill, a ghostly coach and four crashes into a wall. This was the old road to Abergavenny. A phantom hearse is seen in the village prior to the death of an inhabitant.

Continuing south-east you come to:

☻⚰ **Dixton.** The ghost of a tramp with a parcel is seen between the rectory and the river Wye where he was drowned. In the water meadows below the church, the ghosts of a man and a white dog have been seen by a number of people.

☻⚰ **Monmouth** itself seems full of ghosts. A leaping spectre was seen in 1948 at Watery Lane. As this was once a stream, it is thought that it may be the ghost of a man who either jumped or slipped or was pushed into the water and drowned. Some people have felt a fearful sense of evil here, while others have seen a ghostly coach driving over White Hill towards Wonastow Court. Monnow Street is the site of a haunting in which hoofbeats and glaring eyes turn down the side of Chippenham House.

Across the Wye to the east is:

☻⚰ **Hadnock.** Here you may see a hazy blue light in the shape of a woman. The Buckholt, also in this borough, is another haunt of the Cwn Annwn or Hound of Death.

☻ **The Kymin** is a high hill haunted by an eighteenth- or nineteenth-century man who presages death to those who live on its slopes.

South at:

☻ **Penallt** the ghost of a woman in white walks from the 'The Argoed' to the pond near 'The Generals', where she drowns herself, re-enacting her suicide.

☻ **Troy** is the next village, where ghostly dragging footsteps may be heard.

Opposite The gloom of Fyvie Castle in Scotland

Scotland

Scotland, like all Celtic countries, abounds with mysteries; but how should they be listed in a logical order for a tour? If one tries to cover them county by county, one finds miles of trackless moors and mountains separating two sites in the same shire, yet two sites in completely different counties lie within a few miles of each other along the same road. I decided to try, as far as possible, to keep to the counties, but to use as a main line the route my wife and I followed when checking the sites. The road across the border was not a motorway, because we had been visiting sites in Cumberland and Northumberland; but for relief from traffic and variety of scenery I would strongly recommend it. It is the 6318 from Greenhead, near Haltwhistle, to Langholm. You are now faced with a choice. You can turn north to Burnfoot and then east to:

👻💀🗡 **Hermitage** (D.E.), in Roxburghshire, one of the most notorious castles in Scotland. It was the awesome fortress of Lord Soulis, black magician and murderer of children – a sinister Scottish Gilles de Rais. The villagers eventually rose in revolt and threw him into a cauldron of molten lead. His restless spirit, attended by his familiar, Robin Redcap, to whom he entrusted the key of the castle with its buried treasure, still inhabits this gaunt and daunting place.

Alternatively you can turn left at Langholm in Dumfriesshire, and make for:

◉ **Lockerbie.** The Lockerbie Penny was a coin which, placed in a cleft stick and used to stir water, imbued it with the power to cure sick animals. (See Ardvorlich.)

North-west near Millhousebridge is:

👻 **Spedlin's Tower.** You can see the top over the trees from the Templand road. Here, in the time of Charles II, Sir Alexander Jardine imprisoned a miller called Porteous. He then went to Edinburgh forgetting his prisoner, who died of starvation. Porteous' ghost haunted Sir Alexander until, with the help of a Bible, he was able to contain the spirit in the dungeon. Without the Bible, the ghost might still roam abroad, as it did at nearby Jardine Hall (now demolished, although the dower house and gates remain) when the Bible was being rebound. The Jardines sold the house in 1884, but left the Bible to prevent the ghost from roaming. Porteous' voice can still be heard, calling to be

Right The apparition of a miller at Spedlin's Tower is repressed by the presence of a Bible

rescued from the tower.

Dumfries. The County Hotel is haunted by Bonnie Prince Charlie, who stayed here in 1745; and the site of a friary church where Robert Bruce stabbed Red Comyn in 1306 is thought by some to be haunted by Bruce and Kirkpatrick, who was also involved in the murder.

Once again you have a choice. You can go south to:

Arbigland, which lies just north-east of Southerness, Kirkcudbrightshire, and is haunted by the Ghost of the Three Cross-roads. Arbigland belonged to the Craiks. The daughter of the house fell in love with a groom called Dunn, who is said to have committed suicide, but local people thought it much more likely that he had been murdered by one of Miss Craik's brothers. She thought so too, and left her home never to return – except to join her phantom lover as a ghost.

Or you can go north to:

Closeburn Castle. A swan with a bleeding breast is believed to foretell the death of a Kirkpatrick. According to legend, about 150 years ago two swans came every summer and brought good fortune to the family, until Robert Kirkpatrick shot one. After that just one swan, with a blood-stained breast, would visit the place, and then only to herald ill-fortune or death.

North again lies:

Drumlanrig, the home of the Duke and Duchess of Buccleuch, which is haunted by Lady Anne Douglas, who walks with her head in her hand.

South-west, in Kirkcudbrightshire, on the 712 is:

Corsock. From here the old drover's trail used to run to Parton. On Corsock Hill a ghostly piper has been seen and heard playing wild music – a macabre sight because he has no head.

North-west of New Galloway is:

Glenlee House, haunted by Lady Ashburton dressed in rustling grey silk. She was rumoured to have killed her husband who was afflicted with lice, and then to have been murdered by her butler for some valuables. Many guests have seen this ghost, and at least one has seen a male apparition as well.

Near the Wigtown border on the outskirts of Newton Stewart you will find:

Minnigaff. Just before you reach the town, on the New Galloway road, is Larg Farm, where there was once a famous gout well. Coins had to be left; and a piper once took the offerings to pay for a drink at the inn. The gout of all those who had been

cured, descended on him, and he could only be healed by returning the money; and, presumably, adding his own payment. The well was rediscovered in 1900 on the 'brae face' of the deer park belonging to old Mackie Castle of Larg. It was thought to be 600 to 800 years old, and although overgrown, flowed freely. But its situation is not known to the present farmer at Larg. Those who want to solve the mystery may find a clue in the *Galloway Gazette* of 15 December 1900.

Down at the tip of the Mull of Galloway, on the eastern side, are:

Chapel Wells. Three sea-water wells, almost touching, lie 30 yards north-west of the ruins of St Medan's Chapel, at the foot of the cliffs. Just before sunrise on the first Sunday in May, known as Co' Sunday, 'backgaen' or sickly children were immersed head first in the largest well, the afflicted part was dipped in the next well, and the eyes bathed in the third. Offerings were left in the ruins of the chapel. The wells are a little difficult to reach, owing to erosion, but have been described by Sir Herbert Maxwell as the oldest ecclesiastical site in the country.

Sickly children were dipped in the sea-water Chapel Wells

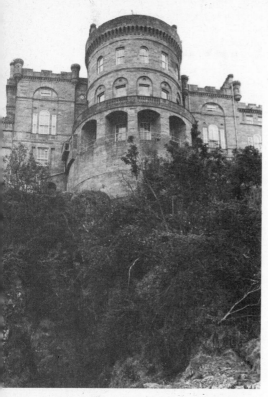

Listen for the phantom piper at Culzean Castle

At Drummore Mr R. McHaffie, a most erudite local historian, told me that St Medan, Modwena, or Etain, was an Irish lady, who fled to the Mull of Galloway to elude the attentions of an importunate lover. He followed her and was on the point of seizing her in his arms when she mounted a rock which promptly put out to sea and crossed Luce Bay, grounding near Monreith. There she founded the Chapel of Kirkmaiden Fernes, named after the parish she had just left. Once again the lover gave chase, and she asked him what made him follow. When he told her it was the beauty of her eyes, she plucked them out and threw them at his feet. Immediately a spring gushed forth which was used as a healing well for whooping cough, not, as one might think, for improving bad eyesight. The water should be drunk from a limpet shell, known in Celtic folklore as the Cup of Mary.

On the west side of the Mull of Galloway is:

☆ **Peter's Paps,** a cave near Port Logan. Once again it is difficult to reach owing to erosion, but those with whooping cough were made to catch in their mouths the drops that fell from the roof.

Further north on the west coast is:

☿ **Caldenoch Castle,** west of Lochnaw Castle. Hauntings are mostly serious, but I hope there is room for one ludicrous ghost. This one took the tenant's grandmother, washed her in the burn and left her naked, cold, and very frightened on its banks. It told the family what it had done, and was finally laid by being outsung in a psalm-singing contest by a man called Marshall. The whole enchantingly ridiculous story can be found in *Highways and Byways in Galloway and Carrick* by C. H. Dick.

North again in Ayrshire is:

☆ **Maybole.** There are two curative wells here. The first is St Murray's about 1½ miles out of the town on the right-hand side of the Ayr road. A mile further on, at Lower Milton Farm, is St Helen's Well which was particularly efficacious for sick children on May Day. It now has a concrete cover.

West on the coast you will find:

☿ **Culzean Castle** (N.T.S.), haunted by the ghost of the Kennedy piper who is heard more often than he is seen. The best place to listen and watch for him is on Piper's Brae, between Happy Valley and the sea, south-west of the walled garden.

West of Glasgow in Renfrew is:

☆ **Kilmacolm.** Two miles to the south-east is the ruined church of St Fillan, together with his curative and wishing well, and his 'chair' on the rock. All lie behind the Old Manse on private ground. Permission should be sought from Mr and Mrs Noad, who are generously informative.

Most of the sites in Argyll lie on or near the A83, A85 and 816, although you will have to take boats to Islay, Mull and Iona. First, as is only befitting in the Duchy, you should drive down the north side of Loch Fyne to:

☿ **Inveraray Castle** (O.P.). Before the death of the Chief of the Clan, or a near relative, a ghostly galley – resembling the ship on the coat of arms born by the Campbells, Dukes of Argyll – appears on the loch, with three people aboard. It passes up the loch and then overland.

The castle is haunted by the ghost of a harper who was hanged at Inveraray by Montrose; but as the house was not built until the mid-eighteenth century, presumably he was hanged on the site which was, in fact, once known as Gallows Foreland Point.

A ghostly harper haunts Inveraray Castle

He has been seen and heard, and his presence felt in Archie's Room, the Blue Room, the Green Library and on the stairs. The description given by those who have seen him might be summed up as dignified deference.

🔮 **Glen Aray** to the north is haunted by a company of redcoats on the march.

Continue along the A83 and the 816 to Bridgend, where a side road will lead you north to:

✡ **Kilmichael.** Near Tibertich Farm is a priest's well, which has miraculous healing powers. This may be the same as St Michael's Well, which my informant, the Revd Thomas Gillies, tells me he visited as a young man when feeling ill. He said a prayer, sipped the water and has 'never looked back since' (in fact, he married for the second time when well over seventy).

Now go back to the A83 and on to Tarbet. Here, if you wish, you can take the car ferry to:

🔮 **Islay.** The distillery just outside Port Ellen is haunted by the ghost of an intruder who, 100 years ago, got drunk and threw himself out of the window. One wonders if he got drunk to summon up enough courage to commit suicide, or if he fell because he was drunk.

From Tarbet go south down the east coast of Kintyre to:

🔮✡ **Saddell Abbey.** In Campbeltown I mentioned the abbey and was told it was haunted. 'By monks?' I suggested. 'I'm nae sure aboot monks,' was the reply, 'but by giants and beasties sairtainly!' Even this did not prepare me for the varied and powerful atmospheres of the place: unhappy but quiescent in the abbey ruins; sinister in the castle; and benign at the charming little wishing well. In the village they say the laird plundered the abbey to build the castle, and used headstones from the graveyard for the fireplaces which make both abbey and castle unquiet places. Then there was a fire seventy years ago, I was told, and a girl perished. The cook at the newer house along the shore has 'seen things'. The long, straight drive to the old castle is marked private, but a villager told me that the private part of the grounds stretches from the inner drive to the left of the old castle. The wishing well lies up a boggy path almost opposite the castle gates.

Now return to Tarbet by the western

The sinister castle north of Campbeltown was built with stones from Saddell Abbey

road, and take the 8024 round the west coast of Knapdale towards Kilberry. Three and a half miles from Torinturk, there is a small graveyard called:

✡ **Kilnaish.** You could easily miss the holy well at the roadside. Miss Marion Campbell of Kilberry Castle, who is a mine of information on the district, says it is usually covered with a sheet of corrugated iron to prevent the sheep from falling in.

Two miles short of:

✡🐎 **Kilberry,** at the crest of the hill near a lay-by, is the Seat of the Cailleach – a witch, or the 'Old Woman whose real name must never be mentioned'. You must throw a stone onto the seat if you want a wish. Two hundred yards away is Slochd na Chapuill – 'The Hollow of the Mare' – and, near Carse, Clac na h'Imuilte – 'The Hollow of the Struggle' – where one clan tried to drag the cailleach from her horse, and a rival clan tried to keep her on its back. It was Miss Campbell who drew the attention of T. C. Lethbridge to these sites. A naked woman riding a horse is a fertility symbol, and this pagan ritual centred round the Great Earth Mother. It is interesting to find that these places lie opposite the Paps of Jura. To find out how this remote Scottish site is linked with Lady Godiva, 'Ride a cock-horse to Banbury Cross', and Wandlebury (see Cambridgeshire) read Lethbridge's *Gogmagog, The Buried Gods*. He relates them to the Epona or Horse People. Rollo Ahmed, in his book *The Black Art*, writes that in Scotland

> there existed a secret society called 'The Horseman's' . . . [which] possessed an inner circle given up to the practices of the black art and the study of spells, incantations and charms.

They were probably the origin of the 'horse-whisperers', who still exist, and can tame the wildest stallion with a word. This may also link up with the Isle of Man horse legends.

North of Kilberry and due west of Kilmichael is Loch Crinan. On a promontory directly facing the Crinan Hotel stands the old castle of:

🔮 **Duntrune or Duntroon** (O.P.A.). In the seventeenth century, 'Left-handed' Coll, wishing to attack the castle, sent his piper to spy out the land. He was captured and imprisoned in a turret room, but managed to warn the invaders by playing 'The Piper's Warning to his Master'. Campbell of Duntroon then chopped off his hands and he died from shock and loss of blood. (Another version says that when the Campbells took Duntroon a piper on a nearby hill played

'The Campbells are Coming' to warn the occupants, but he was too late, and the attackers cut off his hands.)

This branch of the Campbell clan subsequently emigrated to Australia, and Duntroon then came into the possession of the Malcolms. For a long time it remained a ruin, but when it was being restored quite recently they discovered, under the kitchen floor, two skeleton hands. The piper's ghost haunts the tower, and this is where some still hear the sound of his warning.

North, at the top of Loch Craignish, is the broad green valley surrounding:

☻ **Barbreck House.** The ghost of a girl with long hair and a shawl or hood over her head, has frequently been seen. She disappears as soon as anyone comes near.

At the northern end of Loch Awe (which is reputed to contain a monster) a road leads from:

✿☻ **Kilchrenan to Ardanaiseig.** It is bordered on the north side by a wire fence. Just before a turning on the right to Achnacarron Farm, the fence on the left swerves away from a large flat stone, as if skirting it warily, before rejoining the road. This was a sacrificial stone and a monk's ghost has been seen here. He may have been an early Christian, sacrificed by a Druid priest, or perhaps the Druid himself, for the robes of a pagan priest could resemble a monk's habit, and the figure is headless.

You must go north through Glen Nant to reach Bridge of Awe on the A85. Just north is:

☻ **Inverawe House,** haunted by the ghost of Duncan Campbell, whose cousin Donald had been murdered by a Stewart of Appin. The murderer had cunningly taken sanctuary at Inverawe in order to escape. He admitted killing a man, but swore Duncan to secrecy. For three nights Donald's ghost indicted Stewart, but Duncan's devotion to Highland hospitality could not be broken. Finally the ghost said, 'Meet me in Ticonderoga', a phrase which meant nothing to Duncan. Years later, in 1758, when the Black Watch was sent to America, Duncan Campbell went with the regiment. On July 17 he was killed near a fort occupied by the French, called Ticonderoga. His body is buried at Fort Edward on the Hudson.

The other ghost at Inverawe is Green Jean, a young girl with golden hair who,

Left A gallant piper haunts Duntrune Castle, where his severed hands were discovered under the floorboards

according to one family who lived there, put out soap and towels for the guests, and for whom the sheep would stop while the shepherd watched her pass by. Nevertheless, quite recently she terrified workers on the hydro-electric scheme.

North of Oban and Connel lie three sites. First:

Loch Nell Castle which is said to be cursed because the staircase was made of sacred yew from Bernera island, off Lismore. St Columba preached under this holy tree and foretold that when it was cut down by the greed of man, the sin could only be expiated by blood, water and fire. When Campbell of Loch Nell ordered it to be felled for his staircase, the woodcutter was crushed to death; several of those towing it to the mainland were drowned and the house has been burned down several times. The staircase, however, remains unharmed.

The castle is haunted by a 'Brownie', and ghostly or fairy music has been heard by Lord Dundonald and General Elliott among others.

On the banks of Loch Creran to the north is:

Barcaldine Castle (O.P.A.) where the ghost of another Campbell was last seen in 1938. He is believed to be seeking revenge. There is also a Blue Lady who loves music.

South-east is:

Ardchattan Priory (D.E.). Tradition says a nun from Kilmaronaig Convent was smuggled into the priory and hidden under the floor of the oratory, where she remains to this day. If ever there were grounds for a haunting, this poor nun's predicament provides them.

To reach the Islands you will have to consult services and timetables, and make your own decisions as to which ones you wish to visit. From Oban you can get a ferry to:

MULL. You will probably land at Craignure. Take the 849 clockwise round the island, and down Glen More, you will see on your left:

Ben Buie. On these slopes you may see the ghost of Eoghann a' Chin Bhig, or Euan of the Little Head, harbinger of disaster for the Macleans of Loch Buie. When mortal, he was egged on by his wife to rise against his father. Euan, riding recklessly to the attack, had his head cut off, and his horse returned with the headless body. He had been warned that things might go wrong the previous

Right Although Loch Nell Castle has burned several times, its staircase of sacred yew is unharmed

The Campbells foolishly hired guns to shoot phantom intruders at Sunipol

evening by a fairy. (Incidentally, in Mull, fairies are said to have only one nostril.)

🏊 **Loch Poit na h-I,** opposite Iona, is said to be inhabited by a sea-horse.

IONA, across the sound, is still the goal of many Christian pilgrims. St Columba landed here in 563. He did not, however, bring Christianity to Scotland; this had been introduced 200 years previously. There are two wells which have nothing to do with St Mary's Abbey, but remind one that the island was known in Gaelic as the Isle of the Druids. They are to be found at the north end of the island.

☆ **The Well of Eternal Youth,** in which women should bathe before sunrise, is on the north slope of Dun-I.

☆ **The Well of the North Wind** is east of Dun-I, and here sailors made an offering and stirred the water to raise a wind to carry them southwards.

Back in Mull on the 8035 at Balmaneach you will find:

🏊 **Mackinnon's Cave.** He was a piper who went with others, including a dog, into the cave to see if it really led right under Ardmeanach and came out at Tiroran, 4 miles to the south-east. Unfortunately they met an ogress, who killed all except the piper and his dog, saying she would spare his life so long as he continued playing. Those above ground eventually heard the pipes falter and stop. They rushed in and found the bodies of all the men. The dog found the way out to Tiroran, but emerged hairless.

The 8073 will take you round the west

and north of the island. At:

☆ **Calgary** there is a magic stone which fills with water; but more interesting is:

☻ **Sunipol,** reputed to be the home of a Campbell who emigrated to Australia, fell in with Ned Kelly or a similar desperado, and perpetrated many crimes. On his return to Mull, the house was plagued with poltergeist phenomena. Stones from the beach were hurled several hundred yards up to the house. Campbell's two sisters employed men with guns to shoot the 'marauders', but the ghosts remained invisible to all but the Campbell family.

☆ ↗ **Tobermory,** in the north-east, may or may not get its name from Tobar Mhoire – the Well of St Mary. The original well is up by the side of the cemetery, and not the one that lies opposite, which was built to commemorate the coronation of Edward VII. The town's chief interest lies in the Spanish galleon sunk in 1588 with thirty million ducats on board. One of the lesser-known stories is that four of the cannon were cast by Cellini.

THE ISLAND OF SKYE is a short ferry trip from the mainland. First, of course, is:

🏊 **Dunvegan Castle** (O.P.) where the McLeods keep their flag, given them by a fairy, with the promise that it may be waved on three occasions to summon help; but a year and a day at least must elapse between the alarms, otherwise cattle will die, crops fail and women become barren (in other words, this is an infertility curse on those who abuse a sacred or supernatural gift). Some people say that a McLeod married a fairy and that she gave her husband the flag on Fairy Bridge when she had to return to her own people. But however it came into the McLeods' possession it is a powerful talisman. It has been waved with good effect twice: at Glendale in 1490, and at Trumpan in 1580.

It is probable, in fact, that the flag was brought back from a crusade. The Victoria and Albert Museum say that the silk from which it is made was woven in Syria or Rhodes, and may have been the shirt of a saint. More romantic even than this explanation is the story that it accompanied Harald Hardrada on his return from Constantinople. This Norse king died at Stamford Bridge near York in 1066, and is the ancestor of the McLeods through Olaf the Black.

Also on Skye, near Portree, is a hillock called:

☆🏊 **Sithean Beinne Bho'idhich,** the 'Fairy Dwelling of the Pretty Hill'. It is said that music can be heard coming from underground at night. Just to the north is Bonnie Prince Charlie's Cave. The Woman's Loch is inhabited by a monster.

In the north of the island:

☉ **Duntulm Castle** is haunted by a cousin of the Lord of the Isles, who tried to usurp his position. He was walled up in the tower with a piece of salt meat, a loaf and an empty jug. His skeleton was found years later. The local guidebook says that this castle was suddenly abandoned at the beginning of the eighteenth century. One story says that it was haunted, another that a nursemaid accidentally dropped a baby into the sea below, bringing sorrow and bad luck to the place.

EIGG lies south of Skye and south-east of Rhum.

☆ **Five Pennies Well** never fails to cure any person of their first disease, if they drink the water for two or three days. If a stranger lies down in the water it will cause a deformity, but this will not happen to a native of the island.

BARRA is at the southernmost end of the Outer Hebrides. At:

☆ **Castlebay,** near the remains of a Druid temple, there is a well which effects cures and also 'wards off fascination'. It is called Tobar-nam-Buadh – the Well of Virtues.

BENBECULA is another of the Outer Hebrides. On the west coast at:

🐾 **Nunton** is the grave of a mermaid who was killed nearly 150 years ago by a stone thrown at her by a boy.

LEWIS, the most northerly island of the Outer Hebrides, has two wells:

☆ **St Cowstans** (Constantine's) at Garrabost is on the steep slope near the shore. Water from this well was believed to be incapable of boiling any meat.

☆ **St Ronan's Well** is near the Butt of Lewis, at the northern tip of the island. Lunatics were made to walk round it seven times, then sprinkle themselves with the water. They were left all night on the site of the altar in the nearby ruins of a chapel dedicated to St Mulvey (known locally as Teampull Mor). If the patient slept he would regain his sanity, but if he remained awake, no cure could be expected.

When you return to the mainland from Skye, you will land either at Mallaig or Kyle of Lochalsh or, in summer, you can cross Kyle Rhea. Just south of Mallaig, in Inverness-shire, is:

🐾 **Loch Morar,** the deepest loch in Scotland at 1000 feet. It is inhabited by a monster known as Morag. There have been thirty-three sightings since 1887, and Lord Glen-devon had a bite on his line in 1931 which was heavier than anything he had experienced. It took the whole line and the backing vertically down in a few seconds and broke the rod.

🐾 **Arisaig.** The steep woods nearby are haunted by a Phantom Hound, whose story resembles that of Gelert (see Beddgelert, Wales). A child was carried off by a wolf, but the distraught father thought that a collie dog was to blame, and cruelly put it to death.

If you land at Lochalsh:

☆ **Kyle Rhea** leads out of the southern end of the loch. Near here is a cairn called Clann Mhic Crumein, the Cairn of Clan MacCrimmon. The clan came from Glen Elg and were slaughtered by the Mathesons of Loch Alsh. From this cairn the most beautiful fairy music in Scotland is said to come.

Your next site is north at:

☆◉🐾 **Loch Maree.** One of the smaller islands in the loch is Innis Maree. Here, in the middle of a grove of sacred holly trees is an oval dike of stones, enclosing a burial ground of sixty or more graves, which has been used since pagan times.

You will also find St Maelrubha's Well, 'of power unspeakable in cases of lunacy'; (lunatics were also towed round the island and periodically ducked as a cure). St Mourie, Maree or Maelrubha, who gave his name to the place, came from Ireland in 673, and founded a monastery at Applecross to the south-west, opposite Raasay where he is buried. For hundreds of years the saint was known as God Mourie, and on his day, August 25, a bull was sacrificed to him on the island (see Mottistone, Isle of Wight). This continued well into the seventeenth century, one of the last vestiges, perhaps, of the Mithraic cult. It is said that the Innis Maree Well lost its power, either through contact with a mad dog, or because someone took the offerings. When the well dried up, the power was transferred to a tree, and thousands of copper coins are wedged in its trunk. It died, they say, of copper poisoning, but the support and the tree itself still receive the tributes of those who come to wish. Queen Victoria visited the island in 1877, and fixed her offering to the tree. Some say that it was a golden sovereign, and that John Brown returned later to retrieve it. The sanctified calm of the place would, one felt, prevent most people from stealing the offerings.

One does not sense the brutality of sacrificial rites; only a sadness at the graves of Olaf the Norwegian, and the princess he loved. She pretended to be dead to test his devotion, and he was so distraught that he plunged a dagger into his heart, which caused her to kill herself in turn.

We planned our visit on the 1200th anniversary of St Maelrubha's death: 21 April 1972. You may find it difficult to arrange a sudden visit to the island, and well-nigh impossible in the fishing season. Fishing is, after all, a serious business and a ghillie's livelihood.

You can cover the Sutherland sites in a reasonable sequence if you go from Ullapool to Ledmore, then due north up the 837. On this road you will pass near:

🐾 **Loch Canisp** which is inhabited by a monster.

Just north of Inchnadamph is:

👻 **Ardvreck Castle,** on Loch Assynt, where a big tall ghost is to be seen among the ruins. This is not surprising, since Montrose sought refuge here in 1650, after being defeated at Culrain. Neil McLeod of Assynt, who lived at Ardvreck, betrayed him, had him taken to Edinburgh and killed. The Mackenzies took revenge by killing all at Ardvreck and burning down the castle.

Continue along the 837, and a mile before you reach:

🐾 **Clachtoll,** Creag an Ordain hangs over the road by the loch, and a Phantom Hound may appear; 'very fierce', is how a roadman described it.

Follow the road north through almost treeless country to Oldany. On:

👻 **Oldany Island** a mysterious light is sometimes seen.

This road will lead you round to:

👻 **Kylesku Hotel** (The Old Ferry House). A ghost appears at the entrance to the Snuggery. Professor Joad is said to have seen it in about 1950. The Snuggery is now the ladies' lavatory, and the ghost makes his appearance through a trap-door in the ceiling. He is thought to be the brother of Miss Mackay, a famous landlady of the 1890s and a great fiddle player. She was tricked by a policeman from Stoer and lost her licence, as a verse hanging on the wall of the bar records, but her brother's spirit obviously refuses to leave the place. Another version of the story is that the ghost is that of a young man cursed by his father, and doomed to haunt the hotel, but this was not substantiated by the present landlord.

There is also another haunting. Just before the 1914 war, a couple – or some say a sea-captain – set out from the hotel to walk to Inchnadamph, in spite of a warning from the

local seer who had dreamed for three successive nights of a drowning in Lochan Dubh, a small loch on the right of the road travelling south. They were indeed drowned at the spot, and people still fear what they may see if they take that road on a dark night.

Up north, beyond Kinlochbervie (where at Craigmore a mermaid was seen in 1949) is:

👻 **Sandwood Bay,** a very haunted place. The ghost is a figure in sea-boots, reefer jacket and sailor's cap. It has been seen on many occasions in 1949 and 1953, and sometimes appears in a cottage on a high ridge facing Cape Wrath lighthouse. It has been reported that a piece of wood sent from here to Edinburgh resulted in ghostly manifestations of the sailor in the Scottish capital. Another legend tells of a Polish ship driven ashore here 300 years ago, and the headless spectre of one of the crew searching for his shipmates.

The most northerly point of the main road, the 838, is:

👻✡ **Durness.** Here the manse is said to be haunted and was once the scene of mysterious deaths. More romantic is Fraisgell's Cave, on the shores of Loch Eribol, which is often filled with fairy music.

Caithness must have many more mysteries than I have yet discovered. I found only:

🐾🗡 **Duncansby Head** where mermaids are said to guard a cave of treasure.

The car ferry runs from Thurso in Caithness to Orkney.

ORKNEY is a county – as Moray McLaren points out in *The Shell Guide to Scotland* – but it is also a number of islands. Off:

🐾 **Deerness,** on the Orkney mainland, mermaids were seen frequently between 1886 and 1893.

On Westray is:

👻 **Noltland Castle** (D.E.), built by Gilbert Balfour in the sixteenth century on a much earlier site. A ghostly light appears in the ruins to herald births, deaths and marriages of the descendants of the Balfours who once lived here.

On Papa Westray you will find:

✡ **St Tredwell's Loch,** which turns red when some important event involving the royal family is about to take place. Its waters have healing powers. The sufferer walks round the perimeter in silence and offers either clothing or bread.

🦌 **South Ronaldshay.** In the chapel of Lady Kirk there is a four-foot stone, pointed at both ends, with the imprint of human feet on its surface. It is said to be St Magnus' Boat, which he used to cross the Pentland Firth.

In **SHETLAND**:

◉ **Lerwick** has a festival on the last Tuesday in January called 'Up-Helly-Aa', in which a Norse galley is burned. This is probably the remnants of a pagan fire ritual.

On Unst, the most northerly Shetland island, is:

✫ **Loch of Watlee.** Near here is the site of a fine spring, Heljabrun. A pedlar is said to have been murdered and then thrown into Heljabrun. Already famous for its healing powers, after the murder it became even more efficacious. It never failed as long as three stones or pieces of white money were offered in payment.

The first site on the southward route is back in Sutherland, west of Dornoch on the east coast:

☻ **Skibo Castle** is haunted by a murdered woman whose screams are still heard.

The next site is in Easter Ross, north-east of Invergordon:

⚔☻ **Balnagown Castle.** It is said that treasure lies buried here, and it is haunted by the ghost of Black Andrew Monro, a sixteenth-century rapist, who eventually had a rope tied round his neck and was thrown out of a tower window by the Chief of Clan Ross.

The next four places are all connected with the same story. Two miles west of Maryburgh, south of Dingwall, is the present:

👻 **Brahan Castle.** Of the original castle nothing remains, but the courtyard is said to have been big enough to drill a thousand men. As the grounds of the present castle are open to the public, one could inspect the probable site. It was the home of Lord Kintail, whose son, Kenneth Mackenzie, was made Earl of Seaforth. His grandson married Isabella Mackenzie of Tarbat, which is on the shores of Nigg Bay, near Balnagown. When her husband was away, she consulted the Warlock of the Glen, also called Kenneth Mackenzie, who lived at:

👻 **Strathpeffer,** five miles to the north-west. The seer told her in front of witnesses, that her husband was enjoying the company of two young ladies in Paris, one on each knee, or, according to another version, he was on his knees before a French lady. This so incensed Lady Seaforth that she had the warlock burned to death in a barrel of boiling pitch at:

👻 **Chanonry,** near Fortrose on the Black Isle, where a stone marks the spot. As he died he cursed the Seaforth line to sorrow and extinction. Among the many omens which would prove the curse was coming true were that in the days of the last Seaforth, who would

A murdered woman still screams at Skibo Castle

be a deaf-mute, four great lairds, Gairloch, Chisholm, Grant and Raasay would be buck-toothed, hare-lipped, half-witted and have a stammer. Late in the eighteenth century Francis Humberston Mackenzie became deaf and dumb from scarlet fever, though he managed to overcome his dumbness. At the same time Sir Hector Mackenzie of Gairloch was buck-toothed, Chisholm of Chisholm was hare-lipped, Grant of Grant was a half-wit, and McLeod of Raasay stuttered. Furthermore the Seaforth Mackenzies died out.

The Brahan seer foretold many other events which have come true, for example, that ships would sail through what has since become the Caledonian Canal, that Strathpeffer would become a spa, the depopulation of the Highlands and the defeat at Culloden. One prediction has yet to be fulfilled. Into:

👻 **Loch Ussie,** between Maryburgh and Strathpeffer, the seer threw the round-holed stone through which he saw the future, saying that a child would be born with four thumbs and six toes who would discover the stone inside a pike and inherit his powers.

169

On the road to Chanonry, you will pass one of the most vivid examples of belief I have yet come across. If you take the 832, between Tore and the turning to Munlochy, on the south side of the road is:

✫◉ **The Cloutie Well.** For twenty-five yards on either side of the spring the fence is a veritable hedge of rags, left as offerings by those who come to be healed. I saw it in mid-April, but the most auspicious day is the first Sunday in May, when the 'clouties' must run into many thousands.

◉✫ **Munlochy Bay** is the site of a cave, reputedly haunted by two warrior giants called MacCoul, and certainly inhabited within living memory by the Black Colleens, who may have been their descendants, for they were described as not tinkers, but belonging to a broken clan. The peculiarly cold water dripping down from the roof cured deafness.

On the opposite side of the Black Isle is:
✫ **Culbokie,** which means Haunted Nook. The two concentric circles near the lochan were probably an ancient burial ground.

The northernmost tip of the Black Isle is:
✫ **Cromarty.** Near here is the Fiddler's Well. William Fiddler and a companion both had tuberculosis. The friend died, and although

The carved stone in Glen Roy

Fiddler himself was desperately ill, he insisted on going to the funeral. That night he dreamed that the dead man arranged for them to meet at a certain spot, and, still in his dream, he went there. A bee buzzed round his head and seemed to be saying, 'Dig, Wullie, Dig! Dig and drink!' The next day he put his dream into practice. He found the water, drank and was cured. To effect a cure the water must be drunk straight from the well in the early morning.

The last site in Ross and Cromarty lies to the west, on the road from Dingwall to:
◉ **Garve.** In a house, once called Hazelbrae, now a hotel annexe, bells rang mysteriously at the hour when, years ago, a maid, who had been deliberately duped by a jealous mistress, threw herself into the ominously named Black Water. Although the hotel chef, who has slept in the house alone, says he experienced nothing strange, there are still a number of villagers who will not pass that way at night.

Inverness-shire has one of the most famous mysterious sites in Scotland.
🐾◉ **Loch Ness.** Millions of words have been written about the monster that lives in its depths. St Columba saw it in 565. Every year more evidence is produced, photographs printed, sightings recorded. Yet nothing is actually proved. There are, on average, a score of 'sightings' annually, most of them near Urquhart Castle. The astonishing thing to me is why Loch Ness has gained so much fame while other places have been completely ignored. There are at least ten other lochs which are said to be inhabited by monsters – often thought to be water-horses. I have heard on good authority of a giant eel, nine inches in diameter and some nine feet long, being found split open after an underwater explosion during construction of a hydro-electric scheme; and I have seen a photograph of a very strange carcass found on a beach in Mull.

On the north-west shore of Loch Ness is the Aultsigh Inn, haunted by the ghost of Annie Frazer, who was loved by two brothers, one of whom killed the other and then the girl.
🐾 **Loch Oich** to the south is reputed to hold a monster.

I have heard that by the side of the main

Right The bridge near Dunvegan Castle where the fairy gave her husband McLeod a magic flag

Overleaf The extraordinary rag offerings at the Cloutie Well

Fort William/Inverness road here, there is a spring known as:

☆ **Tobar nan Ceann,** or the Well of the Heads, which commemorates the washing of human heads by a man who had avenged a murder and was bringing home the heads of seven Keppochs as proof.

But Loch Ness and Loch Oich are in:

👣 **Glen Mor.** The Goblin of Glen Mor is apparently two feet six inches to three feet high, aggressive, and similar to an elemental. His home is said to be Glen Gloy, which lies between Loch Lochy, and:

☆👁 **Glen Roy.** A road runs along the north bank of the Roy river. Halfway down on the south side of the road there is a stone, and cut in its face one can distinguish a Chalice, Holy Wafer and I.H.S. The place is haunted by a malevolent spectre, once exorcised by a priest. It was a venerated spot; but used for strange rituals 100 years ago.

The A86 leads past Roybridge and on to the A9 and Aviemore. South is:

👁 **Rothiemurchus Forest.** The Grants of Rothiemurchus were warned of an impending death in the family by an apparition known as the Bod-an-Dun. Legend also has it that a bedroom in an old house here is haunted by the ghost of a lunatic who murdered a servant girl and then committed suicide. At the Post Office they thought that this must refer to a then empty house on the 970, known as The Doune.

South again lie the:

👁 **Cairngorms,** and here the high peak of Ben Macdhui is haunted by the Grey Man, who has been studied by students of psychic research from Edinburgh.

I suggest you continue north-east to:

👣 **Loch Pityoulish and Loch Garten,** each reputedly inhabited by a water-horse.

Now take the A9 north-west to Findhorn Bridge. Three and a half miles upriver is:

👁 **Dalarossie Kirk,** where a skull mysteriously appears; and when Christmas Day falls on a Sunday, two ghostly teams of Shaws from Strathnairn and Strathdearn replay a game of shinty in the glebe.

North of the A9 is:

🐎👻 **Moy Hall.** It is the house of the Mackintosh family, and once belonged to the Mackintoshes of Clan Chatten. The legend runs that the Macintoshes patched up their quarrel with the Grants, and swore to maintain the peace. However, they captured two

Copper coins wedged in a tree trunk for wishes on an island in Loch Maree

Bonnie Prince Charlie haunts Culloden House

Grants and then asked the daughter of one, who was betrothed to the other, which should die, her father or her lover. Distraught, she eventually decided to let her father be killed only to see them both murdered in front of her eyes. Not unnaturally she cursed the Mackintoshes of Moy that they should never again have a direct heir. This has not been entirely fulfilled, but Moy has passed rather frequently to a brother or nephew or a cousin during the last 250 years. The Curse of Moy was made famous by Sir Walter Scott. He wrote of the celebrations at the birth of a Mackintosh heir, when the ghost of Margaret Grant appeared and cursed the child:

> For the blast of Death is on the heath
> And the grass yawns wide for the child of Moy.

And sure enough:

> Scarce shone the moon o'er the mountain's head
> When the lady wept o'er her dying boy.

East of Inverness, near the site of the famous battle is:

👁 **Culloden House,** haunted by the ghost of Bonnie Prince Charlie. The site of the battle itself seems drenched in sadness, and many ghosts have been seen here, including an army in the sky.

You are now set for a tour of the counties of Nairn, Moray, Banff and Aberdeen.

👁 **Rait Castle,** three miles south of Nairn,

An apparition in a bloodstained dress stalks the ruins of Rait Castle

belonged to the Cummings (or Comyns). They invited the Mackintoshes to a feast at Rait, intending to murder them – the very antithesis of Highland hospitality. The Mackintoshes were forewarned, and so came prepared. The Chief of the Cummings clan, whose daughter was in love with a Mackintosh, suspected her of the betrayal, and cut off her hands. Distraught with horror, she leaped to her death from the tower. Since then the castle has stood gaunt and silent except for the occasional clash of steel and empty but for the ghost of a girl in a blood-stained dress with no hands.

North-east at:

Burghead on January 13 an old fire ritual, known as 'Burning the Clavie' is still performed. A tar barrel is set alight, carried to the top of a hill and rolled down. If the bearer stumbles it means bad luck for him and the town. Any pieces picked up are considered good-luck tokens, and a protection against witchcraft.

South of Forres and west of Dunphail station are the ruins of:

Dunphail Castle. The clash of steel and groans of the dying are heard, and the severed heads of Alastair Cummings and three or four companions have been seen in spectral form. They managed to escape from the castle while it was being besieged by the Earl of Moray, and threw sacks of meal over the wall to feed the beleaguered members of the clan. They were eventually captured and beheaded; the heads were then thrown over the castle wall with the blood-curdling cry, 'Here's beef for your bannocks!' When,

years later a nearby mound was excavated, five headless skeletons were found.

South again is:

Castle Grant, about two miles north-east of Granton-on-Spey, and surrounded by trees. Here a small benevolent female ghost appears in a bedroom in the tower, washes her hands and darts across the room towards the staircase. She is thought to be the phantom of Barbara Grant, who lived in the sixteenth century and died incarcerated in the tower, imprisoned there by her father because she would not marry a man she did not love.

If you continue along the 939, you will cross Bridge of Brown into Banff. The first turning north will take you to:

Kirkmichael. Opposite the manse, on the wooded slopes of Cnoc Fergan, is Fergan Well. It is rather difficult to find now 'because of the Forestry', but a path leads up to it from Balnedan Farm on the southern slopes. About forty years ago it was much used for healing skin diseases, and crowds would gather there for cattle sales. It was especially efficacious on the first Sunday in May and coins were left. Its healing powers diminished during the summer months, and in September pilgrimages ceased till the following year.

East, across the Glenlivet Forest, between: Knockandhu and Milton of Auchriachan, the 9008 is haunted by a most fearsome Phantom Hound of ill-omen. It leaves tracks in the snow as big as a man's hand.

North near Bridge of Avon is:

Ballindalloch Castle, home of the Macpherson-Grants. It is haunted by a Green Lady who appears nightly.

North-east at:

🌀 **Rothes,** Glen Grant House has been turned into accommodation for distillery workers; but a century or so ago, when 'Old Glen' Grant lived there, there were rumours of strange and tragic events; his spirit is still believed by some to be earthbound.

East on the A96 is:

☆ **Keith.** South of the town, along the road which joins the A96 and the 920, you will find a modern croft called Tobar Chalaich, the Old Wife's Well. It is called after a well near a stone circle up behind the house. I believe that this is the site of a pagan ceremony when the Earth Mother in her old witch phase bathed at a well and once more returned as a young maiden.

If you are travelling east, as we were, the first site in Aberdeenshire is on the 947:

🐎🌀☝ **Fyvie Castle** where, it is said, a secret room in the south-west tower remains closed, because disaster befalls any owner who enters. There are indelible bloodstains, a ghost, and two curses connected with this place. Thomas the Rhymer said that the owners would never inherit for more than one generation until three stones were brought together, which, from an obscure rhyme, would seem impossible. An alternative reading is that the stones must merely be retained. These stones were probably originally part of a church or religious house, but were used in building 'the oldest tower', 'the Lady's bower' and 'the water gate', all secular places. The penalty of such sacrilege has not yet been paid fully, but dearly enough to be considered more than co-incidence.

Almost due east on the coast is:

☆ **Cruden Bay.** In this parish you will find:

> St Olav's Well, low by the sea,
> Where pest nor plague shall never be.

The next site to the south is the capital of the county, on the river Dee. The original sacrifices to the river goddess are commemorated in the rhyme:

> Bloody thirsty Dee
> Each year demands three.

🐾 **Aberdeen** was the scene of a very strange story just over a century ago. On Tuesday 31 May 1859, at 8.30 p.m., the Revd Spencer Nairn saw a Miss Wallis, whom he knew, in Union Street, but when he tried to speak to her she disappeared. In the latter part of July, Miss Wallis saw Spencer Nairn in the same place. Miss Wallis was not there on the first occasion, nor the minister on the second. F. W. Myers, one of the founders of the Society for Psychical Research, is reported

A secret room is sealed in a tower of Fyvie Castle to prevent disaster

to have found it easy to believe that Miss Wallis saw Spencer Nairn *after* he had been there, but difficult to see how Nairn could have seen Miss Wallis before she visited the spot. This surely is tying oneself to the hands of a clock rather than time. Second sight has never been confined to the past. One of the latest theories being developed by Dr Kozynev in Leningrad is that 'time is a form of energy that accomplishes or allows psychic happenings.' (See *Psychic Discoveries Behind the Iron Curtain* by Sheila Ostrander and Lynn Shroeder.)

Now follow the Dee to:

🌀 **Crathes Castle** (N.T.S.), which is in Kincardine. The ghost of a Green Lady moves across a room to an oddly carved fireplace, and lifts up a baby. Some years ago the skeletons of a woman and child were found under the hearth.

Continuing west you come to:

☆ **Aboyne** where 1½ miles from the church, and ½ mile beyond Dykehead Farm, off the Braemar road, are St Munricha's Well and stone cross, which the spirit of the well always brought back if anyone attempted to remove it. It has, alas! fallen into disuse.

Let us hope that the next site, also to the west, will have a big revival:

☆👹 **Pannanich.** Just over 200 years ago, an old woman who lived in Tullich, on the north side of the Dee, and suffered from the King's Evil, found that the water from four springs on the south side cured her. By 1771 they were held in such high esteem that the town of Ballater was built to cater for those who came to be cured of stomach disorders, bladder troubles and scrofula. Now there are two springs (which produce water tasting very strongly of iron) and a delightful small hotel – the original miniature spa – overlooking the Dee, at a spot where a water kelpie is said to be seen, and opposite the site of a Pictish village. Queen Victoria visited this hotel, and in 1971 the Queen Mother came here. The landlord, a retired journalist, hopes to open up the other wells.

North-west on the 939 is Cock Bridge. West of the inn and at the top of the Loinberry Burn is:

✡ **Tobar Fuar,** the Big Cold Well, at the foot of a steep hill. Curiously enough, the innkeeper did not know of its existence, although this group of three springs was once famous, one for curing blindness, one deafness and the third lameness. He did, however, tell me that Mr William Troup, who lives at Colnabaichin, would know; and not only did Mr Troup confirm the well's existence, but also told me of another one, west of Corgaff. In his opinion:

☻ **Corgaff Castle** (D.E.) is haunted, which is not surprising. In November 1571 Margaret Forbes was mistress of Corgaff. She, together with her family and servants, numbering twenty-seven in all, were burned to death in a retaliatory raid by the Gordons, while her husband was away. I cannot believe that their agony did not leave its mark.

☻ **Skellater House,** which is 2 miles to the north-east, is, according to Mr Troup, also haunted. A boy was murdered here over some business of rent-collecting.

South-west on the A93 is:

☻ **Braemar.** At Dubrach the phantom of Sergeant Arthur Davies, who was murdered in 1749, has been seen. Russell gives the reason for the haunting as 'revenge or justice on the murderers'. John Harries says he 'appeared naked, and implored mortals to find his bones and bury them in sanctified ground'.

Between the Braemar Hills and the Forest of Atholl is:

⛺ **Fealaar.** Nearby stands a bothy haunted by a vampire. In the 1920s two poachers experienced the phenomenon and one bore its marks for the rest of his life.

Having visited Crathes Castle on your journey up the Dee, the other sites in Kincardine lie on or near the coast.

☻◉ **Stonehaven** is said to be haunted by a

Green Lady. It is definitely the site of a pagan fire festival survival, when the New Year is ushered in with swinging fireballs carried by young men through the streets.

Just off the A92, on the way to Montrose, you will find:

✡ **Marykirk.** About 2 miles to the north-west is St John's Well in Balmanno Street, which provides a sovereign cure for bad eyes.

Between Montrose and Arbroath in Angus on the coast is:

☻ **Ethie Castle,** haunted by a woman who appears dressed in different clothes in a high-walled garden. She is believed to presage death. The ghost of Cardinal Beaton haunts the narrow staircase which leads to the secret doorway in the Cardinal's Bedroom.

☻ **Arbroath** is on the coast. About 3 miles outside the town a piper called Tam Tyne took shelter in a cave with his dog. They were never seen again, though the pipes are still heard, some say from under the hearthstone at Dickmountlaw Farm.

North-east of Dundee, just off the 961 is:

⚔ **Carmyllie.** On Cairnconan lies a crock of gold. You can, they say, see it shimmering when the sun shines, but no-one has ever reached it.

To the north a triangle lying across the A94 is marked by:

☻ **Careston, Finavon and Aberlemno.** This area is haunted by Jock Barefut who, when alive, cut a stick from a Spanish chestnut in Careston Castle grounds. The laird, known as The Tiger, hanged him from the same tree, which withered and died, but the ghost of the man who swung from its branches remains.

☻ **Finavon Castle:**

> When Finavon Castle runs to sand
> The end of the world is near at hand.

This was the home of Lord Crawford, known as Earl Beardie, who is thought by some to have been one of the card players at Glamis (q.v.) Here is the same story as at Careston, of a man cutting a cudgel and being hanged from the tree and subsequently haunting the place.

A few miles to the north-west is:

⚔⛺ **Fern.** On the north bank of the river Noran are the ruins of the Castle of Vayne, once the home of the Lindsays. There is reputed to be buried treasure, guarded by a monster.

About 3 miles north of Kirriemuir is:

🐕 **Cortachy Castle.** Since 1641 it has belonged to the Ogilvys, Earls of Airlie. A

handsome young drummer is said to have
been caught in a compromising position with
a Lady Airlie. He was sealed in his drum and
hurled from the highest tower. Drumming is
usually heard outside the walls of the castle
before the death of one of the family.

Forfar. When it freezes, the small loch to
the west of the town is haunted by several
ghosts. The bottom half of them is invisible,
for they are the spirits of those who drowned
after the murder of Malcolm II.

Now to the most famous castle of them all.
South of Kirriemuir is:

Glamis (O.P.), which lies across
Dean Water:

> The dowie Dean
> It rins its land
> And ilka seven year
> It takes ane.

Legends concerning the Monster of
Glamis are legion. Only Lord Strathmore,
his heir and the factor are said to know the
secret. Towels have been hung out of every
known window to try to discover the secret
room where, according to some, card
players and revellers including Lord (Beardie)
Crawford (see Finavon Castle), are condemned
to eternal drinking till Judgment Day; or,
others say, the Ogilvys, fleeing from the
Lindsays, sought sanctuary and were starved
to death; or where the vampire monster,
born periodically to the Strathmores, is kept
alive in utter isolation. Whatever the truth,
the fifteenth earl, great-grandfather of Queen
Elizabeth II, is reputed to have said: 'If you
could only guess the nature of the secret, you
would go down on your knees and thank God
it was not yours.'

Those who have come near to solving the
mystery, such as workmen who discovered
a bricked-up door during alterations, have
reputedly been paid large sums to emigrate.
In his *Ghost Book* Lord Halifax has fascinating
details of how in some rooms iron rings
fastened to the stones were covered by coal
stores which the servants were ordered to
keep full; also of the dreams of an archbishop's wife about the Blue Room and the
rusty iron it contained; of the tall dark
figure that passed through a locked door, seen
by the Dean of Brechin and the Provost of
Perth; and of other figures seen by a house-
maid in the Oak Room. More recently it has
been reported that Lady Elphinstone, sister of
the Queen Mother, remembered being very
frightened as a young girl of the sinister
atmosphere in the room where Duncan is
said to have been murdered.

Top A monster guards treasure at the ruined Castle
of Vayne near Fern

Above Supernatural drumming heralds a death at
Cortachy Castle

The latest theory I have heard is that the secret is documentary evidence which incriminates Mary, Queen of Scots. Whatever it is, it remains a mystery. The legend of the monster has rather overshadowed the ghost of Janet, wife of the sixth Lord Glamis, who was burned to death at Castle Hill in Edinburgh in 1537 for witchcraft and plotting to poison James V. She haunts the Clock Tower, and may possibly be the White Lady who flits about the avenue.

The spectre of a man has been seen at Malcolm Stone in the village. Glamis is supposed to be the centre of a fairy region. The Folk Museum in Kirk Wynd is well worth visiting, and may provide more mundane mysteries for visitors. St Fergus' Well is down by the side of the church.

◉ **The river Tay** demanded a coin for luck, or rather to propitiate the goddess Talitha.

☻ **Perth** is at the mouth of the Tay. It takes a lot to put the fear of God into a Highland regiment, but in 1915 this happened to the 2nd/1st Highland Artillery Brigade. The cause was the mysterious manifestations at Belfield House, ½ mile outside the town, where they were quartered.

☻ **Huntingtower Castle** (D.E.) lies 2 miles west of Perth. It is haunted by the ghost of 'Milady Greensleeves', a benevolent apparition, who has saved an old man, reputedly a miser, from dying, cured a sick boy, and warned another man of impending death. The Maiden's Leap is the gap between the two towers.

✿ **Dunsinane Hill** is to be found about 8 miles to the north-east, near King's Seat. Below the hill is Lang Mari's Grave, marked by a long stone at the roadside. Some people believe that the original Stone of Destiny still lies here, where it was hidden by the monks of Scone, and that Edward I took away nothing but a counterfeit.

To the north the A93 crosses:

☂ **Lunan Burn** where you will find the Witches Pool. Witches were tried here by ducking.

Continue north to Blairgowrie where:

☻☂☙ **Newton Castle** lies high up on the west side of the town, overlooking the Sidlaw Hills. It is haunted by the Green Lady Jean, who was jilted by her lover. She consulted a witch, who told her to wear fairy clothes of green. To obtain these she had to sit all night on the 'Corbie's Stane', among other things. The experiment failed and she died and was laid out on the bridal bed. On All Hallowe'en, at midnight, her gravestone turns three times and the Green Ghost walks.

The Witches Pool at Lunan Burn

Dogs, ordered to chase a phantom beast on the A93, between Blairgowrie and Bridge of Cally, whimper and cringe with their tails between their legs.

A few miles to the east is Alyth. On Barry Hill is the site of:

☗ **Dunbarre Castle,** setting of an Arthurian legend. When King Arthur was fighting on the continent, Modred, his nephew, carried off Guinevere (or Varnorna). But Modred was defeated by the Picts and Scots, and the queen was incarcerated here. She was killed by wild dogs and buried at Meigle. Her tombstone is in the museum (D.E.) there, and you can see the carving of a figure being attacked by animals. Some people prefer to think that it is not Guinevere being attacked by dogs (or wolves), but Daniel in the lion's den; but why should this scene be depicted on a tombstone?

North-west again on the 924 is Kirkmichael. At:

☻☂ **Ashintully Castle,** which lies north-east of the village, there are three ghosts. A

Spalding of Ashintully hanged a tinker for trespassing. The tinker laid a curse that the family would die out, which it did. His ghost haunts the avenue of trees in which he was hanged, together with a second ghost, Crooked Davie, a hunchback servant, killed by another Spalding. The third ghost is Green Jean, at one time owner of the castle, who, while wearing a green dress, was murdered by an avaricious uncle. Her footsteps are still heard and her ghost appears in the private burial ground, among the dank, dark pines. This is supposed to be the most haunted house in Scotland, and an underground passage is said to lead from Ashintully to Whitefield Castle (now in ruins).

The Old Manse at Kirkmichael is built on the site of a temple used by the Druids. The spectral figure of a man in long flowing robes, with a chaplet of flowers on his head and a golden sickle in his hand has been seen here, and screams have been heard.

Logierait lies to the south-west on the 827. Three miles west of the town, you will find the site of a *cause célèbre*:

⊙⅋ **Ballechin House** was rented by the Marquess of Bute to have its peculiar manifestations investigated by the Society for Psychical Research. The organizer was Miss Adah Freer, and between February and May 1897 a number of apparitions were noted, including a nun and her companion, a limping man, a shuffling man, a black dog, a priest, two old women (one without legs), and the spirit of a living man. The house had belonged to a Major Steuart who had sworn to return after death in the form of his favourite black spaniel. His twenty-seven-year-old housekeeper died in strange circumstances the year before him, in 1873. His sister Isabella became a nun and died in 1880. The house was left to John Steuart, a Catholic, and a priest lived in the grounds. The whole story is recorded by Eric Russell, who says:

> Unlike Borley, no overwhelming accusation or trickery regarding Ballechin has ever been made, much less substantiated . . . [but] the task of assessing the reliability of individual testimony is rendered almost impossible.

Miss Freer was subsequently proved to be a most unsatisfactory psychic investigator; but the manifestations cannot be wholly attributed to her utter lack of objectivity.

Continue up the A9 and you will pass through Glen Garry with:

🐇 **Loch Garry** to the south, near the border of Inverness. A curse was uttered by Donald Macdonald (who after Culloden accompanied Bonnie Prince Charlie to France) on

> any of my race who puts his foot on British soil and my double curse on he who submits to a Guelph [the original name of the Royal House of Windsor], and my deadliest curse on him who may try to regain Loch Garry.

Some of his descendants did try to regain this property, but the ghostly disturbances were too great and they gave up.

You can make your way south by secondary roads passing:

⅋ **Schichallion** supposed to be a stronghold of the Little People, to:

☆ **Kenmore** where a spring achieves a very rare cure – of toothache.

Again taking the secondary roads westwards you can travel up:

⅋ **Glen Lyon.** There is a burn here called Inbhirinneoin, and beside it there once lived an Urisk, or fawn, whose footprints can still be seen (see Ben Doran and Ben Venue).

⊙ **Meggernie Castle** is nearby. It is haunted by a ghost which appears sometimes as head and shoulders, and sometimes as trunk and legs. A man, who once lived here, murdered his wife and cut her up in this way (Russell dates the killing 1862). A touch of her fingers causes a burning pain, but no blister appears.

To the south, at the western end of Loch Tay, is:

🐐⊙ **Killin.** The church is dedicated to St Fillan. Nearby are stones and pebbles used by the saint to protect man and beast against

Protective stones in a mill at Killin

Loch Katrine

the torrent which rushes into the loch. They are kept in a niche of the eastern gate of a mill. Every Christmas stones are taken out and placed on a bed of *pulled* – not cut – rushes.

North of Tyndrum, before you reach Bridge of Orchy in Argyll, is:

Ben Doran or Beinn Dorain. This mountain is haunted by a Urisk, half-man and half-goat, banished there by St Fillan.

South-west of Lochearnhead, on Loch Voil, is:

Balquhidder. St Angus came here, and the stone on which he sat is now in the gable of the farm buildings at Easter Auchleskine. The turn in the road, where the beauty of the valley first struck St Angus is still called Beannachadh Aonghais, or Angus' Blessing. For hundreds of years men raised their hats and blessed the saint here. Angus settled below the present kirk, near a stone circle. Another stone circle in a haugh below the manse is the site of the market or fair held in April on Angus' Day. In the grounds of

Edinchip is a healing well. The whooping cough well is beside the burn Alt Cean Dhroma. This is a pot-hole in the limestone, ten to twelve inches in diameter and six inches deep. It is overshadowed by a large, flat moss-covered boulder some seven feet in diameter. Children were given this water from the horn of a living cow.

South-west are the Trossachs and:

Ben Venue. Coire nan Irisgean is the most famous haunt of the Urisks.

Loch Katrine has the Goblin's Cave.

Now go back to Lochearnhead and take the road on the southern side of the loch to:

Ardvorlich. The Stewarts of Ardvorlich have a lineage that goes back to the first Duke of Albany, third son of Robert II of Scotland, who married in 1361. Somewhere along that line, perhaps on the Crusades, they acquired a talisman of rock crystal set in silver. It is known as Clach Dearg or Red Stone, although it is clear and colourless. Alexander Stewart, Younger of Ardvorlich, tells me that one theory is that it got its name by being used as a burning glass to light fires; but its main use was in healing sick animals. People would bring water to the laird's wife. She would dip the stone in the water moving it in the direction of the sun, while repeating a Gaelic spell. The water was then given to the cattle (see Lockerbie). Unfortunately the incantation is lost, and for several generations the wives of the lairds have not spoken much Gaelic.

At the eastern end of the loch is:

St Fillans. The saint's name seems to dominate this part of the country:

St Fillan's Blessed Well
Whose springs can frenzied dreams dispel
And the crazed brain restore . . .

is supposed to have moved from the summit to the foot of the hill. It was held in great respect as both a healing and a wishing well. It was especially good for curing barrenness.

Above the well, at the top of Dunfillan, is a rocky seat where the saint sat and blessed the country. Anyone who suffered from rheumatism in the back sat in St Fillan's Chair and then lying on his back was dragged down the hill by his legs. The sick either walked or were carried sunwise three times round the pool on May 1 and August 1, then drank the water and bathed in it. Finally they

The hideous monster at Glamis remains a secret

threw a pebble on Fillan's Chair, or left a rag as an offering.

Between Muthill and Auchterarder is:

✩◉ **Tullibardine** where there are two sites marked by stones, and near the smaller one is a well. On Beltane morning (May Day) one should walk round it nine times before drinking the water, then walk nine times round the stones to bring good fortune.

Whether you start your tour of Fife, Clackmannanshire and Stirlingshire by continuing eastward from the last site, or set off from any other point, the sites follow a reasonably clockwise sequence. If you take a small road due south of Newburgh in Fife, it will lead you to:

☻ **Macduff's Cross.** This is a block of freestone 3·5 feet high, 4·5 feet long and 4 feet wide. It was the pedestal of a cross destroyed at the Reformation. It provided sanctuary for anyone claiming kinship with Macduff, Earl of Fife, even if he or she had committed murder in hot blood, as this could be atoned by the payment of nine cows and a heifer. However, if kinship were not proved, any murderer was killed there and then. The place is haunted by those who have been so slain, and their shrieks have often been heard. Nine Wells, the spring nearby, was where the slaughterers washed their hands of blood.

Near Logie – not the one on the coast but south of the 914 and about 5 miles northeast of Cupar – is:

☻☝ **Airdit Farm,** haunted by the ghost of a witch in the shape of a familiar, commemorated in the rhyme:

> Here I am and there I am
> Sometimes I dinna ken what I am,
> But they that catch me
> Pray let me gang
> For the Laird of Airdit's hare I am.

The next site lies to the north-east. At:

✧ **Scotscraig** another rhyme tells of buried treasure here:

> Here I sit and here I see
> Bro'ty, St Andrews and Dundee
> And neath me as much as would buy all these
> In a kist.

To the south:

☻ **St Andrews Bay** is reported to be haunted by a phantom coach.

South-east at Crail:

The Clach Dearg, preserved at Ardvorlich, holds the magic of a Gaelic spell

☻ **Balcomie Castle** is haunted by the ghost of a boy who was starved to death 400 years ago. A general apparently punished a boy for whistling, and whistling is now heard coming from the keep, but whether the two manifestations are related has not been established.

Round the north side of the Firth of Forth you next come to:

☻ **Buckhaven,** where the college is said to be haunted, and at:

☻ **West Wemyss,** the ubiquitous Green Jean appears in the castle.

Just north of the Kincardine road bridge is:

🏰 **Tulliallan Castle.** 'The Lady's Purse' was the Luck of the Blackadders of Tulliallan. This was a cauldron which hung from the rafters in the Great Hall, and may perhaps have served as a safe in which jewels and money were kept. When it fell, the legend said, the House of Blackadder, too, would fall; and fall it did. The castle became a ruin, the family died out. According to Charles R. Beard, this talisman measured just over eight inches across and five and a half inches deep, and was dug out of the ruins by a neighbouring tenant, who continued to revere it.

In Clackmannan the most famous site is:

☝ **Alloa Tower.** The Curse of Mar is a really strange prediction. The Erskines were

Green Jean is one of several spectres at Ashintully Castle

Lords of Mar, and the prophecy – which is too long to quote in full – include these main points: the family would go into eclipse; their lands would be given to strangers; the place where a king was reared would be burned and a mother perish in the flames; three of her children would never see the light; horses would be stabled in the Great Hall; and a weaver would throw his shuttle in the Chamber of State; but when an ash sapling should spring from the top of the ancient tower the troubles would be over and a kiss of peace be given. This and much more was foretold before 1571, some say by Thomas the Rhymer, others by the Abbot of Cambuskenneth. After the Battle of Sheriffmuir in 1715, the Erskines' title was forfeited and their lands confiscated. A fire broke out in Alloa Tower, where James VI had lived as a child, and Mistress Erskine was burned to death, leaving among others, three blind children. Early in the nineteenth century a detachment of cavalry was stabled in the Great Hall. In 1810 a party of visitors were most surprised to see a weaver working at a loom in what was once the Chamber of State. Between 1815 and 1820 an ash sapling grew on top of the tower. George IV restored the earldom to the grandson of the Erskine who had been deposed, and finally his granddaughter-in-law was kissed by Queen Victoria. So after 300 years the 'weird dreed out' and the doom of Mar ended.

North-east of Alloa is:

Tillicoultry, the scene of another curse. In the seventh century, St Serf cursed the laird for killing his favourite ram, saying that no heir to the estate would enjoy its possession. In 200 years, fourteen different families owned it.

Tullibody is north-west of Alloa. Here you will find the Maidenstone. In 1449 Martha Wishart, daughter of the Laird of Myreton, was seduced and abandoned by Peter Beaton, priest of Tullibody. She pined away, and on her death bed asked her parents to enshrine her 'lifeless body in solid stone and place it above ground by the pathway leading to the church'. The stone stands there to this day, hollowed in the form of a human body, but the three blocks which covered it have gone.

There are three sites in Stirlingshire:

Stirling has the ghost of a Pink Lady. A young girl dressed in pink silk and surrounded by a pink light walks between the castle (D.E.) and the church, near Lady's Rock, once the point of vantage where the womenfolk watched their men jousting.

Top Balcomie Castle, scene of a child murder and the haunt of a boy spectre

Above The Curse of Mar laid on Alloa Tower was ended by a kiss from Queen Victoria

To the south-west is Touch Muir and on top you will find:

☆ **St Corbet's Well.** Whoever drinks this water on May 1 before sunrise will live another year.

South at:

☆ **Kilsyth,** on the road leading over the hills to Stirling, is Kitty Frist Well, which is said to be 'noxious'.

The final tours in Scotland can be based on Edinburgh. First:

🌐☆🐟👥♿ **Edinburgh** itself. In Holyrood Palace (O.P.) the bloodstain outside the Queen's Apartment, where Rizzio was murdered, is thought to be indelible.

There are several well sites. St Anthony's Well in the Queen's Park is still used for healing. The ancient hermitage and chapel of St Anthony were under the overhanging crags of Arthur's Seat. St Margaret's Well in the Queen's Park was once at Restalrig. St Bernard's Well lies in the valley below the Dean Bridge close to the Water of Leith. It is sulphurous and the waters are said to give one a good appetite for breakfast. South of the city, on the ridge of Liberton (originally Leper-town) Hill, is St Catherine's Balm Well, whose surface has a layer of oil and is said to be most efficacious in skin diseases. It was cleaned out and restored by James VI (James I of England), destroyed by that arch-iconoclast Cromwell, and once again restored and allowed to flourish.

The most notorious ghosts are the Devil, who drives a coach drawn by headless horses up Lawnmarket and into the Bow, and his disciple Major Weir who rides back home inside. Major Weir, who was born in Lanark in 1600, informed the astounded citizens of Edinburgh in 1670 that he had committed incest with his sister from the age of sixteen to the time he was fifty; adultery with his wife's daughter; fornication with the maid for twenty years; and bestiality with his horses and cows. He was tried and found guilty on all charges, but the fact that he had been a warlock all his life seems to have been ignored.

More pleasant ghosts haunt Ann Street. There are many stories about these charming little houses. One concerns a Mr Swan who, having been sent to sea at a tender age, died of homesickness in some far-off land, and could never rest till he was re-united with his home and family at No. 12. An exorcism took place and Mr Swan remained quiescent for many years till new owners moved into the house in 1936; something then caused

The stone hollowed in the form of Martha Wishart at Tullibody

him to reappear. He was a familiar figure there for more than three years, and various children referred to 'the little man in black who comes to say goodnight'. Charlotte Square boasts of four apparitions, a monk, a sad-looking beggar, a woman in eighteenth-century dress, and a phantom coach.

For the first trip out of Edinburgh I would suggest that you tour the counties of West Lothian, Peebles, Selkirk and Roxburgh, returning by Midlothian; and the second one will take you through East Lothian and Berwickshire and thus over the border.

☆ **Torphichen** in West Lothian was the chief seat of the Templars in the twelfth century. The ruins of the preceptory (D.E.) can still be seen, and once provided sanctuary up to a radius of one mile. To the east of the ruins, on the hill, is St John's Well, reputed to heal and charm.

Nearby and well signposted is:

☆ **Cairnpapple Hill** (D.E.). A steep climb leads to this strange and awe-inspiring place, used for worship and burial from 2500 B.C. to A.D. 100. The burial place under the cairn has been excavated and one can enter it. It seems full of mystery, and this, with the strange stone circles and monoliths above the ground, give one a sense of complete time-lessness.

In Peeblesshire you will find the:

◉ **River Tweed** which demanded heavy

sacrifices. Salt was thrown into it and over the fishing nets to appease the river gods. At the confluence of the Tweed and Drumelzier Burn is:

🐾 **Merlin's Grave.** The day that James VI was crowned King of England a flood made the old Scots rhyme come true:

When Tweed and Pawsayl meet at Merlin's Grave
Scotland and England shall one monarch have.

But Drumelzier is south of our first site:

☆ **West Linton** where, on the Rutherford estate, is Heaven Aqua Well.

Due east of Drumelzier on the Selkirk border, at the head of the Brora Burn is:

☆ **Minch Muir** where the Cheese Well demands the strange recompense after which it is named.

South-east in Roxburghshire is:

◉ **Hawick.** Although Riding the Commons is supposed to commemorate the Scottish victory at Hornshole Bridge, it also includes pagan rites, for instance, a sunrise procession, and the chorus of one song is an invocation to two Norse gods: 'Terribus-ye Ter-y-Odin' originally meant 'Thor, keep us, both Thor and Odin'.

South-east again is:

👁 **Bonchester Bridge.** From here to Chesters on the 6088 phantom Roman cohorts can be seen on the march.

North-east is the site of:

🐾 **Jedburgh Castle** (for the last 150 years the county jail), the original setting of E. A. Poe's *Masque of the Red Death*. At the wedding breakfast of Alexander III (1249–1285) held here, a tall gaunt figure appeared, shrouded and masked. Shroud and mask were torn away to reveal – nothing; and when the king and his attendants looked round, the vestments too had vanished.

To the north, on the way back to Edinburgh, there is a cluster of sites around:

☆ **St Boswells** where in the well-brae wall is the Hare Well, St Boswell's very own, but if it is the one that we found, then it is in a sorry condition.

👁 **Maxton** lies to the south-east and the inhabitants benefited from the ghost who haunted Littledean Tower on the banks of the Tweed. This was the spirit of a former rapacious owner who told a servant girl where his gold was hidden and instructed her to see that it was divided between the new owners and the poor of Maxton.

To the north is:

🐾 **Bemersyde.** The thirteenth-century seer Thomas the Rhymer wrote:

Tide what e'er betide
Haig will be Haig of Bemersyde.

The Haigs, who were originally of the same family as the Hays of Yester (q.v.), lived here before 1200; and when the house was sold in 1921, it was given to Field Marshal Earl Haig who was a distant cousin of the last owners.

North-west at:

👁♿ **Galashiels** in Selkirkshire is Buckholm Tower where the ghost of a Pringle, who murdered two Covenanters, is seen in June. An indelible bloodstain on a beam marks the scene of the murder. The baying of spectral hounds is heard, doomed forever to hunt down the spirit of the man, who once set his own dogs upon innocent people.

Sir Walter Scott thought that:

👁 **Abbotsford,** (O.P.), his nearby home, was haunted by George Bullock who died while in charge of building alterations.

Continuing north the road into Midlothian between:

👁 **Stow and Heriot** is haunted by a phantom lorry.

👁 **Borthwick Castle,** near Tynehead in Midlothian, is haunted by a boyish-looking ghost who is really Mary, Queen of Scots. She lived here after marrying Bothwell in 1566, and escaped to Cakemuir Castle disguised as a page.

🐾 **Arniston.** The Luck of Arniston can be traced back to Catherine, daughter of the third Lord Oliphant, who married the seventeenth Dundas of Dundas. Before she died on 12 December 1612 she had saved enough money to leave her son the estate of Arniston and with it a Venetian glass cup, with the warning that if it were lost or broken, misfortune would follow. There have been twelve Dundases of Arniston, but the family no longer lives there.

🐾✏ **Roslin Chapel and Castle.** Read Sir Walter Scott's 'Lay of the Last Minstrel'. A sleeping lady is said to guard a million pounds or more in the castle vaults, and there is a prediction that a knight named Wilson will break the charm with a trumpet call. The chapel appears to be on fire when there is about to be a death in the family of the St Clair Erskines, Earls of Rosslyn.

The legend of the Prentice Pillar is well known, but worth repeating. While his master was in Rome, a young apprentice produced such a beautifully carved figure that the master, on his return, killed the boy for his presumption. The Revd J. C. Carrick says that every piece of carving in the chapel is a Masonic symbol, deliberately designed as

The ruin of Buckholm Tower, Galashiels

a monument to Freemasonry by Lord St Clair, Grand Master in 1450.

Woodhouse Lee. The ruins of the old house were haunted by the ghost of a distraught woman in white, carrying the body of her murdered child. When the new house was built, material from the old was incorporated, and the woman still appeared.

Travelling east out of Edinburgh you come first to:

Musselburgh. Here is the Well of Our Lady of Loretto, which has a curious history. It is a curative well, and after the Reformation stones from the walls of the baptistry were used to build a jail. For this offence the citizens of Musselburgh were excommunicated annually till the end of the 1700s.

Continuing east you will enter East Lothian.

Penkaet Castle or Fountainhall House, south-east of Tranent, is haunted. John Cockburn murdered a man called Seton here. The ghost is heard 'hummocking about' and dragging something across the floor. It is also haunted by the ghosts of Charles I and a beggar called Alexander Hamilton who caused the death of the owner by witchcraft, and was hanged for it in Edinburgh.

At the foot of the Lammermuir Hills is the village of Gifford, where you will find:

Yester House. This was the home of the Tweeddales until the eleventh Marquis died. Hugh de Gifford, Lord Yester, was a warlock who, with the help of Merlin, is said to have built the mysterious Goblin Ha' or Bo-Hall in one night. This is not the hotel in the village, but lies up behind Yester. Hugh de Gifford had a daughter, Joanna, who in the mid-fourteenth century married Sir Thomas de Haya. The warlock is said to have imbued a pear with magical properties, and it was this pear which Jean or Marion, third daughter of the second Lord Hay of Yester, brought as part of her dowry when she married George Broun of:

Colstoun, which is a few miles to the north. The Colstoun Pear is supposed to keep the family lands intact and is still in the Broun-Lindsay family who alone can lay eyes on it.

Bibliography

Ashe, Geoffrey, ed., *The Quest for Arthur's Britain*, London, 1968

Bardens, Dennis, *Ghosts and Hauntings*, London, 1965

Beard, Charles R., *Lucks and Talismans*, London, 1934

Bergamar, Kate, *Discovering Hill Figures*, Tring, 1968

Betjeman, John, and Piper, John, ed., *Shell Guide* (to various counties), London, 1935–72

Braddock, Joseph, *Haunted Houses*, London, 1968

Bray, Mrs A. E., *The Borders of the Tamar and the Tavy*, London, 1879

Burke, Sir John Bernard, *Family Romances*, London, 1853

Chambers's Encyclopaedia, vol. 2, London, 1888

Chetwynd-Stapylton, M., *Discovering Wayside Graves and Memorial Stones*, Tring, 1969

Courtney, M. A., *Cornish Feasts and Folklore*, Penzance, 1890

Day, James Wentworth, *A Ghost Hunter's Game Book*, London, 1958

———, *Here are Ghosts and Witches*, London, 1954

———, *In Search of Ghosts*, London, 1969

Dyer, T. F. Thistelton, *The Ghost World*, London, 1893

———, *Strange Pages from Family Papers*, London, 1895

Elder, Abraham, *Tales and Legends of the Isle of Wight*, London, 1839

Frost, Thomas, *Life of Thomas, Lord Lyttelton*, London, 1876

Gascoigne, Margaret, *Discovering English Customs and Traditions*, Tring, 1969

Gordon, Ruth E. St Leger, *The Witchcraft and Folklore of Dartmoor*, London, 1965

Hadfield, John, ed., *The Shell Guide to England*, London, 1970

Lord Halifax's Ghost Book, London, 1936

Hallam, Jack, *The Ghost Tour*, London, 1967

Harland, John and Wilkinson, T. T., *Lancashire Folklore*, London, 1867

———, *Lancashire Legends*, London, 1882

Harper, Charles G., *Haunted Houses*. (This classic, illustrated by the author, was first published in 1907 and revised and enlarged in 1924. By great good fortune I managed to acquire the author's corrected copy, with MS notes for a further revised and enlarged edition due to be published in 1936.)

Harries, John, *The Ghost Hunter's Road Book*, London, 1968

Hole, Christina, *English Folklore*, London, 1940

———, *Haunted England*, 2nd edition, London, 1950

Hopkins, R. Thurston, *Adventures with Phantoms*, London, 1946

Hutchins, Jane, *Discovering Mermaids and Monsters*, Tring, 1968

Ingram, John H., *The Haunted Homes and Family Traditions of Great Britain*, London, 1905

Jones, Francis, *The Holy Wells of Wales*, Cardiff, 1954

Kitchener, P., and Leaf, V., *Catholic Wayside Guide to the West Country and Wales*, Hartland, 1964

Lang, Andrew, *The Book of Dreams and Ghosts*, London, 1899

Leather, Ella Mary, *The Folklore of Herefordshire*, (new ed. of 1912 ed.), Wakefield, 1970

Legg, Rodney, *A Guide to Dorset Ghosts*, Bournemouth, 1969

Lethbridge, T. C., *Ghost and Divining Rod*, London, 1963

———, *Ghost and Ghoul*, London, 1961

———, *Gogmagog: The Buried Gods*, London, 1957

Lockhart, J., *Curses, Lucks and Talismans*, London, 1938

MacGregor, Alasdair Alpin, *The Ghost Book*, London, 1955

MacKenzie, Andrew, *Apparitions and Ghosts*, London, 1971

———, *Frontiers of the Unknown*, London, 1968

Mackinlay, James M., *Folklore of Scottish Lochs and Springs*, Glasgow, 1893

McLaren, Moray, *The Shell Guide to Scotland*, 2nd edition, London, 1972

Norman, Diana, *The Stately Ghosts of England*, London, 1963

O'Donnell, Elliott, *The Screaming Skulls and other Ghost Stories*, London, 1964

Owen, A. R. George, and Sims, Victor, *Science and the Spook*, London, 1971

Porteous, C., *The Beauty and Mystery of Well Dressing*, Derby, 1949

Porter, Enid, *Cambridgeshire Customs and Folklore*, London, 1969

Quiller-Couch, M. and L., *Ancient and Holy Wells of Cornwall*, London, 1894

Rudkin, Ethel, *The Black Dog*, Gainsborough, 1936

———, *Lincolnshire Folklore*, Gainsborough, 1936

Russell, Eric, *Ghosts*, London, 1970

Sampson, C., *Ghosts of the Broads*, London, 1931

Saunders, W. H. Bernard, *Legends and Traditions of Huntingdonshire*, London, 1888

Sikes, Wirt, *British Goblins*, London, 1880

Spence, Lewis, *The Fairy Tradition in Great Britain*, London, 1948

Stead, W. T., *Real Ghost Stories*, London, 1892

Steer, Francis William, ed., *Sussex Archaeological Collections*, Chichester, 1963

Timbs, J., *Abbeys, Castles and Ancient Halls of England and Wales: Their Legendary Lore and Popular History*, London, 1925

Underwood, Peter, *Gazetteer of British Ghosts*, London, 1971

Walford, Edward, *Chapters from Family Chests*, 2 vols, London, 1886

———, *Tales of our Great Families*, 4 vols, London, 1877–80

List and Sources of Black and White Illustrations

The following abbreviations are used in the list:

BTA – British Tourist Authority
John Freeman – John R. Freeman & Co. (Photographers) Ltd
Mansell – The Mansell Collection, London
NPG – The National Portrait Gallery, London
RE – Photographs by Robert Estall

14–15 Forde Abbey. *RE*
16 Launceston churchyard. *Mansell*
19 Top: Tintagel. *RE*
19 Bottom: Dupath Well. *RE*
20 Top: The Nine Maidens. *RE*
20 Bottom: Roche Rocks and St Michael's Chapel. *Mansell*
23 Top: Phantom Ship. *The Harry Price Library, University of London*
23 Bottom: Mermaids. *Associated-Rediffusion Picture Library*
25 Top: Knill Monument. *RE*
25 Bottom: Veryan Church clock. *RE*
27 Top: Berry Pomeroy tower. *RE*
27 Bottom: The Black House. *RE*
29 An exorcism. *Mansell*
30 Squire Cabell's tomb. *RE*
32 The Spinsters' Rock. *RE*
34 Top: Tomb in Lapford churchyard. *Photo: Antony Hippisley Coxe*
34 Bottom: St Nectan's Well. *From 'The Life of St Nectan' by Rev. Gilbert H. Doble, D.D., Polypress Ltd, Bideford/Photo: John Freeman*
37 Tetcott Church. *RE*
38 Taunton Castle. *BTA*
39 The Tudor Tavern. *RE*
40 Sir Francis Drake, an engraving attributed to J. Hondius, *c.* 1583. *NPG*
41 Walford's Gibbet. *RE*
43 James Scott, Duke of Monmouth and Buccleuch (1649–1658), copy after Wissing, *c.* 1683. *NPG*
44–5 Sherborne Castle. *RE*
46 Top: Sandford Orcas Manor. *RE*
46 Bottom: The Chilton Cantelo skull. *RE*
47 Battle fought by Jasper, Earl of Pembroke, and James Butler, Earl of Ormond and Wiltshire, against Edward, Earl of March, 1461, during which multiple suns appeared in the sky. From John Speed's Atlas. *Courtesy of the Royal Geographical Society/Photo: John Freeman*
48 The Caratacus Stone. *RE*
50 A dragon. *From 'Traditional Cornish Stories and Rhymes' by Donald R. Rawe; illustrations by Morgelyn; Lodenek Press, Padstow/Photo: John Freeman*
51 Top: Cannard's Grave Inn sign. *RE*
51 Bottom: Puck's Well, Rode. *RE*
55 Beaminster churchyard. *Mansell*

56 Top: The Cross and Hand. *RE*
56 Bottom: Wolfeton gatehouse. *Crown copyright*
57 Top: Bryanston. *Mansell*
57 Bottom: The drive at Eastbury. *RE*
58 Top: Lulworth Castle. *Mansell*
58 Bottom: T. E. Lawrence by A. John. *NPG*
59 Athelhampton Hall cellar. *BTA*
60 The Demon Drummer of Tedworth. *Mansell*
62 The modern Westbury White Horse. *BTA*
62 Inset: The original horse of Bratton Hill. *From 'English Folklore' by Christina Hole; courtesy of B. T. Batsford Ltd/Photo: John Freeman*
63 Top: A lane in Braishfield. *RE*
63 Bottom: The Rufus Stone. *Mansell*
64 Netley Abbey. *Mansell*
65 Jane Seymour, after Holbein. *NPG*
66 Bramber Castle. *RE*
67 Top: La Belle Chauffeuse by Sir William Nicholson, 1904. *National Gallery of Victoria, Melbourne, Australia*
67 Bottom: Herstmonceux Castle. *From 'Haunted Houses' by Joseph Braddock; illustrated by Felix Kelly; courtesy of B. T. Batsford Ltd/Photo: John Freeman*
68–9 Gladwish Wood. *RE*
70 St Dunstan and the Devil. *The Harry Price Library, University of London*
73 Rochester Castle. *RE*
74 Canterbury Cathedral. *RE*
75 Scotney Castle. *BTA*
76 Sir Philip Sidney, artist unknown. *NPG*
77 Puttenden Manor. *RE*
79 Downe Court Manor. *Courtesy of Mr Brian Thompson*
80 Kensington Palace. *RE*
81 The Adelphi Theatre. *RE*
82 Oliver Cromwell by R. Walker, *c.* 1649. *NPG*
83 Vine Street Police Station. *RE*
85 Hughenden Manor, interior. *BTA*
86 Herne the Hunter by George Cruikshank. *Mansell*
87 The Uffington White Horse. *Aerofilms Ltd.*
91 The Maharajah's Well. *Courtesy of the Trustees of the Maharajah's Well at Stoke Row, and H.H. The Maharaja Banaras/Photo: John Freeman*
92 Hanham Court. *RE*
94 The Coningsbury Hound. *Hereford Times*

95 Top: Raggedstone Hill. *RE*
95 Bottom: Prior's Court. *RE*
96 Charlecote Park. *BTA*
97 The effigy of Sir Walter Trayli in Woodford Church. *RE*
98 Little Gaddesden Manor. *RE*

100 Top: Salisbury Hall. *RE*
100 Bottom: Lady Anne Grimston's grave. *RE*
101 The Minsden Chapel ghost. *From 'History of Hitchin' by Reginald Hine, Allen & Unwin, reprinted by Eric T. Moore; courtesy of Mrs Florence Hine and the Trustees of Hitchin Museum/Photo: T. W. Latchmore, 1907*
102 The Cluniac Priory. *RE*
103 Left: Spirit-writing from Borley Rectory. *Harry Price Library, University of London*
103 Right: Borley Rectory after the fire. *Harry Price Library, University of London*
104 Matthew Hopkins and two witches. *Mansell*
105 The Druid's Stone. *RE*
106 Westwood Lodge. *Photo: East Anglian Daily Times*
109 Fred Archer by 'C.W.S.', 1888. *NPG*
110 Top: Dr Butts. *Courtesy of The Master, Fellows and Scholars of Corpus Christi College, Cambridge/Photo: Edward Leigh*
110 Bottom: Mary I by Hans Eworth, 1554. *NPG*
111 Sawston Hall. *BTA*
114 Left: Walsingham monastery. *BTA*
114 Right: The Brown Lady of Raynham Hall. *Harry Price Library, University of London*
115 Castle Rising. *RE*
116 Top: Catherine of Aragon, artist unknown. *NPG*
116 Bottom: The Ferry Boat Inn, interior. *RE*
117 Woodcroft Castle. *RE*
118 Stoke Dry Church. *RE*
119 Bosworth Hall. *RE*
120 Left: Boatswain's tomb, detail. *BTA*
120 Right: The Garland King at Castleton. *Courtesy of Derbyshire Countryside Ltd/Photo: C. Eric Brown*
121 Castleton Church tower. *Courtesy of Derbyshire Countryside Ltd/Photo: C. Eric Brown*
122 Top: The Lumsdale Wishing Stone. *RE*
122 Bottom: St Anne's Well, from John Speed's Atlas. *Courtesy of the Royal Geographical Society/Photo: John Freeman*
123 Tamworth Castle, interior. *RE*
124 Chester Wishing Steps. *RE*
128 Top: Bunbury Image House. *RE*
128 Bottom: Wardley Hall. *RE*
129 Smithills Hall. *RE*
130–1 Thirwall Castle. *RE*
132 Bamburgh Castle. *RE*
133 Lindisfarne, from John Speed's Atlas. *Courtesy of the Royal Geographical Society/Photo: John Freeman*
134 Littleburn colliery. *RE*
135 Anne Griffith: detail from a painting by Marc Gheeraerts. *Courtesy of Mr Marcus Wickham-Boynton/Photo: Richard Tillbrook, Jarrold Colour Publications*
136 The Rocking Stone. *RE*
137 Whitby Abbey and Church. *RE*
138 Top: The Hand of Glory. *Mary Evans Picture Library*
138 Bottom: Epworth Rectory, interior. *From 'Real Ghost Stories' by W. T. Stead, c.1890/Photo: John Freeman*
140 Left: Doddington Hall. *RE*
140 Right: Robert Cooke's tomb. *RE*
142 Castle Rushen. *Courtesy of The Manx Museum*
146 Kidwelly Castle. *RE*
147 St Govan's Well. *RE*
149 Devil's Bridge. *RE*
150 The Nanteos Cup. *Pickford Photography*
151 Top: Bala Lake. *RE*
151 Bottom Ff. Enddwyn. *RE*
152 Top: Dinas Emrys. *RE*
152 Bottom: Cwm Pennant. *RE*
153 Llanddaniel Fab. *RE*
154 Gwydir Castle. *RE*
157 Fyvie Castle. *RE*
158 Top: Spedlin's Tower. *Mansell*
158 Bottom: Spedlin's Tower. *RE*
159 Chapel Wells. *RE*
160 Culzean Castle. *RE*
164 Duntrune Castle. *RE*
165 Loch Nell Castle. *RE*
166 'Shooting a ghost', from The Supernatural by Weatherley and Maskelyne. *The Harry Price Library, University of London*
169 Skibo Castle. *RE*
170 The carved stone, Glen Roy. *RE*
175 Prince Charles Edward Stuart by David. *National Galleries of Scotland/Photo: Annan*
176 Rait Castle. *RE*
177 Fyvie Castle. *RE*
179 Top: Castle of Vayne. *RE*
179 Bottom: Cortachy Castle. *RE*
180 The Witches Pool. *RE*
181 Stones in a niche at Killin mill. *RE*
182 Loch Katrine. *Mansell*
185 The Clach Dearg. *RE*
186 Top: Balcomie Castle. *RE*
186 Bottom: Alloa Tower. *RE*
187 The Tullibody Maidenstone. *RE*
189 Buckholm Tower. *RE*

Front jacket illustration: Ghostly moonlit landscape by Sebastian Pether, oil on canvas, $17\frac{1}{2} \times 16$ in. (44·5 × 40·7 cm.). *Collection Mr John Hadfield/Photo: Derrick Witty*
Back jacket illustration: The Screaming Skull of Bettiscombe. *RE*

Index

Names in roman type indicate **bold** headings in the text
Numbers in **bold** indicate illustrations

Key to Map Pages

Reference to Counties

ABERDEENSHIRE	70
ANGLESEY	47
ANGUS	72
ARGYLL	60
AYRSHIRE	58
BANFFSHIRE	69
BEDFORDSHIRE	19
BERKSHIRE	12
BERWICKSHIRE	80
BRECKNOCKSHIRE	52
BUCKINGHAMSHIRE	11
CAITHNESS	64
CAERNARVONSHIRE	46
CAMBRIDGESHIRE	23
CARDIGANSHIRE	44
CARMARTHENSHIRE	42
CHESHIRE	32
CLACKMANNANSHIRE	75
CORNWALL	1
CUMBERLAND	35
DENBIGHSHIRE	48
DERBYSHIRE	29
DEVON	2
DORSET	4
DUMFRIESSHIRE	55
DUNBARTONSHIRE	85
DURHAM	37
EAST LOTHIAN	82
ESSEX	21
FIFE	74
FLINTSHIRE	49
GLAMORGAN	41
GLOUCESTERSHIRE	14
HAMPSHIRE	6
HEREFORDSHIRE	15
HERTFORDSHIRE	20
HUNTINGDONSHIRE	25
INVERNESS-SHIRE	61
ISLE OF MAN	40
KENT	8
KINCARDINSHIRE	71
KINROSS-SHIRE	84
KIRKCUDBRIGHTSHIRE	56
LANARKSHIRE	83
LANCASHIRE	33
LEICESTERSHIRE	27
LINCOLNSHIRE	39
LONDON	10
MERIONETHSHIRE	45
MIDLOTHIAN	77
MONMOUTHSHIRE	53
MONTGOMERYSHIRE	50
MORAY	68
NAIRNSHIRE	67
NORFOLK	24
NORTHAMPTONSHIRE	18
NORTHUMBERLAND	36
NOTTINGHAMSHIRE	28
ORKNEY ISLANDS	65
OXFORDSHIRE	13
PEEBLES-SHIRE	79
PEMBROKESHIRE	43
PERTHSHIRE	73
RADNORSHIRE	51
RENFREWSHIRE	59
ROSS AND CROMARTY	62
ROXBURGHSHIRE	54
RUTLAND	26
SELKIRKSHIRE	81
SHETLAND ISLES	66
SHROPSHIRE	31
SOMERSET	3
STAFFORDSHIRE	30
STIRLINGSHIRE	76
SUFFOLK	22
SURREY	9
SUSSEX	7
SUTHERLAND	63
WARWICKSHIRE	17
WEST LOTHIAN	78
WESTMORLAND	34
WIGTOWNSHIRE	57
WILTSHIRE	5
WORCESTERSHIRE	16
YORKSHIRE	38

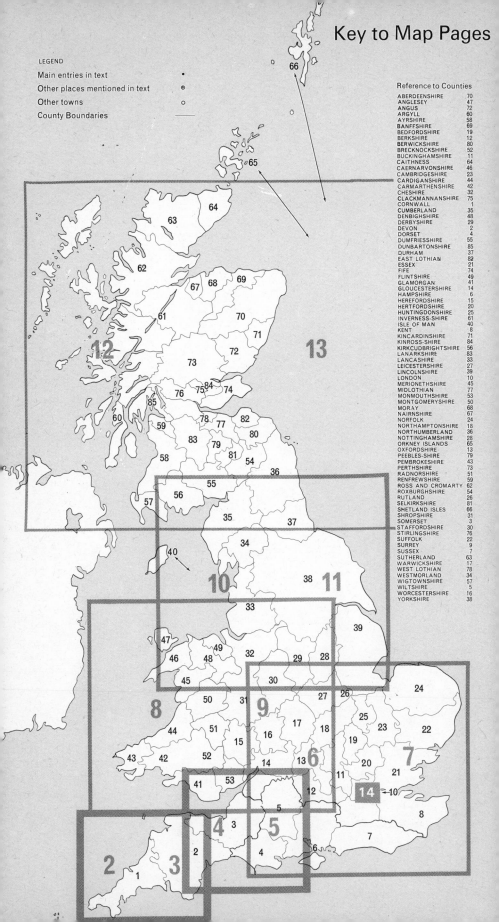

2

4

0 miles 10 miles

0   10 miles
0   15 kilometres

See Map 8-9

WALES

○ Clevedo

Brockle

○ Weston-super-Mare

Ca
Ca

Wring

Locking

Do
Hi

Banwell

Shute Shelve Hill

○ Lynton

Porlock Weir ○   ○ Selworthy
   ● Porlock   Minehead

● Burnham

Horner ●   ● Luccombe   Dunster   Watchet   ○ Wick Moor
   Timberscombe ●   Carhampton   ● St Audrie's
● Pinkworthy Pond   Cleeve ●   Farm ● Dowsborough   Stogursey

Hawkecombe   Cutcombe   Hill   ● Shervage   ● Combwich
Head ●   ● Chetsford Water   Withycombe   Staple ● Wood   Cannington
Challacombe ○   Williton   Weacombe ● Walford's   Park
   ● Simonsbath   Rodhuish ●   Nomansland   Holford ● Gibbet ● Fiddington   ○ Edington
   ● Exford   Nether   Glast
      Heddon Oak   Stowey
      Combe Sydenham ●   ● Stogumber   Wembdon ●   Bridgwater
   ● Wambarrows   ● Sedgemoor
               ● Westonzoyland
aple   S O M E R

   ● The Caratacus   ● Cothelstone
      Stone
         Bishop's Lydeard ●
   ● Dulverton   ● Kinston St Mary   Langpo
● Chittlehampton   Friends'   ● Taunton   Mulc
   ● South Molton   Burial Ground ○   ● Milverton   Abbe
      Bathealton ●
● Challditch Cross   Langford
   Budville
Moor   Park Farm ●   ● Duddlestone   ● Curry Mallet
      ● Wellington   ● Corfe
          ● Holmans
          Clavel
oworthy ●   ● Lapford   Churchstanton ●   ● Robin Hood's   ○ Ilminster
ckditch Cross ●   ● Stogate Cross   Butts
   Downe St Mary ●   ● Copplestone   ● Whitestaunton   M
                     ● Chard   Cr
         ● Tiverton
         ○ Cullompton
                     ● Forde
                     Abbey
   V   O   N   Bro
● kehampton   Crediton ○   ● Dunkeswell   Beamir
   The   ● Honiton
   Spinster's ● Drewsteignton   DEVON   Marshwood ●   ● Bettiscombe
● Throwleigh   Rock ●
   ● Wonson Manor   Well
   ● Gidleigh   Fil
● Scorhill Circle   ● Exeter   Uplyme ●   Fa
         ● Moretonhamstead   ○ Lyme Regis
● Shapley Common   Seaton ●   Bridpor
rren House Inn ● Merripitt   ● Manaton   Exton ●
aw Gully ● Hill   Jay's   ● Nutwell Court
ood ●   Grave ● Great Hound   Sidmouth
● Postbridge   ● Cator Common Tor   Bovey Tracey   Exmouth ●
Tor ●   ● Widecombe in the Moor ● Chudleigh Knighton
   DARTMOOR
● Bel Tor ●   Buckland in the Moor   Little
● Poundsgate ●   New Bridge ●   Kingsteignton   Haldon
   Childe's   ● Newton
well Tomb ● Holne   Abbot
or   The Abbot's Way   ● Buckfastleigh
         Dartington   Torquay
● Dean Combe ●   Shiners ● Hall   Compton
   Bridge ●   Castle
○ Cornwood   ● Berry Pomeroy
● Fardel Hall   ● Totnes   ● Paignton
   ● North Huish
         ● Brixham
   ● Dartmouth
   ● Bigbury-on-Sea
h Island   ● Kingsbridge

● Salcombe

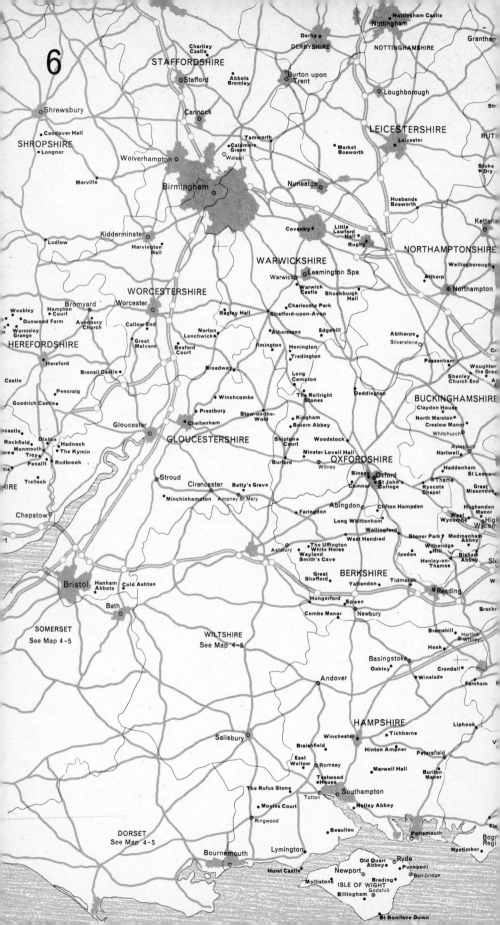

Map 10-11

Boston

LINCOLNSHIRE

Spalding

Hannath Hall

Wisbech

Etton
Woodcroft
Castle

HAMPTONSHIRE   CAMBRIDGESHIRE

undle

CAMBRIDGESHIRE

Huntingdon St Ives
HUNTINGDONSHIRE   Holywell

Kimbolton
Great
Staughten

Madingley
Hall

FORDSHIRE

CAMBRIDGE

Grantchester

Harston

Sawston Hall

Bedford

Steeple
Morden

Hinxworth Ashwell Royston
Place

Bygrave
Ho
Baldock

Barkway

Brent
Pelham

Letchworth
High Down

Hitchin Little Wymondley

Stevenage

Abbey
Minsden
Chapel
Luton

HERTFORDSHIRE

Knebworth
Datchworth
Old Clibbon's
Post
Bramfield

Hill
Redbourn
Hemel
Hempstead
Salisbury
Hall
St Albans
Kings Langley
Abbots
Langley

Tewin

Campfeld

Hatfield
House

Cheshunt

Watford

Waltham Abbey

LONDON
See Map 14

Loughton

Thames Ditton
eet
Brooklands
Cobham

SURREY

ton Place
dford

Reigate

Dorking

The Silent
Pool

Horsham

St Leonard's
Forest

Knepp
Castle

SUSSEX

Amberley
rundel Castle

Poling

Worthing

Shoreham

Brighton

Hunstanton
Hall

Houghton
Hall

Castle Rising

Sandringham

King's Lynn

Swaffham

Walsingham

Syderstone

Fakenham

Raynham Hall

Stiffkey
Binham

Aylmerton
Felbrigg Hall

Mannington

Blickling Hall

Cromer

Happisburgh
Waxham
Hall
Stalham
Hickling
Broad
Potter
Heigham

Cottishall
Wroxham Horning
Salhouse
Ranworth
South
Walsham

St Benet's
Acle

Norwich

Great Melton

NORFOLK

Breckles Hall

Attleborough

Ely

Thetford

Hoxne

Burgh Castle

Burgh
St Peter Oulton
Bungay Beccles
Oulton
Broad

Harleston
Redenhall
Lush's Bush

Covehithe

Wangford
Reydon
Southwold
Blythburgh

Spinney Abbey
Unware
Beck Row
Holywell Row
The Boy's or
Gypsy's Grave

Christ's College
St John's College
Jesus College
Trinity College
Corpus Christi
The Old Abbey Ho
25 Montague Road
Trumpington Street
Addenbrookes Hosp.
Gog
Magog Hill
Balsham
Wratting
Horseheath

Newmarket

Bury St Edmunds

Woolpit

Rushbrooke

Rougham
Green

Stowmarket

SUFFOLK

Bildeston

Great Bealings

Woodbridge

Kesgrave

Long Melford

Borley

Sudbury

Hadleigh

Hintlesham
Hall

East
Bergholt

Thorington Hall

Ipswich

Seafield Bay

Dugwich

Westleton

Leiston

Coggeshall

Colchester

Great Leighs Faulkbourne

Layer
Marney

Langenhoe

Brightlingsea

St Osyth

Clacton

Mersea Island

Bishop's
Stortford

ESSEX

Chelmsford

Springfield

Barn
Hall

Beeleigh
Abbey

Tolleshunt
D'Arcy

Bradwell-juxta-Mare

Woodham
Ferrers

Maldon

Ingatestone

Rettendon

Latchingdon &
Snoreham
Cold Norton

Stock

Canewdon

Billericay

Wickford
Roundabout

Hockley

Rochford Hall

Pitsea

Southend

Rainham

Canvey

Tilbury

Hall
Place

Northfleet

Southfleet

Rochester

Meopham

Chatham

Margate

Ramsgate
Cliffsend

Faversham

The Shipwright's
Arms

Cleve
Court

Richborough
Castle
Sandwich

Canterbury

Deal

Wrotham

Combe
Bank

Sundridge

Maidstone

Hollingbourne

Ightham
Mote

W.
Peckham

Diamond's
Cottage

Leeds
Castle

Charing

Ashford

KENT

Ringwould
Oxney Court

The Goodwin
Sands

Leigh Tonbridge

Chiddingstone Castle
Penshurst Place

Hever

Lingfield

Puttenden
Manor

Tunbridge Wells
Bayham
Bell's Yew
Green
Scotney Castle

Pluckley
Smarden

Cranbrook

Saltwood

Dover Castle

Folkestone

Lympne Castle

Hythe

Forest Row

Ashdown
House

Hook Green

Wych
Cross

Rotherfield

Best
Beech

Cuckfield

Buxted

Uckfield

Mayfield Burwash

Warbleton

Brede
Place

Rye

Winchelsea

Pyecombe

Lewes

Sherrington
Manor

The Long Man
Alfriston

Willingdon

Battle
Abbey

Michelham
Priory

Herstmonceux
Castle

Bexhill

Hastings

The Crumbles

Eastbourne

0   25 miles
0   40 kilometres

8

10

See Map 12-13

CUMBERLAND

Workington

Penrith   Eden Hall

Thirlemere   Lowther
Castle

WESTMORLAND   The
Spit

Calgarth   Grasrigg
Hall

Muncaster
Castle   Kendal   Nappa Hall Wo

LANCASHIRE   Levens
Hall

Warton

Lancaster   Clapdale Hall

Settle

Rainsber
Scar   Gisburn

Bashall Eaves   Clitheroe   Colne   Wycol

Chingle   River   Wyre
Hall   Ribble

Blackpool   Samlesbury Hall   Burnley
Parish Church

Preston   Blackburn

LANCASHIRE

Southport   Chorley

Smithills Hall   Oldham

Maghull   Wigan   Bury
Bolton

St Helen's   Manchester
Wardley   Manchester
Hall

Wallasey   Liverpool   Newton-le-
Willows

Hoylake   Leasowe   Handforth   Mari
Castle   Warrington   Rostherne
Thurstaston   Bromborough   Mere   Alderley   Lyme
Hall   Walton   Edge   Park
Hall

Parkgate   Knutsford   Macclesfield

Holywell   Weaversham   Lower   Capesthorne
Premerchion   Peover   Hall
Phil   Delamere
Forest

FLINTSHIRE   Chester   CHESHIRE

Llandudno   Rhyl

Tarporley   Crewe
Llangelynin   Utkinton Hall
Church   Llanelian   Bunbury   Barthomley
Bwlch-y-   Llanbedr-y-cennin   Horley's   Spurstow
Ddeufaen   Henllan   Bath

Lake Dulyn   Lianrwst   Farndon   Stoke-on-
Llyn   DENBIGHSHIRE   Trent
Caernarvon   Ogwen   Llyn   Ruthin Castle   Shocklach
Llyn   Cowlyd   Hotel   Combermere
Idwal   Abbey   Staffo

CAERNARVONSHIRE   Llandegla

Beddgelert   Wrexham
Cwm   Dinas   Char
Pennant   Emrys   Llangollen   Cas

STAFFORD:
Ffestiniog
Parish   Llyn Arennig-Fawr
ath   Maes-y-Neuadd

MERIONETHSHIRE   Bala
Lake
Llanenddwyn
Ff. Badrig   Treferid   St Melangell's
Llanfachreth   Shrine

Dolgellau

Shrewsbury

Treferid

Welshpool   Condover Hall
MONTGOMERYSHIRE

Machynlleth   Montgomery   SHROPSHIRE   Longnor   Wolverhampton

Lodge Park   Birmingha

Llandre   Morville

beryswyth   Kidderminster

Pen-parcau   Nanteos   Devil's
Bridge   Ludlow
Ff. Trisant

St Patrick's
Well

Chibbyr Pherick

Ramsey   Maughold
Ballig Wonder
Glen Roy   Well
Peel   Laxey
Peel Castle   ISLE OF MAN   Chibbyr Nigius

Crosby

Earystane
The Fairy Stone   Douglas

Castletown
panish Head

0   25 miles
0   40 kilometres

Fab

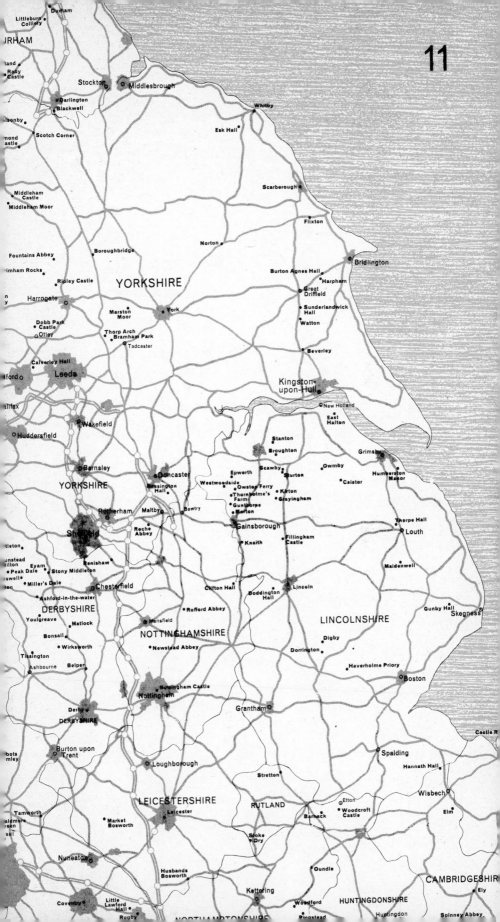

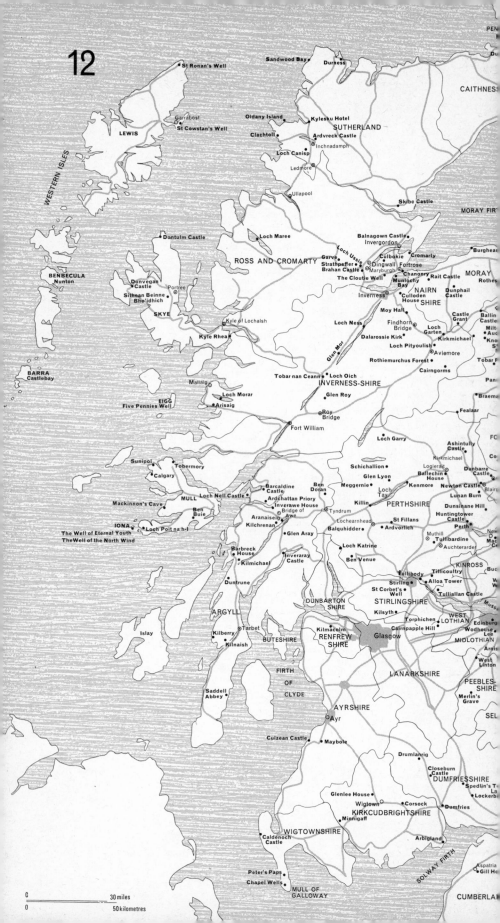

12

St Ronan's Well

Sandwood Bay • Durness

CAITHNESS

Garrabost
St Cowstan's Well

Oldany Island
Kylesku Hotel
SUTHERLAND

LEWIS

Clachtoll
Ardvreck Castle

Loch Canisp • Inchnadamph

MORAY FIRTH

Ledmore

Ullapool

Skibo Castle

Duntulm Castle

Loch Maree

Balnagown Castle
Invergordon

Burghead

WESTERN ISLES

Loch Ussie
Cromarty
Fortrose

Garve
Culbokie
MORAY

ROSS AND CROMARTY
Strathpeffer • Dingwall
Maryburgh
Chanonry
Rait Castle

BENBECULA
Nunton

Brahan Castle
The Cloutie Well
Munlochy
Bay

Rothes

Dunvegan
Castle
Portree
Sithean Beinne
Bho'idhich
SKYE

Inverness
Culloden
House
NAIRN
SHIRE
Dunphail
Castle

Moy Hall

Loch Ness
Findhorn
Bridge
Loch
Garten
Castle
Grant
Ballin
Castle

Kyle of Lochalsh

Dalarossie Kirk
Kirkmichael
Milt
Kno
S

Kyle Rhea

Loch Pityoulish
Aviemore

BARRA
Castlebay

Glen Mor

Rothiemurchus Forest
Cairngorms

Tobar F

Tobar nan Ceann • Loch Oich
INVERNESS-SHIRE

Mallaig

Glen Roy

Pani

EIGG
Five Pennies Well
Loch Morar
Arisaig

Roy
Bridge

Braema

Fealaar

Fort William

Loch Garry

Ashintully
Castle

Sunipol
Tobermory

Schichallion
Kirkmichael
Logierait
Dunbarre
Castle

Calgary

Glen Lyon
Ballechin
House
Newton Castle
Blair

Mackinnon's Cave
MULL

Barcaldine
Castle
Ben
Doran
Meggernie
Loch
Tay
Kenmore
Lunan Burn

Loch Nell Castle
Ardchattan Priory
Inverawe House
Killin
PERTHSHIRE
Dunsinane Hill
Huntingtower
Castle

Ben Buie
Aranaiseig
Bridge of
Awe
Tyndrum
Lochearnhead
St Fillans
Perth

IONA
Loch Poit na h-I
Kilchrenan
Balquhidder
Ardvorlich
Muthill
New

The Well of Eternal Youth
The Well of the North Wind
Glen Aray
Tullibardine
Auchterarder

Barbreck
House
Loch Katrine
KINROSS

Kilmichael
Inveraray
Castle
Ben Venue
Tillicoultry

Duntrune
Tullibody
Stirling
Alloa Tower

St Corbet's
Well
Tulliallan Castle

ARGYLL
DUNBARTON
SHIRE
STIRLINGSHIRE
Muss

Kilsyth
WEST
LOTHIAN
Edinburgh

Islay
Kilberry • Tarbet
BUTESHIRE
Kilmacolm
RENFREW
SHIRE
Glasgow
Torphichen
Cairnpapple Hill
Wodhouse
Lee
MIDLOTHIAN

Kilnaish

FIRTH
OF
CLYDE
LANARKSHIRE
West
Linton

Arnis

PEEBLES-
SHIRE

Saddell
Abbey
AYRSHIRE
Merlin's
Grave

Ayr

SEL

Culzean Castle • Maybole

Drumlanrig

Closeburn
Castle
DUMFRIESSHIRE
Spedlin's T
La
Lockerb

Glenlee House
Wigtown
Corsock
Dumfries

KIRKCUDBRIGHTSHIRE
Minnigaff
Arbigland

WIGTOWNSHIRE

Caldenoch
Castle

Peter's Paps
Chapel Wells
MULL OF
GALLOWAY
SOLWAY FIRTH
Aspatria
Gil Ho

CUMBERLA

0 ____ 30 miles
0 ____ 50 kilometres

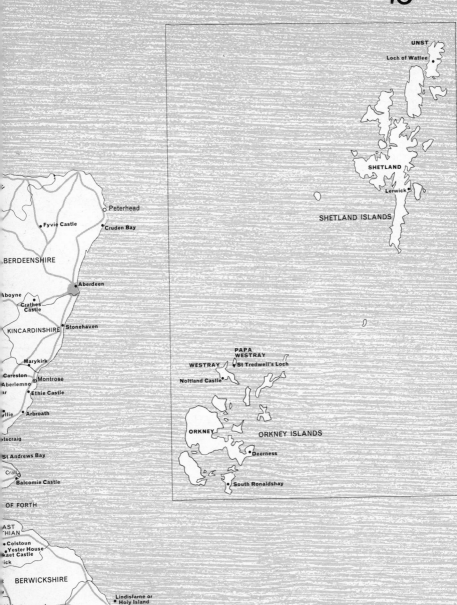

13

UNST
Loch of Watlee

SHETLAND
Lerwick

SHETLAND ISLANDS

Peterhead
• Fyvie Castle
• Cruden Bay

BERDEENSHIRE

Aboyne
• Aberdeen
• Crathes
Castle

KINCARDINSHIRE   • Stonehaven

• Marykirk

Careston
Aberlemno   • Montrose
ar   • Ethie Castle

llie   • Arbroath

tscraig

St Andrews Bay

Crail
• Balcomie Castle

OF FORTH

AST
HIAN
• Colstoun
• Yester House
aet Castle
ick

BERWICKSHIRE

Lindisfarne or
Holy Island

hiels Bemersyde
• St Boswells
• Maxton

Bamburgh
• Wooler

Craster

• Jedburgh Castle
ROXBURGHSHIRE   • Alwinton
k
• Bonchester
Bridge

• Elsdon
rmitage

NORTHUMBERLAND
• Wallington Hall

• Black Heddon
Stamfordham

Thirlwall
Castle   • Bellister Castle   Corbridge
land   Haltwhistle   Willington Gut
eenhead
Blenkinsop   • Featherstone   Dilston
Castle   Castle   Hedley
Newcastle-upon-
Tyne
• The Marsden Grotto
Hylton
Castle

rby
astle
oglin   Blanchland   Langley Hall   Finchale
ange   Neville's Castle   • Abbey
Littleburn Colliery   • Durham

Penrith
• Eden Hall

See Map
10-11   DURHAM

**PAPA
WESTRAY**
WESTRAY   St Tredwell's Loch

Noltland Castle

ORKNEY   ORKNEY ISLANDS

• Deerness

• South Ronaldshay

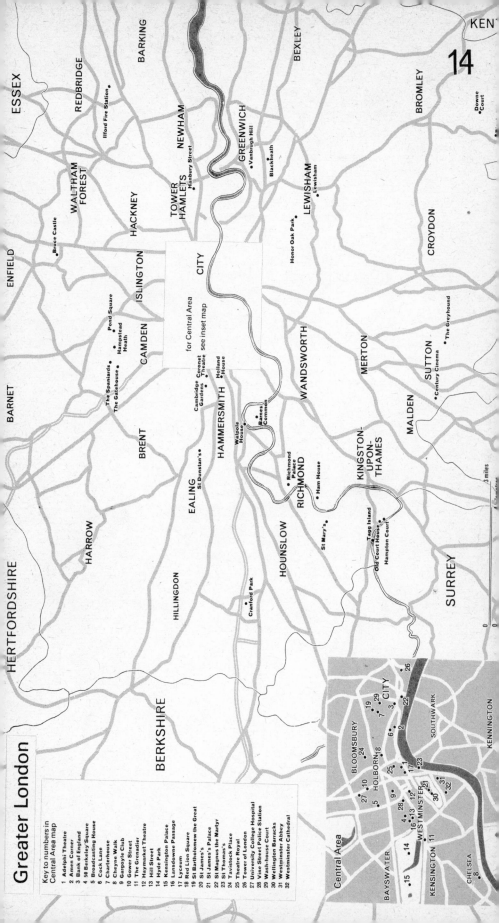

Greater London

14

KEN[T]

Key to numbers in Central Area map

1 Adelphi Theatre
2 Amen Corner
3 Bank of England
4 50 Berkeley Square
5 Broadcasting House
6 Cock Lane
7 Charterhouse
8 Cheyne Walk
9 Gargoyle Club
10 Gower Street
11 The Grenadier
12 Haymarket Theatre
13 Hill Street
14 Hyde Park
15 Kensington Palace
16 Landsowne Passage
17 Lyceum
18 Red Lion Square
19 St Bartholomew the Great
20 St James's
21 St James's Palace
22 St Magnus the Martyr
23 St Thomas's
24 Tavistock Place
25 Theatre Royal
26 Tower of London
27 University College Hospital
28 Vine Street Police Station
29 Wash-house Court
30 Wellington Barracks
31 Westminster Abbey
32 Westminster Cathedral

ESSEX

HERTFORDSHIRE

BARNET

ENFIELD

REDBRIDGE
Ilford Fire Station

WALTHAM FOREST

BARKING

NEWHAM

HACKNEY
Bruce Castle

TOWER HAMLETS
Hanbury Street

GREENWICH
Vanbrugh Hill
Blackheath

BEXLEY

BROMLEY
Downe Court

CAMDEN
Pond Square
Hampstead Heath
The Spaniards
The Gatehouse

ISLINGTON

CITY

for Central Area
see inset map

LEWISHAM
Lewisham

Honor Oak Park

CROYDON

BRENT

HARROW

EALING
St Dunstan's

HAMMERSMITH
Cambridge Gardens
Coronet Theatre
Holland House

Walpole House

Barnes Common

WANDSWORTH

MERTON

MALDEN

SUTTON
Century Cinema
The Greyhound

BERKSHIRE

HILLINGDON

HOUNSLOW
Cranford Park

RICHMOND
Richmond Palace Theatre
Ham House
St Mary's

KINGSTON-UPON-THAMES
Tagg Island
Old Court House
Hampton Court

SURREY

3 miles
Kilometres

Central Area

BAYSWATER

BLOOMSBURY

HOLBORN

CITY

SOUTHWARK

KENNINGTON

WESTMINSTER

KENSINGTON

CHELSEA